Digital Teaching, Learning and Assessment

CHANDOS

INFORMATION PROFESSIONAL SERIES

Series Editor: Ruth Rikowski
(Email: rikowskigr@aol.com)

Chandos' new series of books is aimed at the busy information professional. They have been specially commissioned to provide the reader with an authoritative view of current thinking. They are designed to provide easy-to-read and (most importantly) practical coverage of topics that are of interest to librarians and other information professionals. If you would like a full listing of current and forthcoming titles, please visit www.chandospublishing.com.

New authors: We are always pleased to receive ideas for new titles; if you would like to write a book for Chandos, please contact Dr. Glyn Jones on g.jones.2@elsevier.com or telephone þ 44 (0) 1865 843000.

Chandos Information Professional Series

Digital Teaching, Learning and Assessment
The Way Forward

Edited by

UPASANA GITANJALI SINGH
University of KwaZulu-Natal, Durban, South Africa

CHENICHERI SID NAIR
Victorian Institute of Technology, Melbourne, VIC, Australia

SUSANA GONÇALVES
Polytechnic Institute of Coimbra, Coimbra, Portugal

ELSEVIER

CP
CHANDOS
PUBLISHING
An imprint of Elsevier

Chandos Publishing is an imprint of Elsevier
50 Hampshire Street, 5th Floor, Cambridge, MA 02139, United States
The Boulevard, Langford Lane, Kidlington, OX5 1GB, United Kingdom

Notices
Knowledge and best practice in this field are constantly changing. As new research and experience broaden our understanding, changes in research methods, professional practices, or medical treatment may become necessary.

Practitioners and researchers must always rely on their own experience and knowledge in evaluating and using any information, methods, compounds, or experiments described herein. In using such information or methods they should be mindful of their own safety and the safety of others, including parties for whom they have a professional responsibility.

To the fullest extent of the law, neither the Publisher nor the authors, contributors, or editors, assume any liability for any injury and/or damage to persons or property as a matter of products liability, negligence or otherwise, or from any use or operation of any methods, products, instructions, or ideas contained in the material herein.

ISBN: 978-0-323-95500-3

For information on all Chandos Publishing publications
visit our website at https://www.elsevier.com/books-and-journals

Publisher/Acquisitions Editor: Glyn Jones
Editorial Project Manager: Naomi Robertson
Production Project Manager: Anitha Sivaraj
Cover Designer: Miles Hitchen

Typeset by MPS Limited, Chennai, India

Working together
to grow libraries in
developing countries

www.elsevier.com • www.bookaid.org

Contents

List of contributors   *xiii*

Preface   *xvii*

Editorial   *xix*

**1. Supporting virtual student research opportunities: the Holistic
     Foundry Undergraduate Engaged Learners program experience   1**

Andrea Arce-Trigatti, Steffano Oyanader Sandoval, Pedro E. Arce and
J. Robby Sanders

   1.1 Background and literature   2
      1.1.1 The digital divide   2
      1.1.2 Digital support for students during the pandemic   3
      1.1.3 Lasting digital tools for student success   3
   1.2 The Holistic Foundry Undergraduate Engaged Learners program   4
      1.2.1 Foundry innovation   5
      1.2.2 Description of the program   6
      1.2.3 Digital learning focus   7
      1.2.4 Illustrated examples of implementation   10
   1.3 Evaluative analysis   12
   1.4 Evaluative findings   13
      1.4.1 Skill development through digital knowledge acquisition and
           transfer   13
      1.4.2 The digital development of a prototype of innovative technology 14
   1.5 Implications   15
      1.5.1 As an innovative delivery approach   15
      1.5.2 For student learning   16
   1.6 Summary and concluding remarks   17
   Acknowledgments   19
   References   19

**2. Digital education for a resilient new normal using artificial
     intelligence—applications, challenges, and way forward   21**

Anju Kalluvelil Janardhanan, Kavitha Rajamohan, K.S. Manu and
Sangeetha Rangasamy

   2.1 Introduction   21
   2.2 Technology-enhanced learning—a paradigm shift   23
   2.3 Emerging need for digital education   24

2.4   Technologies for digital education   25
    2.4.1   Internet of things   25
    2.4.2   Artificial intelligence   26
2.5   Role of artificial intelligence in education   28
    2.5.1   Intelligent assistance for education   28
    2.5.2   Applications of artificial intelligence   35
2.6   Strengths, weaknesses, opportunities, and challenges of digital education   38
    2.6.1   Strength   39
    2.6.2   Weakness   39
    2.6.3   Opportunities   40
    2.6.4   Challenges   40
2.7   Digital education—the way forward   40
2.8   Conclusion   41
References   42

3.   Endured understanding of learning in online assessments: COVID-19 pandemic and beyond   45

Fay Patel

3.1   Endured understanding of learning in online assessments: enabling learning and learners   45
3.2   Alternative paradigms in online learning design   46
3.3   The United Nations Educational, Scientific, and Cultural Organization   46
    3.3.1   (UNESCO) 2030 Sustainability Development Goals   46
3.4   Literature review   48
3.5   Diffusing online learning   50
3.6   Online learning: pedagogy before technology   52
3.7   Authentic assessment   53
3.8   Endured understanding of learning   53
3.9   McTighe and Wiggins test to confirm essential question   54
3.10 Essential questions should inspire endured understanding of learning   55
3.11 COVID-19 pandemic—essential questions   56
    3.11.1   General   56
    3.11.2   Health   56
    3.11.3   Education   57
    3.11.4   Management and leadership   57
    3.11.5   Employment and labor law   57
3.12 Apple Inc and Coca Cola—essential questions   57
3.13 Apple Incorporated   58
3.14 Apple Inc—essential questions   58
3.15 Coca Cola company   59

3.16 Coca Cola   59
3.17 Recommendations, dilemmas, and challenges   59
3.18 Recommendations   59
3.19 Limitations of the study   61
3.20 Conclusion   62
References   62

**4. Transformative course design practices to develop inclusive
online world language teacher education environments from a
critical digital pedagogy perspective   65**

Giovanna Carloni

4.1 Introduction   65
4.2 Developing a course design pedagogy   66
    4.2.1 Open educational resource—enabled pedagogy   67
    4.2.2 Critical digital pedagogy   67
    4.2.3 Design Justice   68
4.3 Conclusion   73
References   74

**5. New teaching and learning strategies during the COVID-19
pandemic: implications for the new normal   79**

Hanoku Bathula, Patricia Hubbard and Tae Hee Lee

5.1 Introduction   79
5.2 Context of the programs   81
5.3 Preparation and delivery challenges   83
5.4 Reflections on delivering classes during COVID-19 lockdowns   87
5.5 Reshaping assessments   90
5.6 Implications for future delivery of higher education programs   92
5.7 Conclusion   95
References   96

6. Birley Place: a digital community to enhance student learning   99

Kirsten Jack, Ryan Wilkinson, Eleanor Hannan and Claire Hamshire

6.1 Introduction   99
6.2 Background   100
    6.2.1 Building Birley Place—digital community development   102
    6.2.2 Case study one—interactive digital placements   105
    6.2.3 Case study two—interprofessional education   107
6.3 Evaluating Birley Place—methodology   108

6.4 Evaluation findings   109
    6.4.1 Theme 1—authentic learning experiences   109
    6.4.2 Theme 2—digital place-based education   110
    6.4.3 Theme 3—opportunities for collaboration   111
    6.4.4 Theme 4—flexibility and convenience   112
6.5 Discussion and conclusions   114
6.6 The future   115
Acknowledgment   116
References   116

7. Assessment: higher education institutions' innovative online assessment methods beyond the era of the COVID-19 pandemic   121

Mercy Dube, Reason Masengu, Sinothando Sibanda and Lucia Mandongwe

7.1 Introduction   121
7.2 Background to the study   122
7.3 Literature review   123
    7.3.1 Online learning and assessment   123
    7.3.2 Higher education institutions' online assessment: the evolution and the paradigm shift   125
    7.3.3 Innovative formative assessment adopted during the COVID-19 pandemic   126
    7.3.4 Summative assessment currently adopted and their future use in the education sector   127
    7.3.5 Blended learning and blended assessment during and post the COVID-19 era   129
7.4 Research methodology   130
7.5 Discussion of findings   131
    7.5.1 Learning and assessment in higher education institutions   131
7.6 Innovative formative assessment adopted in higher education institutions during and post the COVID-19 pandemic   140
7.7 Summative assessment currently adopted and their future use in higher education institutions   140
    7.7.1 Recommendations   141
7.8 Conclusion   142
References   143

8. Formative assessment in hybrid learning environments   147

Natalia Auer

8.1 Introduction   147
8.2 A relevant model for implementing online formative assessment in ways that increase self-regulation by learners   148

8.3   The need for a conceptual framework   148
8.4   Formative assessment and online formative assessment   149
8.5   Using formative assessments online   150
8.6   Key concepts   151
8.7   Hattie and Timperley's feedback model   152
   8.7.1   Examples of the three feedback questions   153
8.8   Applying Hattie and Timperley's model to hybrid learning environments 154
   8.8.1   Dialog   155
   8.8.2   Time and immediacy of response   155
   8.8.3   Learning outcomes   156
   8.8.4   Individual learning   156
   8.8.5   Design considerations   156
8.9   Conclusion   157
References   157

9. Student experience of online exams in professional programs: current issues and future trends   161

Nga Thanh Nguyen, Colin Clark, Caroline Joyce, Carl Parsons and John Juriansz

9.1   Introduction   161
9.2   Literature review   162
   9.2.1   Online exams   162
   9.2.2   Learners' experiences of online exams   163
   9.2.3   Challenges faced and trends in transforming traditional exams   164
   9.2.4   Theoretical framework   165
9.3   Methodology   165
   9.3.1   Study setting   166
   9.3.2   Data collection and analysis   167
9.4   Results   167
   9.4.1   The fear of being disadvantaged   168
   9.4.2   Online exams: an uncomfortable experience   170
   9.4.3   Students need for authenticity in online exams   171
9.5   Discussion   174
9.6   Conclusion   176
References   176

10. E-textbook pedagogy in teacher education beyond the COVID-19 era   179

Orhe Arek-Bawa and Sarasvathie Reddy

10.1   Background and introduction   179

10.2 Literature review   180
10.3 Theoretical framework   184
10.4 Research methodology   185
10.5 Data presentation and discussion   186
    10.5.1 Before the pandemic   186
    10.5.2 During the pandemic   187
    10.5.3 Beyond the pandemic   192
10.6 Conclusion   194
Acknowledgment   195
References   196

11. The death of the massification of education and the birth of personalized learning in higher education   199
Shamola Pramjeeth and Sarina C. Till

11.1 Introduction   199
11.2 Literature review   201
    11.2.1 Online learning   201
    11.2.2 Personalized learning   203
11.3 Research methodology   204
    11.3.1 YouTube analytics   204
    11.3.2 Online surveys   205
    11.3.3 Informal WhatsApp chats   205
    11.3.4 Focus groups   206
    11.3.5 Qualitative data analysis   206
    11.3.6 Quantitative data analysis   206
    11.3.7 Ethical considerations   206
11.4 Results and discussion   207
    11.4.1 Student learning: when?, what time?, using what device?   207
    11.4.2 Student learning: which resources?   210
    11.4.3 Student learning: support-seeking behavior   211
    11.4.4 Student learning: how they blend technology, resources, platforms, and content to create their personal braid   212
11.5 Student-centric framework for personalized learning   215
11.6 Implications and the way forward   216
11.7 Conclusions   217
11.8 Limitations   218
References   218

12. New online delivery methods beyond the era of the pandemic: varied blended models to meet the COVID-19 challenges   221

Shravasti Chakravarty

12.1 Background to the study   222
12.2 Blending the classroom: established norms   223
12.3 The half-and-half model   225
12.4 Case 1: the English class   226
    12.4.1 Components of the syllabus   226
    12.4.2 Classroom processes   227
    12.4.3 Sample task from the English class   228
12.5 Case 2: the information and communication training class   228
    12.5.1 Components of the syllabus   228
    12.5.2 Classroom processes   229
    12.5.3 Sample task from the information and communication
            training class   230
12.6 Case 3: the mathematics class   230
    12.6.1 Components of the syllabus   230
    12.6.2 Classroom processes   231
    12.6.3 Sample task from the mathematics class   232
12.7 Results and discussion   233
    12.7.1 Using different digital tools simultaneously   233
    12.7.2 Interaction with other learners   233
    12.7.3 Access to the resources   234
    12.7.4 Movement of the teacher in the classroom   234
    12.7.5 Greater involvement of online learners   234
    12.7.6 Limited exposure to learners   235
    12.7.7 Motivating students   235
    12.7.8 Aversion to new technology   236
    12.7.9 Mode of instruction   236
    12.7.10 In-class practices   236
12.8 Conclusion   237
Conflict of interest   238
Acknowledgment   238
References   238

13. Digital teaching and learning: the future of ophthalmology education   241

Tony Succar, Virginia A. Lee, Hilary Beaver and Andrew G. Lee

13.1 Introduction   241

13.1.1 Digital teaching program one: an academic ophthalmology
curriculum for preprofessional students   244

13.1.2 Digital teaching program two: a virtual COVID-19
ophthalmology rotation   246

13.2 Clinical knowledge   247

13.3 Morning report   247

13.4 Grand rounds   248

13.5 Research experience   248

13.6 Patient encounters   249

13.7 Oral examination   249

13.8 Conclusions   250

References   251

Further reading   251

**14. "Online education which connects" adopting technology to
support feminist pedagogy—a reflective case study   253**

Upasana Gitanjali Singh

14.1 Introduction   253

14.2 Background   254

14.2.1 The South African context   254

14.3 My positionality   254

14.4 Literature   255

14.5 My journey—an exploration of my teaching through the lens of
critical feminist pedagogy   257

14.6 Methodology   257

14.7 Analysis and discussion   260

14.8 Implications   265

References   265

Index   *267*

List of contributors

Pedro E. Arce
Department of Chemical Engineering, Tennessee Technological University, Cookeville, TN, United States

Andrea Arce-Trigatti
Tallahassee Community College, Office of Institutional Effectiveness, Tallahassee, FL, United States

Orhe Arek-Bawa
Higher Education Studies, School of Education, University of KwaZulu-Natal, Pinetown, Durban, South Africa

Natalia Auer
Faculty of Education and Society, Malmö University, Malmö, Sweden

Hanoku Bathula
University of Auckland, Auckland, New Zealand

Hilary Beaver
Department of Ophthalmology, Blanton Eye Institute, Methodist Hospital, Houston, TX, United States

Giovanna Carloni
University of Urbino, Urbino, Italy

Shravasti Chakravarty
General Management, Xavier School of Management (XLRI), Delhi-NCR, India

Colin Clark
Western Sydney University, Sydney, NSW, Australia

Mercy Dube
Department of Information and Marketing Sciences, Faculty of Business Sciences, Midlands State University, Gweru, Zimbabwe

Claire Hamshire
University of Salford, Salford, United Kingdom

Eleanor Hannan
Faculty of Health and Education, Manchester Metropolitan University, Manchester, United Kingdom

Patricia Hubbard
University of Auckland, Auckland, New Zealand

Kirsten Jack
Faculty of Health and Education, Manchester Metropolitan University, Manchester, United Kingdom

Anju Kalluvelil Janardhanan
Southern Cross Institute, Parramatta, NSW, Australia

Caroline Joyce
Western Sydney University, Sydney, NSW, Australia

John Juriansz
Western Sydney University, Sydney, NSW, Australia

Andrew G. Lee
Department of Ophthalmology, Blanton Eye Institute, Methodist Hospital, Houston, TX, United States; Departments of Ophthalmology, Neurology, and Neurosurgery, Weill Cornell Medicine, New York, NY, United States; Department of Ophthalmology, University of Texas Medical Branch, Galveston, TX, United States; Department of Ophthalmology, University of Texas MD Anderson Cancer Center, Houston, TX, United States; Department of Ophthalmology, University of Iowa Hospitals and Clinics, Iowa City, IA, United States

Tae Hee Lee
University of Auckland, Auckland, New Zealand

Virginia A. Lee
Department of Ophthalmology, Blanton Eye Institute, Methodist Hospital, Houston, TX, United States

Lucia Mandongwe
Department of Accounting, Manicaland State University of Applied Sciences, Mutare, Zimbabwe

K.S. Manu
School of Business and Management, CHRIST University, Bangalore, Karnataka, India

Reason Masengu
Department of Management Studies, Middle East College, Knowledge Oasis Muscat, Oman

Nga Thanh Nguyen
Western Sydney University, Sydney, NSW, Australia

Carl Parsons
Western Sydney University, Sydney, NSW, Australia

Fay Patel
Independent International Higher Education Consultant, Sydney, NSW, Australia

Shamola Pramjeeth
The IIE Varsity College, School of Management, Durban, South Africa

Kavitha Rajamohan
School of Sciences, CHRIST University, Bangalore, Karnataka, India

Sangeetha Rangasamy
School of Business and Management, CHRIST University, Bangalore, Karnataka, India

Sarasvathie Reddy
Higher Education Studies, School of Education, University of KwaZulu-Natal, Pinetown, Durban, South Africa

J. Robby Sanders
Department of Chemical Engineering, Tennessee Technological University, Cookeville, TN, United States

Steffano Oyanader Sandoval
Department of Chemical Engineering, Tennessee Technological University, Cookeville, TN, United States

Sinothando Sibanda
Department of Marketing, Zimbabwe Open University, Harare, Zimbabwe

Upasana Gitanjali Singh
University of KwaZulu-Natal, Durban, South Africa

Tony Succar
Massachusetts Eye and Ear, Harvard Medical School, Boston, MA, United States; Department of Ophthalmology, Faculty of Medicine and Health, The University of Sydney, Sydney, Australia

Sarina C. Till
The IIE Varsity College, School of Information Technology, Durban, South Africa

Ryan Wilkinson
Lifelong Learning Centre, University of Leeds, Leeds, United Kingdom

Preface

While causing the greatest disruption in human history, Covid-19 has also resulted in the global community embracing distance and online learning almost overnight. In a recent study of students in South Africa, 95% of respondents agreed that online teaching had become the dominant mode after the onset of the pandemic. However, the same report confirmed the uneven distribution of devices and lack of connectivity, where more than 40% students relied on sharing devices with friends and family members. The study also revealed that more than 65% of the institutions surveyed had utilized online modalities for formative assessments and in most cases for summative assessment (<85%), with no proctoring or online invigilation. This situation is not just limited to South Africa but prevails in most countries around the world. It is clear that governments and institutions need to invest more in digital infrastructure and provide free connectivity. There is also an urgent need to revisit assessment methods and adopt authentic approaches. This can be achieved by building the capacity of teachers in developing digital assessments and offering micro-credentials for greater flexibility.

The future of learning is flexible and blended, where technology must be "domesticated" to leave no one behind. Technology must be appropriate, affordable, and accessible. While the promise of many digital tools, including AR/VR, and blockchain is covered in this book, we must also be aware of the potential perils so as not to widen the existing divides. Both teachers and learners need to be empowered to integrate quality and equity in the teaching–learning process. The ACTIONS model proposed by Tony Bates—accessibility for learners, cost structure, teaching applications, interactivity or ease of use, organizational impact on the educational institution, novelty, and speed with which courses can be developed through the use of technology—can provide a useful framework.

Similarly, the recent Transforming Education Summit organized by the United Nations called for urgent action on providing "digital learning for all." This emphasizes attention to three aspects—content, capacity, and connectivity—all can be achieved through openness and collaboration. One of the biggest lessons of the pandemic has been the realization of how interconnected and interdependent we are. The Commonwealth of Learning has been a leader in the Open Educational Resources movement and built the capacity of partners to develop policies, adopt open licenses, and share quality content for making learning opportunities accessible to all.

The pandemic has also shown that it is time to seize this moment to refresh, rethink, and redesign our policies and processes to make education relevant to the needs of the 21st century. It is imperative to prepare learners for employability and global citizenship. This will require a balance between theory and practice; a focus on hard as well as soft skills, a curriculum that addresses the needs of the labor market. The future must also consider the role of parents and siblings in the teaching and learning ecosystem. The pandemic created a momentum for self-directed learning. How can we build on this experience to promote lifelong learning for all? It is time to build on the lessons learned during the pandemic to transform our systems of education so that they are prepared to deal with future uncertainties and disasters.

This publication edited by Dr. Upasana Gitanjali Singh, Prof. Chenicheri Sid Nair, and Prof. Susana Gonçalves could not have come at a more opportune moment. The valuable experiences and perspectives from 10 different countries capture the essence of how the global community addressed the various challenges encountered during this difficult time. The lessons learned and the insights gained will provide a concrete roadmap for both policy makers and practitioners to integrate technology for more effective teaching and learning. It will also contribute to enriching the ongoing discussions on digital teaching, learning, and assessment. The journey beyond is an exciting one as it has implications for shaping the future of coming generations.

Kanwar Asha
President and CEO, Commonwealth of Learning

Editorial

This book is the result of the continuous discussion taking place in the teaching and learning space of what the future holds for academics and their main stakeholder, the students post the pandemic. The editors of this book work in the teaching and learning domain and consider such discussion critical to ensure that students are well serviced by all concerned. This book brings such discussions to one platform where academics, administrators, and other stakeholders like researchers and regulatory bodies ponder over the ideas and practices presented in this book on how the digital world will dominate and change the teaching and learning space.

Digital teaching and learning has shifted from a just an option to delivery to busy executives in most cases to a development where education revolves around the delivery primarily on a digital platform. This, however, has arisen due to the COVID-19 pandemic. This book provides the target audience with a futuristic look at the new digital world. Of importance would be how practitioners perceive this new era and for administrators to have a glance at the possibilities of teaching and learning of the future. Regulatory bodies would benefit from having this glimpse as they try to find how QA would be for such teaching and learning that deviates significantly from didactic approaches.

The primary audience for the work will be "Academics and management staff of HEIs." The book should reach teachers and administrators in HEIs globally. It could also become an essential for reader in graduate certificate programs on higher education teaching, regulatory bodies (such as national and regional higher education officials), professional bodies, and quality assurance oversight bodies or regulators.

This book brings together a rich global collection of 14 chapters reflecting and exploring the digital stratosphere of teaching and learning. Chapters in this book come from Denmark, South Africa, New Zealand, Sweden, Italy, India, Zimbabwe, Australia, the United States, and Oman.

Chapter 2 explores the developments in artificial intelligence (AI) in the field of education with specific emphasis on teaching, learning, and assessment.

Chapter 8 presents a framework for implementing online formative assessment in hybrid learning environments. The conceptual model adopted by the authors to achieve this looks at how the teacher designs and shares the learning outcomes with students, students' responses, and the learning outcomes that fit students' needs. The model adopted promotes self-regulatory processes.

Chapter 3 presents a diffusion of innovations theoretical perspective supporting the rapid rate of diffusion of online learning during the outbreak of the COVID-19 pandemic. This chapter is focused on endured understanding learning as a critical component of learning design. The author identified essential questions to interrogate the impact of COVID-19 and other life events. The author argues, "endured understanding utilizing essential questions requires educators and learners as partners in the co-construction of learning, and as open-minded educators, creative thinkers, and courageous innovators."

Chapter 11 brings forth the realization to lecturers that each student is very different, with very different learning needs and behaviors, a key finding borne out of the COVID-19 pandemic. This chapter reflects on the lessons learnt during the emergency remote teaching and learning (ERTL) as a result of COVID-19 pandemic. The chapter postulates a personalized framework for higher education based on observed students learning behavior and literature, catering to the newly realized student and learning environment post the pandemic.

Chapter 7 outlines the need for innovative summative assessments that minimize chances of cheating or other irregularities. The author argues the need for different technologies to address connectivity and the access to knowledge and information in higher education.

Chapter 5 reflects on the challenges and changes that were incorporated into the COVID-19 pandemic. This chapter reflects on the integration of assessments, online tools of teaching and learning, active interactions, and the constructivist/progressive practices in the programs.

Chapter 4 outlines course design pedagogy for fostering the development of inclusive online world language teacher education environments. This chapter expounds on a problem-based approach, design thinking.

Chapter 1 describes the *Holistic Foundry Undergraduate Engaged Learners (FUEL)* program as an innovative and socially impactful platform and approach to virtual learning focused on STEM areas and aimed at the students underrepresented in those areas. The evaluation studies of this technological prototype allowed the authors to reach some conclusions about effective teaching and learning practices in the field of STEM using digital technologies to improve teacher–student interaction and enhance the effects of exposure to online digital resources and their applications.

Chapter 13 describes two innovative digital teaching platforms in the field of medicine (ophthalmology), which aim to mitigate the difficulties in the education of undergraduate and graduate students in medicine. The first platform aims to increase students' motivation and contribute to their practical exposure to basic clinical, research, and educational domains in ophthalmology using strategies such as virtual training, didactic lectures by external experts, active research projects, presence at local conferences, and encouraging the publication of student studies; in addition, supporting and encouraging postgraduate students to create short videos for YouTube focused on topics relevant to their colleagues from previous years. The second platform was developed and applied during the pandemic to allow medical students to continue remotely their education in ophthalmology, in both virtual and hybrid learning environments. This platform, of proven effectiveness and about to be replicated in other disciplines, consists of a virtual environment designed to carry out and present research projects from home, allowing students to interact with teachers. Resources of this nature demonstrate that in many aspects of the curriculum, it is possible to replace face-to-face learning with virtual learning environments without loss of quality.

Chapter 10 is focused on digital transition. The context is a South African university and the study considers the adoption of electronic textbooks in virtual learning platforms by accounting science teachers in their online pedagogical practice and their perception of the effectiveness and value of these resources, when compared with the traditionally used and still dominant printed academic manuals. The results indicate that although they continue to have paper textbooks in virtual learning spaces, these teachers believe in the effectiveness of these materials for teaching and learning accounting, recognize the self-efficacy of the Internet, and consider the hedonic factors and the cost of textbooks as crucial determinants in adopting e-textbook pedagogy beyond the pandemic era. Moreover, the value of the e-learning manual appears to be even greater in poor socioeconomic contexts, ensuring quality and accessible education for all in the midst of a digital transformation. As anticipated by the authors, these conclusions, similar to those of other studies with the same focus, could lead publishers to adapt e-textbook offerings to meet the needs and demands of the students and allow a smooth transition to online learning.

Since the pandemic, technological advances, which are increasingly holistic, have been widely integrated into traditional classroom teaching practices. In the longitudinal study reported by Chakravarty in Chapter 12, these developments are analyzed, taking in particular the modality of flipped classroom in a "Foundation international program" in Uzbekistan and, more specifically, in topics such as maths, ICT, and English as a foreign language. During a whole school year, the research gathered data through classroom observation, questionnaires, and semi-structured interviews with teachers and students and found positive effects of the flipped classroom on student motivation, digital awareness, and communication skills.

Chapter 9 focuses on the current and relevant theme, given the concerns about the academic integrity of online exams, comparing supervised and unsupervised exams. The study asks how emerging trends associated with online exams are perceived by Australian students enrolled in two professional disciplines with different assessment regimes. For data collection, interviews and surveys to focus groups were carried out. The results indicate that, while understanding the vulnerability of online exams, students perceive surveillance, especially when carried out by external security guards, as a source of stress, the origin of several technical challenges, and an invasion of privacy. This study suggests the need to find credible and rigorous ways of administering the assessment/examinations without resorting to invigilation.

Chapter 6 reviews the development, use, and evaluation of Birley Place, a virtual community. This platform aims to facilitate learning about socioeconomic influences on health and well-being in undergraduate health and social assistance. The program aims to help students understand the link between socioeconomic status and health and well-being in an inclusive and supportive way. The health statistics and population distribution and lifestyles used in this virtual community replicate publicly available data from the large British metropolitan city (Manchester), the context in which this study is based, which is a guarantee of authenticity in the learning. This program is a resource that well illustrates the virtues of digital technology to support high-quality learning experiences and overcome the challenges associated with limited on-campus resources or access to quality professional internships, by offering students authentic learning experiences, digital place–based learning, opportunities for collaboration and flexibility, and convenience.

Singh highlights the journey of a South African female academic during the pandemic in her transition from the face-to-face delivery method to a fully online delivery for final year students of an IT module at a public South African higher education institution, in Chapter 14. Lessons learned include the need to create social spaces, develop trust with students, guide them on the effective use of technology for engagement and collaboration, and allow the "student voice" to be projected and heard.

Taken together, these chapters present a coherent overview of recent developments in the context of the increasing digitalization of education and reflect global concerns of the academic community on how to ensure que quality of higher education by making the most of the potential and opportunities inherent in digital technologies.

The chapters included in this book address crucial questions that include or depart from a reflection on the challenges and changes on higher education resulting from the COVID-19 pandemic and the emergency online teaching and learning. Topics covered include the followings:

- technological dimensions focused on smart and immersive technologies in education, including the use of AI and innovative digital teaching platforms;
- pedagogical and didactic dimensions, such as learning design and personalized learning, innovative online assessment, and new online delivery methods beyond the era of the pandemic (such as blended models of teaching and learning like flipped classroom or the role and design of e-textbook);
- social dimensions, such as the effect of social spaces and virtual communities on student learning and engagement and inclusive and innovative and socially impactful approaches to virtual learning.

This is a seminal collection of interest to all who are concerned with innovation and the effectiveness of higher education.

Upasana Gitanjali Singh
Chenicheri Sid Nair
Susana Gonçalves

CHAPTER 1

Supporting virtual student research opportunities: the Holistic Foundry Undergraduate Engaged Learners program experience

Andrea Arce-Trigatti[1], Steffano Oyanader Sandoval[2], Pedro E. Arce[2] and J. Robby Sanders[2]

[1]Tallahassee Community College, Office of Institutional Effectiveness, Tallahassee, FL, United States
[2]Department of Chemical Engineering, Tennessee Technological University, Cookeville, TN, United States

This contribution offers insight into the development and implementation of a fully virtual undergraduate student research and mentoring opportunity entitled the Holistic Foundry Undergraduate Engaged Learners (FUEL) program. Due to the pandemic, the design of the program was intentionally virtual and leveraged different online platforms that facilitated student training, mentoring, collaboration, and research development either in a virtual or hybrid capacity. Led by a group of seven interdisciplinary leaders—including four faculty, two graduate students, and a university administrator—the conception of this program was rich in the integration of community projects, student participation, engagement in research, and the continuation of student mentoring as an additional aspect of their program of study. Delving deeper into the aspects that made this virtual program successful, the purpose of this work is to highlight best practices from the Holistic FUEL program that provide evidence and support to the use of online delivery methods as effective measures in learning and engagement that go beyond the era of the pandemic.

As part of this contribution, we present the Holistic FUEL program as a virtual learning experience that can be replicated after the era of the pandemic as an effective strategy to engage students in extracurricular research opportunities. As this program focused on the recruitment of

Digital Teaching, Learning and Assessment
DOI: https://doi.org/10.1016/B978-0-323-95500-3.00008-0

underrepresented student populations in Science, Technology, Engineering, and Mathematics (STEM) disciplines specific to the region served by the institution (e.g., females in STEM, Hispanic/Latinx, first-generation, and low socioeconomic status/rural), this allowed the authors to observe the engagement of these students in activities relevant for their professional development in the program. We begin by outlining the design and implementation of the program, focusing on the virtual platforms and digital learning aspects that students leveraged as part of their engagement in the program. This overview is supplemented with selected, illustrative examples of digital learning experiences and student data from the evaluative aspects of this program that provide insight into the effectivity of a completely virtual, extracurricular research program for undergraduate students. Preliminary analysis provides insight into the ways in which the benefits of face-to-face interaction in these types of programs were maintained or paralleled as part of this virtual learning experience.

1.1 Background and literature

1.1.1 The digital divide

Scholars van Dijk and Hacker (2003) describe the digital divide as a gap that expands beyond the availability and access to technological supports in training, education, and professional development. In particular, the digital divide, more recently, extends to more complicated social issues than one of access, enveloping challenges related to training, exposure, and experience with the use of digital technology for learning (van Dijk, 2020). This type of multifaceted challenge exposes student learning issues associated with sociocultural and socioeconomic factors related to several distinct components impacting digital learning. These include, for example, physical access to digital technology, the type of usage opportunities, the degrees of motivation to integrate technology, the type of skills developed, and the differences in levels of support. Variations in these types of digital divisions, in turn, influence the type of inequality or inequity experienced within digital learning environments that were not only present before the onset of the pandemic but were also exposed and exacerbated by the pandemic and the diverse learning environments that were created as a response to this global health crisis (van Dijk & Hacker, 2003; van Dijk, 2020).

1.1.2 Digital support for students during the pandemic

During the pandemic, postsecondary institutions found themselves transitioning quickly to online learning environments (Arce, Jorgensen, Sanders, & Arce-Trigatti, 2021). For facilitators of learning, this meant leaning on the literature and best practices espoused by experts in the digital field to help facilitate this transformation, as acknowledged by scholars reflecting on their own experiences during the early stages of the pandemic (Hedges, 2021; Iqbal, Umar, Gomez, & Umar, 2022). Quickly, it was recognized that these types of digital learning tools, if not utilized effectively, were platforms for more transactional communication, but not necessarily the tools necessary to help implement or enhance engaging experiences for students that were on par with traditional learning settings (Zha & He, 2020). As Hedges (2021) notes, "The problem was that the transition did not align with the original instructional design" of traditional digital learning practices (p. 1). This was particularly the case in laboratory or field-based disciplines, like STEM, which require students to transfer knowledge to hands-on activities, or clinical practices, that are requisite in their field (De Souza, Ochotorena, Self, & Cooper, 2021; Ramsey, 2021).

Moreover, in terms of the digital divide, it became evident that gaps relating to digital divisions and equity were becoming exacerbated in digital learning environments (Arce-Trigatti, Kelley, & Haynes, 2022; Iqbal et al., 2022). Scholars turned to digital learning to address such issues with pedagogical solutions, including, for example, flexible learning strategies, reflection-based practices, lab simulations, the use of varied technological tools as part of class, and peer-assisted small group learning (Arce et al., 2021; De Souza et al., 2021; Hedges, 2021; Zha & He, 2020). However, a study by De Souza et al. (2021) found that albeit students appreciate the opportunity to continue to learn in pandemic-era digital transitions, they also noted challenges with building community in the classroom, decreased motivation, and increased stress levels. Further, Iqbal et al. (2022) identified the limitations of digital learning in terms of the effectivity of "knowledge transfer, learning outcomes, hands-on skills, professionalism, and students' career readiness" (p. 1).

1.1.3 Lasting digital tools for student success

As Ramsey (2021) explains, the difference between such *emergency remote teaching* (ERT) as was evidenced during the early phases of the pandemic and *online delivery methods*, as an established body of best practices and scholarship related to intentional digital design structure, lies in the intentions and purpose of its use. Although several pandemic-based ERT practices were effective, the utility of such practices for engaging student learning, specifically within the digital divide, needed to be both intentional and aligned with larger learning objectives (Hedges, 2021). Specifically, several key digital practices became cornerstones of students' success during the pandemic, leading to effectivity and promise beyond the pandemic. For example, Hedges (2021) identifies the following: collaborative group activities facilitated by online platform communication, use of video resources to support student learning, the use of both synchronous and asynchronous activities, and providing a variety of different online course content for engagement.

As is clear in the literature, pandemic-based best practices that are both relevant and carry promise beyond the pandemic address the major challenges associated with these digital tools as they relate to the digital divide, equity, and intentional student learning. In the case of the Holistic FUEL program, several components related to digital learning success are inherently integrated. For example, the challenges related to knowledge transfer (Hedges, 2021) are addressed using the iterative functions of the knowledge acquisition and transfer paradigms within the Foundry pedagogical platform (Arce et al., 2015; Sanders, Arce-Trigatti, & Arce, 2020). Further, learning outcomes, professionalism, and career readiness (Iqbal et al., 2022) are embedded in the program's training curriculum, which features the development of students' skills towards research-based learning, as well as critical thinking, problem identification, and collaborative-learning techniques (Jorgensen et al., 2020; Arce-Trigatti, Jorgensen, Sanders, & Arce, 2020; Jorgensen, Arce-Trigatti, Sanders, & Arce, 2019). As an extracurricular research-focused program, the purpose of Holistic FUEL embedded hands-on and community-based exposure through various digital and virtual opportunities that not only addressed various issues associated with the digital divide, but also provided opportunities for students to gain exposure, and learn skills, relevant to their academic success.

1.2 The Holistic Foundry Undergraduate Engaged Learners program

As noted, the underlying objective of the Holistic FUEL program sought to recruit underrepresented students studying in STEM fields specific to the region served by the institution (e.g., females in STEM, Hispanic/ Latinx, first-generation, and low socioeconomic status/rural), to become part of one of five research groups on campus tasked in developing a prototype of innovative technology that was socially impactful (Arce et al., 2015). The opportunities offered by the program opened a space in which undergraduate students could engage in meaningful research activities while sharing significant personal experiences in their postsecondary training as underrepresented students in STEM. This mission aligned with key strategic planning initiatives in the region which focused on enhancing the engagement of rural and economically disadvantaged student populations (Department of Labor & Workforce Development DLWD, 2019). These populations are considered to have varying levels of access to educational opportunities concerning college readiness and preparation, access to resources that would help better prepare students for postsecondary options, and exposure to diverse professional opportunities and experiences (Potter, 2019).

1.2.1 Foundry innovation

The Holistic FUEL program was conceived as an opportunity to explore the value of more nontraditional programs, the role of mentorship, and the connections students make to research which may be valuable for underrepresented student populations in STEM. As a program designed to be intentionally virtual due to the pandemic, this also afforded the opportunity to connect students in ways to technologically based learning that was previously unavailable or unfamiliar to this population. Extant research has established that employing a pedagogical framework consistent with key concepts (e.g., knowledge acquisition, mentoring, professional skills, sense of belonging, and disciplinary identity) that help students connect their content knowledge to professional outcomes enhances motivation and confidence that supports sustained persistence (Fakayode et al., 2019; Winfield, Hibbard, Jackson, & Johnson, 2019). The Holistic FUEL program thus provided students with opportunities to engage in academic best practices that fostered comprehensive strategies for success as developed and communicated in a fundamental research project (Arce et al., 2015).

To leverage unique aspects opened by this primarily virtual learning environment, the pedagogical components of the Holistic FUEL curriculum were founded in the Foundry model. As a detailed description of the

Foundry is not within the scope of this contribution, we offer a summary in the following. The Foundry is an innovation-driven learning platform, anchored on constructivist and constructionist approaches to learning that help students navigate iterative phases of knowledge acquisition and transfer to construct new knowledge towards the development of a prototype of innovative technology (Arce et al., 2015). The pedagogical platform integrates six elements as part of the student learning experience that includes the identification of a student-driven learning challenge, organizational tools, learning cycles, resources, the linear engineering sequence, and the development of a prototype of innovative technology (Arce et al., 2015). As noted, these elements are anchored in two major cognitive processes—knowledge acquisition and knowledge transfer—that, when used iteratively, help students work collaboratively towards the design of a novel prototype of innovative technology (Arce et al., 2015). The Foundry, in tandem with the curricular learning outcomes of the Holistic FUEL program, allowed for the use of digital tools to be intentionally guided by best practices for the creation of an effective virtual learning environment.

1.2.2 Description of the program

The Holistic FUEL program was designed as a learning opportunity to invite undergraduate students into research as well as create an open environment conducive to the integration of digital tools that enhanced the experiences of students. As noted, although designed intentionally as a virtual program, with selected, integrated hybrid experiences, the Holistic FUEL program offered ways to create virtual learning environments coupled with the Foundry model that moved beyond the pandemic. The implementation phase of the program lasted one semester and comprised eight training sessions and multiple research-group and community-immersion sessions. The eight training sessions constituted the core of the curriculum and paralleled the knowledge acquisition and transfer phases of the Foundry. For example, four sessions focused on the acquisition of knowledge regarding research practices, professionalism, diversity in STEM, and other important topics, wherein the transfer of knowledge sessions focused on collaborative team efforts that applied skills learned to the development of a prototype of innovative technology (e.g., research posters and presentations) (Oyanader, Arce-Trigatti, Arce, & Sanders, 2022; Oyanader et al., 2021). Throughout the implementation of these sessions, digital tools were leveraged to help immerse, connect, and build community engagement among students in the program.

1.2.3 Digital learning focus

Guided by the Foundry, there was a motivation to integrate the prospective undergraduate researchers to the digital era. During the planning phase of the Holistic FUEL program, which occurred the semester before implementation, thoughtful and provocative conversations resulted in identifying key discerning points for success in the project as the viability of interactions was associated with higher retention rate within the student research groups. Two of the larger goals that would align with the Foundry model used to plan the research projects were anchored in the knowledge acquisition and knowledge transfer paradigms and integrated in the resultant training sessions within the curriculum (Oyanader et al., 2021). To successfully implement these goals, a thorough planning of the application of the available digital tools needed to be incorporated. Table 1.1 provides selected, illustrative examples of how digital tools were paired with Foundry model elements and learning outcomes of the curriculum to implement core aspects of the program.

For example, one learning outcome of the Holistic FUEL program was to introduce students to professional development and presentation skills, research etiquette, skills related to identification of research opportunities, teamwork practices, culturally relevant and community-based strategies in STEM. This learning outcome within a Foundry-guided approach was aligned with the knowledge acquisition paradigm and offered an opportunity for students to engage in learning cycles related to each of these components as part of the first half of the program. In the implementation of these components, students took part in both bimonthly training sessions (i.e., "town-hall" meetings) involving everyone in the program as well as private research meetings between the project leader(s) and the undergraduate researchers. In terms of the digital components leveraged for this aspect of the program, several virtual tools were integrated, including virtual conference platforms (e.g., Zoom, Teams), Internet or electronic resources (e.g., PowerPoint presentations, online guides), and collaborative digital tools (e.g., shared documentation, Google Docs, SharePoint). The integrations of these tools with the Foundry-guided aspects of the program were aligned with several best practices in the field, including the practice of building or expanding

Table 1.1 Selected, illustrative examples of digital tool applications in the Holistic Foundry Undergraduate Engaged Learners (FUEL) program.

Learning outcome	Foundry element	Program implementation	Digital tools	Best practice indicator
To introduce Holistic FUEL students to professional development and presentation skills, research etiquette, skills related to identification of research opportunities, teamwork practices, culturally relevant and community-based strategies in STEM.	Knowledge acquisition (learning cycle)	Bimonthly training sessions (i.e., "town-hall" meetings) involving everyone in the program. Private research meetings between project leader and undergraduate researcher	Virtual conference platforms (e.g., Zoom, Teams). Internet or electronic resources (e.g., PowerPoint presentations, online guides). Collaborative digital tools (e.g., shared documentation, Google Docs, SharePoint)	Build community engagement through exposure to experts in various areas. Easy access to shared resources eliminating barriers to resource availability. Exchange of resources, ideas, information by a diverse group of people
To engage Holistic FUEL students in conducting research activities, implement presentation and professional communication skills, interact with community leaders, and facilitate culturally relevant dialogue.	Knowledge transfer (linear engineering sequence)	Bimonthly training sessions (i.e., "town-hall" meetings) involving everyone in the program. Private research meetings between project leader and undergraduate researcher	Using virtual conference platforms (Zoom, Microsoft Teams, or Discord). Virtual lab simulations. Hybrid meeting practices with lab environments. Collaborative digital tools (e.g., shared documentation, Google Docs, SharePoint)	Research groups were able to discuss and collaborate on their distinctive projects. Digital platform allowed access to a neurodiverse group of underrepresented individuals in STEM, including individuals outside of the institution to be represented

To develop prototypes of innovative technology through collaborative and knowledge construction methods guided by the Foundry.	Both knowledge acquisition and knowledge transfer	Private Research meetings (both with mentor and student-led meetings) Regional and national opportunities to engage in research practices Exposition of student-led research	Using virtual conference platforms (Zoom, Microsoft Teams, or Discord) Collaborative digital tools (e.g., shared documentation, Google Docs, SharePoint) Leveraging virtual conference and research exhibitions available to students	Different venues allowed for students to understand research in diverse settings Held virtually for each individual and their respective invitees to celebrate collaboration and completion of research projects—linked to community engagement

STEM, Science, technology, engineering, and mathematics.

student exposure to community (Iqbal et al., 2022; Zha & He, 2020), the facilitation of access to shared resources in a timely and efficient manner (van Dijk, 2020), and the practice of having students actively exchange resources, ideas, and information as a diverse group of learners (De Souza et al., 2021; Hedges, 2021).

Other examples are offered in Table 1.1 to illustrate the use and alignment of digital tools within the Holistic FUEL program to best practices in the field. What can be inferred from these examples is how the digital tools paired with the Foundry offer an advantage over face-to-face learning with respect to the immediacy of information shared, convenience of access to resources, and integration of different perspectives in the conversation. For instance, these digital tools helped students in their progress to develop a prototype of innovative technology by facilitating a seamless integration of different virtual venues (e.g., virtual conferences and online research exhibitions), allowing for students to understand how research is communicated in diverse settings at their own pace. Overall, the program was useful to better understand the value that digital tools bring to student learning when connected to the Foundry model.

1.2.4 Illustrated examples of implementation

In addition to Table 1.1, the selected examples of the use of the technology for effective private research meetings are also offered. These examples expand on how the use of digital tools and platforms helped to facilitate student learning and research development as part of the Holistic FUEL program, as aligned to best practices in digital learning. These examples are written from the perspective of a graduate student mentor and a faculty mentor that participated in the program.

1.2.4.1 Research project example 1

A team of one graduate student mentor and one undergraduate student researcher was interested in investigating the modeling of drug delivery to wound healing processes. As part of the knowledge acquisition phase, both team members engaged in the use of Zoom, Microsoft Teams, and Discord to correspond and collaborate on identifying viable ideas within this field of research to further explore, leveraging videos, available electronic documents, and local expertise throughout the Holistic FUEL program. In the knowledge transfer phase of the program, the team planned to meet on a virtual platform weekly; however, with ongoing scheduling changes and life demands, each was able to relay to the other availability and coordinate a block of time to complete their tasks via digital platforms that facilitated communication and continuity. Since the research was specifically bound to digital technology and proprietary software, students were each able to work from the comfort of their own home and complete tasks at their own pace in a collaborative manner. The digital tools used allowed this team to develop an electronic poster that was submitted to a virtual, regional conference featuring their efforts.

1.2.4.2 Research project example 2

A team of two faculty mentors, a graduate student mentor, and three undergraduate student researchers was interested in exploring a research project related to the availability of wastewater treatment plants located in a specific region of the state in which they were residing. As part of the knowledge acquisition phase, digital platforms were used to provide information-rich discussions with the team members, as well as electronic-based resources helpful for better understanding the project. The prototype of innovative technology as created by the students was the formulation of a table containing information about types of treatment plants, locations, sizes, and contaminants treated as part of the contributions to public information regarding wastewater treatment. This prototype was developed using digital sharing platforms, including Microsoft Teams and SharePoint, which was then easily developed into a digital abstract and poster for a virtual, regional research conference.

1.2.4.3 Research project example 3

A team of two faculty mentors and six undergraduate students engaged in a project focused on connecting biomedical-related opportunities to local communities. As part of the knowledge acquisition phase, information was shared with students regarding the dermal wound healing process (which is an area of active research in the faculty mentors' lab) and certain connections to various disease conditions. Compromised wound healing that can occur in diabetics was pointed to as a prominent issue that can lead to limb amputation. The prevalence of diabetes was discussed; online resources were explored, and each student was tasked with the challenge to identify the prevalence of diabetes in their home county. This was followed by sharing of information at a subsequent meeting and discussions speaking to the prevalence of diabetes, health disparities (e.g., the lack of medical facilities), and the difficulties in wound repair under these conditions which provided an opportunity to make more direct connections to the work occurring in the research lab. Subsequent meetings occurred routinely using simultaneous virtual formats and hybrid/in-person opportunities that included the sharing of research data by faculty and graduate students. The use of both available digital platforms and technology to share both information and ideas ultimately helped students to begin the process of identifying a more detailed research project with the program.

1.3 Evaluative analysis

An evaluative analysis of data collected for the Holistic FUEL program was conducted for the purpose of understanding aspects of student success as aligned to the primary learning outcomes described earlier (Caffarella, 2002; Patton, 2002). These data included student responses from various survey polls incorporated as part of the eight training sessions, artifacts from student work reflective of research and training activities (e.g., completion of worksheets, online tasks), pre- and postsurveys regarding student experiences in the program, and general observations from faculty incorporated into recorded meeting notes. The student responses from various survey polls included typically 5−10 open- and closed-ended questions related to the training session for the day, wherein the pre- and postsurveys comprised approximately 20 open- and closed-ended questions, as well as reflective essay questions, regarding student demographic information, research interests, retention, persistence, achievement outcome items, and experience in the program. As part of these data, the experiences of students and faculty as they engaged in the digital aspects of the program were salient, allowing for an exploration of student satisfaction with the program, overall learning, and completion of objectives to be evaluated (Caffarella, 2002). A general content analysis of this data, which was both quantitative and qualitative in nature, allowed for general themes regarding student experiences to be identified (Patton, 2002).

The evaluative data used for this analysis were collected as part of the first cohort of the Holistic FUEL program. In total, 28 undergraduate students comprised the sample population for this data. Students represented a variety of disciplines, including chemical engineering, biology, chemistry, nursing, and STEM education, as well as a variety of grade levels (11 freshmen, 16 sophomores, and 1 junior). Within this sample, 12 males and 16 females were represented, reflective of various underrepresented student populations characteristic of the region served by the institution (e.g., females in STEM, Hispanic/Latinx, first-generation, and low socioeconomic status/rural). In terms of ethical considerations, the approval of the Institutional Research Board was sought and given for the purpose of this study. Further, to ensure confidentiality in this study, the data were intentionally disaggregated and deidentified as part of the original evaluative process.

1.4 Evaluative findings

The following provides an overview of the results of the content analysis of the evaluative data described previously. Both quantitative and qualitative data support the general themes found as associated with the learning outcomes of the Holistic FUEL program.

1.4.1 Skill development through digital knowledge acquisition and transfer

Through the abovementioned strategies, a cohesive mentoring and research-driven program provided students an opportunity to explore STEM research using a myriad of different potential projects, research teams, and training seminars. This was documented primarily through the creation and implementation of a comprehensive training program that included eight training sessions, four around research strategies, and four centered on leadership training. Throughout the course implementation, the eight sessions were planned, implemented, and evaluated through student responses from polls taken during the debriefing sessions of every training, the end-of-program exit survey, and qualitative responses during the general focus group session.

Overall, the responses captured from students expressed an appreciation for the content and deeper connections to the topics. For example, in one poll after a research-based training session, 100% (18/18) of students present indicated "Yes" when asked, "Within your research groups, do you see connections to your expressed interest?" In another end-of-session poll for leadership training, students expressed their appreciation for the content in open-ended responses, indicating appreciation for the content. This included the following responses:

Thank you for sharing your knowledge and advice!

So many success principles spoken today for not only STEM, but for life! Thank you all so very much for speaking with us today!!! I really enjoyed it!

Thank you all! This was so inspirational:)

Student responses to questions about their understanding of research in the internal metrics also revealed the value of a comprehensive training program using the Foundry. In a close-ended question, 76% of respondents indicated that they either agreed or strongly agreed with the statement: "I understand what research is." Survey results also indicated that over half of participants envisioned themselves as researchers and more than two-thirds envisioned themselves continuing to conduct research as part of their program of study.

1.4.2 The digital development of a prototype of innovative technology

In terms of the research participation aspects of this program, the major metric was the completion of a research project which could be finalized in various forms (e.g., research paper, poster, project, presentation, and data collection). With respect to the completion of research activities, all participants were afforded integration in one of their top two interests, offered full participation in the knowledge acquisition and transfer activities related to their research, and given the opportunity to become a coauthor in one of the various forms of research as developed in the program. In total, nine different final research projects were presented as part of the final virtual event for the Holistic FUEL program which consisted of two panel sessions, two presentations, and five poster presentations. The projects represented a diverse array of topics related to socially impactful research applications, biomedical research, environmental research, and agricultural applications.

Below is a summary of all project topics that were presented, as well as a summary of all research team participants:

- WCTE PBS Cohort (panel session): five students, one faculty mentor
- CARES Act Research (presentation): one student, one graduate mentor, one faculty mentor
- Electro-Assisted Wound Healing (poster session): one student, one graduate mentor, and two faculty mentors
- Drug Transport and Cancer Treatment (poster session): one student, one graduate mentor, one faculty mentor
- Featured Biomedical Research (presentation): two students, one faculty mentor
- Biomedical Cohort (panel session): six students, two faculty mentors
- Wastewater Treatment Plant (poster session): Biodigester: one student, one graduate mentor, two faculty mentors

- Photocatalysis in Water Treatment (poster session): two students, one faculty mentor
- Wastewater Treatment Plant—Survey (poster session): four students, one graduate mentor, one faculty mentor

All Holistic FUEL participants had a team of at least three research members, including a faculty mentor or a combination of faculty mentors and a graduate student mentor. All poster sessions had a graduate student mentor as a coauthor, and those projects were submitted to virtual, regional research conferences and competitions as a showcase of their learning. In addition, the socially impactful research application projects were presented at various community outlets, including a virtual, local event that offered a monetary award to help students patent their work. Furthermore, applications of the panel session have formed the basis of larger research projects, including applications in experimental and theoretical thesis projects.

Survey results collected as part of the evaluative analysis of the Holistic FUEL program also indicate that students were able to see the value of the digital experiences as part of their research development. In an open response, students offered the following as part of their digital learning experiences: "finding different solutions," "key tool in engineering," "learning new concepts," "formulating research questions," "inspirational." In one posttraining survey, over 90% of students positively affirmed that they agreed that research was valuable to their academic career. When asked on another posttraining survey, over 95% of students positively affirmed that research experiences would help them develop learning strategies.

1.5 Implications

In implementing and delivering the Holistic FUEL program, several implications can be identified with respect to this being an innovative delivery approach applicable beyond the era of the pandemic and one that enhances student learning and success.

1.5.1 As an innovative delivery approach

Three major implications are highlighted with respect to this program as an innovative delivery approach that moves beyond the pandemic. The first involves the use of online delivery methods to purvey opportunities for research outside of students' program of study. These opportunities are valuable in terms of the flexibility they provide for student populations juggling several different work, life, and school responsibilities as noted in the selected illustrative examples in this contribution. The second implication highlights the coordination between the design and delivery of the program as the program is enhanced with the use of technology (i.e., streamlined approach to communication). In addition, we noted that the use of digital technology as part of extracurricular research programs increased options for opening students to exposure to different worlds and external stakeholders.

These implications also highlight important intersections between the use of digital technology and the type of learning environment that can be offered to underrepresented students, in particular those characteristic of the populations served by the institution. For example, the digital platforms leveraged by the Holistic FUEL program allowed students a flexible research environment that worked around their schedules and would be otherwise impossible. With respect to the streamlined approach to communication, because the delivery method was digital, the focus could be maintained more readily, and integrated with other online resources, than in a traditional classroom setting. Moreover, different platforms could be combined (e.g., chat, email, collaborative electronic documents, Internet resources) in a quicker, effective method as all students interacted in the same digital setting. In terms of exposure to other stakeholders, holding digital venues and meetings allowed for connections beyond the immediate community and facilitated the external sharing of program outcomes and ideas (e.g., research conferences and research showcases). In effect, the use of digital technology to enhance student learning as part of this research opportunity offered different ways to engage and expand upon shared ideas.

1.5.2 For student learning

Three additional implications can also be identified in terms of student learning with respect to the digital aspects of the Holistic FUEL program. For example, we found that opportunities for exploration into different research avenues could be leveraged using digital technology in tandem with innovative pedagogical platforms like the Foundry model. Students' ability to share ideas, research projects, and experiences was also facilitated by use of a digital delivery method as noted in the students' reflections from the preliminary evaluation. In addition, students' exposures to the use of digital technology in new ways outside of the classroom that was also connected to vital components of their learning processes were also noted.

For student learning, the use of digital technology in the Holistic FUEL program was intertwined with the success of their experience in the research components of the delivered training. Drawing from the teams' individual areas of expertise, research topics covering biomedical applications, water and wastewater treatment, and community engagement were ultimately chosen, also reflecting student interest. The use of the digital integrative approach allowed each group to make real-time progress and to explore different points of view that may have been limited in a more constrained environment. This digital integration also connects to students' ability to exchange ideas, research projects, and experiences as Holistic FUEL resources were readily available in digital mediums allowing for more effective sharing. Thus there was a seamless integration of technology into the Holistic FUEL program that is potentially otherwise not available or allowed in traditional learning spaces. The availability of this type of seamless integration, in turn, offered students exposure to the use and utility of technology and digital learning mediums that they could leverage in their academic programs of study, as useful resources beyond the program, and as tools in the overall student success practices.

1.6 Summary and concluding remarks

The purpose of this contribution was to present the Holistic FUEL program as a virtual learning experience that can be adopted as an innovative approach beyond the pandemic that employs the use of digital learning paired with an innovation-driven learning platform. As part of this effort, we observed that the integration of the Foundry with effective digital delivery methods enables an inclusive and comprehensive strategy to engage students in extracurricular research opportunities, relevant to underrepresented students who participated in the program. Specifically, the design and implementation of the Holistic FUEL program incorporated the use of virtual platforms and digital learning aspects that students could utilize to explore different avenues of research, engage with relevant resources, and make connections to their own research interests. The program examples and student data from the evaluative aspects of this program offered more information concerning the effectiveness of hybrid, virtual, extracurricular research programs for undergraduate students. Lessons learned from this program include how best practices in digital technology can help enhance the interaction of faculty and students within an extracurricular research experience, the benefits associated with more exposure to online digital resources and their applications, as well as the learning processes associated with using this technology in tandem with the Foundry.

In particular, there were several components of the digital tools leveraged in this program that can be linked to best practices as described in the extant literature. The use of digital and conference platforms, Internet resources, and digital tools for collaboration, for example, in helping students to gain professional, research, and teamwork skills can relate to scholarship reinforcing the benefits of digital community building (Ramsey, 2021), effective access to shared resources (Iqbal et al., 2022), and the exchange of resources, ideas, and knowledge (Hedges, 2021). The use of virtual lab simulations and hybrid meeting practices with lab environments additionally provided students with ability to discuss and collaborate on their distinctive projects with a neurodiverse group of underrepresented individuals in STEM (De Souza et al., 2021; Iqbal et al., 2022). Leveraging virtual conferences and research exhibitions also allowed for students to use diverse technical skills (van Dijk, 2020) allowing them to navigate avenues where research was presented to better understand research implications in diverse settings.

This strategy is promising to attract and engage students from underrepresented populations, particularly those representatives of areas like the one in which this program was implemented. The example of the Holistic FUEL program as applied to these particular student populations builds on other literary work that provides information on how Foundry-guided approaches coupled with the use of digital tools offer a potential avenue to build skills related to student success (Arce et al., 2021; Oyanader et al., 2021). Specific to the Holistic FUEL program, as the digital divide typically brings challenges to the use, familiarity, and availability of digital learning and resources to rural areas, the data from this study suggest that the scaffolding approach through the use of the Foundry can potentially attenuate these challenges (Oyanader et al., 2021; van Dijk, 2020). For instance, students were able to interact, explore, and exchange ideas not only with one another, but also with faculty, graduate students, and other members of the learning community that were facilitated through the use of a digital medium that allowed for easier coordination and increased communication opportunities (e.g., via chat and virtual conversations). In leveraging these tools a wonderful opportunity for learning exchanges occurred in organic ways through the integration of digital tools that were connected via the Internet and the digital platforms used. Acknowledging these digital gaps is therefore an important aspect of designing and delivering these programs, and then integrating effective tools to provide necessary scaffolds for student success is needed to achieve a larger, common goal as related to research.

Acknowledgments

We would like to thank all the members of the Holistic FUEL Directorship team, including Dr. Stephanie Jorgensen and Michael Aikens, all student partners who participated in the Holistic FUEL program, and all affiliated community partners. We also appreciate the generous support of the Tennessee Board of Regents, via the Student Engagement, Retention, and Success Grant program.

References

Arce, P. E., Jorgensen, S., Sanders, R. J., & Arce-Trigatti, A. (2021). Only two weeks: The lived experiences of four engineering educators transitioning to virtual learning during the 21st century pandemic. *American Educational History Journal, Special Edition*, 163–171.

Arce, P. E., Sanders, J. R., Arce-Trigatti, A., Loggins, L., Biernacki, J., Geist, M., … Wiant, K. (2015). The Renaissance Foundry: A powerful learning and thinking system to develop the 21st century engineer. *Critical Conversations in Higher Education*, *1*(2), 176–202.

Arce-Trigatti, A., Jorgensen, S., Sanders, J.R., & Arce, P.E. (2020). Constraining the landscape: Unpacking the inquiry learning aspects of the foundry model for the purpose of curriculum design. In: *Proceedings from the American society for engineering education southeastern conference*. March 6–10, 2020. Auburn, Alabama.

Arce-Trigatti, A., Kelley, J., & Haynes, A. (2022). On new ground: Assessment strategies for critical thinking skills as the learning outcome in a social problems course. *New directions for teaching and learning* (Vol. 2022, pp. 83–97). Special issue: International perspectives on university teaching and learning. Spring. Available from https://doi.org/10.1002/tl.20484.

Caffarella, R. S. (2002). *Planning programs for adult learners (2nd edition)*. Jossey-Bass.

De Souza, N., Ochotorena, M., Self, B.P., & Cooper, L.A. (2021, July). Sudden shift to online learning: COVID-19 impact on engineering student experiences. In: *2021 ASEE virtual annual conference content access, virtual conference*. Available from https://peer.asee.org/37784.

Department of Labor and Workforce Development [DLWD]. (2019). *Millions of dollars earmarked for Tennessee's rural communities*. Newsroom. Retrieved from https://www.tn.gov/workforce/general-resources/news/2019/8/9/millions-of-dollarsearmarked-for-tennessees-rural-communities.html.

Fakayode, S. O., Davis, J. J., Yu, L., Meikle, P. A., Darbeau, R., & Hale, G. (2019). Transforming STEM departments for inclusion: Creative innovation, challenges, adaptation, and sustainability at the University of Arkansas-Fort Smith. In Z. S. Wilson Kennedy, G. S. Byrd, E. Kennedy, & H. T. Frierson (Eds.), *Broadening participation in STEM* (pp. 73−105). Emerald Publishing Limited.

Hedges, K. E. (2021, July). The COVID-19 pandemic: The hallmarks of online and hybrid teaching in the engineering classroom. In: *2021 ASEE virtual annual conference content access*, virtual conference. Available from https://peer.asee.org/37845.

Iqbal, U., Umar, A., Gomez, J., & Umar, M. (2022). Impact of COVID-19 pandemic on engineering education: Evaluation of limitations and recommendations for effective teaching. In: *2022 ASEE southeast section conference proceedings*. Available from https://sites.asee.org/se/wp-content/uploads/sites/56/2022/03/2022ASEESE88.pdf.

Jorgensen, S., Arce-Trigatti, A., Sanders, J. R., & Arce, P. E. (2019). Promoting innovative learning strategies: A collaborative curricular re-design at the undergraduate level. In: *Proceedings from the American society for engineering education southeastern conference*. March 10−12, 2019. Raleigh, North Carolina.

Jorgensen, S., Arce-Trigatti, A., Sanders, J. R., & Arce, P. (2020). A focus on functional-based teams in the development of prototypes of innovative technology: Observations from a QEP grant implementation at Tennessee Tech. In: *Proceedings from the American society for engineering education southeastern conference*. March 8−10. Auburn, Alabama.

Oyanader, S., Hevia, L., Arce-Trigatti, A., Jorgensen, S., Sanders, J. R., & Arce, P. (2021). 'Role of the graduate student mentors in the successful recruitment and mentoring of underrepresented minorities in STEM research initiatives.' In: *14th annual Tennessee STEM education research conference* [virtual conference due to COVID-19]. January 16−17.

Oyanader, S., Arce-Trigatti, A., Arce, P. E., & Sanders, J. R. (2022). The Holistic F.U.E. L. program: A Renaissance Foundry-designed mentoring approach for diverse and historically excluded populations. *Journal on Excellence in College Teaching, 33*(4), 37−58.

Patton, M. (2002). *Qualitative research and evaluation methods* (3rd edition). Sage Publications.

Potter, D. W. (2019). *Integrated versus traditional curriculum: moderating effects of gender and aptitude on high school ACT mathematics achievement* [Doctoral dissertation]. Cookeville, TN: Tennessee Tech University, ProQuest.

Ramsey, H. (2021, April). Lessons from listening to students during the COVID-19 pandemic: Using self-determination theory to contextualize course evaluations and best practices for online teaching. In: *2021 ASEE pacific southwest conference − "Pushing Past Pandemic Pedagogy: Learning from Disruption"*, virtual. Available from https://peer.asee.org/38239.

Sanders, J., Arce-Trigatti, A., & Arce, P. (2020). Promoting student problem-identification skills via a jeopardy-inspired game within the Renaissance Foundry. *Education for Chemical Engineers, 30*, 49−59.

van Dijk, J. (2020). *The digital divide*. Wiley & Sons.

van Dijk, J., & Hacker, K. L. (2003). The digital divide as a complex and dynamic phenomenon. *Information Society, 19*(4), 315−326.

Winfield, L. L., Hibbard, L. B., Jackson, K. M., & Johnson, S. S. (2019). Cultivating agency through the chemistry and biochemistry curriculum at Spelman College. In: Broadening Participation in STEM (Diversity in Higher Education), (Vol. 22, pp. 153−181). Emerald Publishing Limited.

Zha, S., & He, W. (2020). Pandemic pedagogy in online hands-on learning for it/is courses, communications of the association for information systems. *Communications of the Association for Information Systems, 44*(1), 124−131.

CHAPTER 2

Digital education for a resilient new normal using artificial intelligence—applications, challenges, and way forward

Anju Kalluvelil Janardhanan[1], Kavitha Rajamohan[2], K.S. Manu[3] and Sangeetha Rangasamy[3]
[1]Southern Cross Institute, Parramatta, NSW, Australia
[2]School of Sciences, CHRIST University, Bangalore, Karnataka, India
[3]School of Business and Management, CHRIST University, Bangalore, Karnataka, India

2.1 Introduction

Over the years, the education system has been transformed according to the increasing demands of contemporary society, advances in technology, changing student personality traits, and requirements of Industry 4.0. The education system is perceived as an important tool for the development of individuals, families, businesses, society, and the economy. Educators are using digital tools and technologies to be innovative in teaching, learning, and assessing students. Hence it is observed that digital education is becoming more ubiquitous in the educational system and replacing traditional education following the COVID-19 pandemic. Previously, digital education was a trend only in institutions that provided higher education. Still, it is now becoming a staple of the education system and displacing traditional schools or lecturing in classrooms. Technology-enhanced learning (TEL) environment combines digital technologies (Law, Niederhauser, Christensen, & Shear, 2016) and strategies to facilitate teacher—student interaction in online education and other types of Internet-supported mediums of learning (Tsai, 2017). Smart classes emerged as a new TEL environment that enables teachers to use digital technology for teaching and assessment. However, the growing pace and popularity of digital technology show that even the educational ecosystem needs to undergo further change to make teaching, learning, and assessment resilient in the new normal. Advances in big data analytics, Internet of things (IoT),

Digital Teaching, Learning and Assessment
DOI: https://doi.org/10.1016/B978-0-323-95500-3.00001-8

artificial intelligence (AI), machine learning (ML), deep learning (DL), virtual reality (VR), etc. are making a great revolution by transforming all aspects of education in terms of teaching, learning, assessment, and feedback. AI consists of computer systems that can carry out human-like functions such as adapting, learning, synthesizing, correcting, and utilizing a variety of data required for processing complex calculations (Popenici & Kerr, 2017). AI has created a plethora of new prospects and challenged academics in the education sector (Silander & Stigmar, 2019). There are many supporting tools such as Grammarly, SchooLinks, Quizlet, and MobyMax that were developed using ML and DL algorithms.

There are a significant number of studies that highlighted the impact of AI on all dimensions of the education sector. AI-powered systems provide opportunities to enhance the overall productivity of the education sector by designing adaptive learning systems, creating analytical dashboards, establishing classroom monitoring systems, implementing simulated models with the help of augmented and VR, and using robots for teaching (Vorst & Jelicic, 2019). An application of AI is the support of intelligent tutoring systems (ITSs) in personalized learning (Chaudhry & Kazim, 2021). Students can use teaching assistants (interactive chatbots) to learn virtually (Sharma, 2021) and to understand students' behavior and emotions (sentiment analysis). An AI-powered writing assistant helps to find out mistakes in the text and suggests easier and more effective learning processes. Further, AI helps to automate manual tasks in education like attendance handling and other inventory management works. A pilot study was done on a digital chatbot to support medical education at Warwick Medical School, United Kingdom (Kaur, Singh, Chandan, Robbins, & Patel, 2021). The function of the developed chatbot is to work as a virtual consultant in a diabetes clinic to learn about patients during pandemic situations. AI incorporated a cooperative hand gesture learning model developed to work as a tutor for disabled people (Banerjee, Lamrani, Hossain, Paudyal, & Gupta, 2020). This expert gesture model teaches students and gives feedback to the learner for their improvement. To maximize the benefit of using AI, it is important to create an appropriate plan with AI governance by the education system. Hence it is essential to understand the applications and challenges of using AI for digital education. This chapter discusses the paradigm shift in TEL, the emerging need for digital education, and technologies used in digital education. To achieve the study objectives, a comprehensive evaluation of the contributions of AI is conducted in the areas of teaching, learning, and assessment. AI-integrated learning analytics help management, teachers, students, parents, and other stakeholders to gain insight into their performance to understand the impact of AI on the process. The analysis and discussions are presented along with strengths, weaknesses, opportunities, and challenges (SWOC) and the way forward.

2.2 Technology-enhanced learning—a paradigm shift

Communication and interaction across the globe have been transformed by the digital revolution at the turn of the century. Education has evolved in modern times to include a wide range of technological tools and to offer students access to online classes regardless of their geographical location. TEL is more than bringing technology into the learning spaces, it is about linking the educational and technological divides. In the wake of the COVID-19 pandemic, TEL became more prevalent worldwide because students heavily resorted to technology for their course learning and social connections. Due to the rapid development of Information and Communication Technologies (ICTs), the landscape of education and training has undergone a significant transformation in the past decade. Universities aim for offering simple teaching and learning online from anywhere in the world via the Internet while companies want to train employees anywhere anytime. Education using technology has transformed into an integral part of learning with distance education, Massive Open Online Courses, and smart devices in the classroom. During the COVID-19 pandemic, educational institutions and students depended on digital technologies as the primary medium of education (Mustapha, Van, Shahverdi, Qureshi, & Khan, 2021). Digitization of teaching, learning, assessment, and administrative processes in the educational environment has become essential for all higher education institutions (HEI) in the new normal. Teachers and students are optimistic about these developments due to the change in lifestyle, work culture, stakeholders' expectations, and the ongoing requirement for quality and efficiency. Adapting the curriculum for a digitally connected future is a major challenge for higher education along with transforming pedagogy to keep pace with the digital age. As digital technology continues to bring rapid changes, the content and intent of a curriculum for the coming digital age should also reflect these shifting paradigms. Industrial Revolution (IR) 4.0 is built on AI and it will be able to shift the working environment from task-oriented to human-centered characteristics such as understanding the user, application of multidisciplinary skills and perspectives in the task environment. In the last three decades, AI applied to education has generated effective learning experiences and rewarding interactive experiences for students. The ITS encompasses most AI topics and has proven to be a reliable measure for formalizing cognitive theories. Smart content, personalized learning, ML, admin tasks, voice assistants, virtual learning knowledge representation, intelligent tutoring, natural language processing, and DL are some of the most common AI applications in the educational industry.

2.3 Emerging need for digital education

In the context of IR 4.0, higher education is a challenging and exciting opportunity that has the potential to represent a paradigm shift in society. As the digital native generation is inspired by TEL, digital education is considered to be the apex of modern education. The growing digital transformation makes information technology skills imperative for schools, universities, and businesses. To be successful in future employment, students will need the appropriate digital education. Furthermore, digital education will help businesses stay competitive. To put it another way, Industry 4.0 necessitates Education 4.0. There is a need to dramatically shift how and what students learn as a result of the digital transformation because digital skills have become an inevitable competency along with reading, writing, communication, mathematical reasoning, and critical thinking. AI technology can be used to improve human productivity and promote human intelligence. The ability to adjust curriculum and approaches to students' unique requirements is now attainable due to the new alternatives available in AI for analyzing data. ITSs can monitor their development and determine which topics have been learned and which still require additional training. Precision education is the new challenge faced in the application of AI due to the advances in transfer learning (Yang, 2021). In precision education, the content may be tailored to meet the needs of individual students while also concentrating on their overall development. It is a unique and innovative technique to identify students at risk. Correct identification is critical for the success of precision education. But it is very difficult to recognize students with low academic performance or low engagement or poor learning behavior and provide timely support to improve their learning and performance. Also, to improve teaching quality, teachers have to identify areas or topics of concern and provide constructive feedback to overcome the issues. Students also require training to identify their gaps in skills and knowledge to take responsibility for their learning. This will facilitate more personalized learning and help students to meet their educational goals. With the help of smart evaluation, precision education can be made more effective. The benefits of digital education are better management of time, learning from any place, promotion of newer educational pedagogies, and learning at own pace (Ozga, 2016). For digital education to become a reality, the focus of educational training given to teachers must also be changed. Digital education necessitates well-trained teachers who can communicate relevant knowledge to students, trainees, and college students via digital platforms.

2.4 Technologies for digital education

Nowadays, it is essential to follow the trends and developments in the education sector. One among these is digital learning, combining technology with education to create high-quality teaching and learning practice that results in better outcomes. Digital education includes digital learning, education technology, online education, virtual learning, eLearning, and blended learning (Paul, 2021). There are many technologies such as IoT, blockchain, AI, big data, learning analytics, gamification, VR, and AR that are the backbone of digital education. Of all these technologies, AI plays an important role in digital education by automating all the basic activities such as virtual tutors and smart evaluation.

2.4.1 Internet of things

IoT is a complex network where thousands of smart devices are connected to sense the environment using sensors and share the data to investigate and make decisions in real time. This technology is used to change the physical world environment to an automated world environment which is controlled by smart devices. Automated attendance recording, supporting disability, interactive learning using mobile applications, smart devices, smart boards, and integrated alarms for safety in school buildings are a few examples of applications of IoT in education. Although the IoT technology is in early-stage implementation in the education field, it shifts the teaching and learning process from traditional to digital education in the form of connected smart classrooms.

2.4.2 Artificial intelligence

For more than three decades, AI has been involved in education to investigate the traditional classroom to support lifelong learning. AI is a powerful tool which helps to understand the "block box of learning" (trying to understand the outer process where the detail process is complex to understand) of a student and this understanding can be used by teachers for effective classroom management. AI is computer software which mimics human intelligence and is made up of different algorithms such as decision support system (DSS), ML, DL, and reinforcement learning (RL). These algorithms are used to produce models which represent knowledge about the real world. In digital education, models are developed to understand the knowledge and expertize of the teacher (teaching), comprehend the subject being learned (learning), and evaluate the knowledge of the learner (assessment). As mentioned in Fig. 2.1, digital learning is developed by AI and AI consists of different algorithms such as DSS, ML, DL, and RL. These algorithms are helping in the teaching, learning, and assessment process in terms of learning analytics and knowledge dissemination, adaptive learning and personalized learning, and feedback analysis and course assessment.

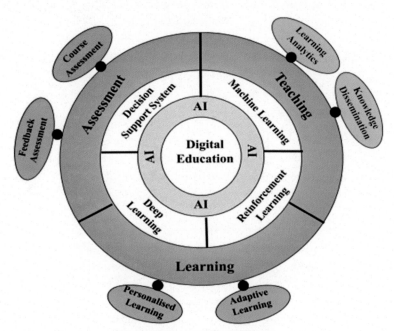

Figure 2.1 Role of AI in education. *AI*, Artificial intelligence.

2.4.2.1 Decision support system

DSS is built for providing solutions to problems that are generally solved by experts in particular areas. This system is made up of models like case-based reasoning or expert systems.

Generally, these models provide solutions in five stages (Ragan & McFarland, 1987):

1. identification: determining problem characteristics,
2. conceptualization: finding concepts to represent knowledge,
3. formalization: designing structures to organize knowledge,
4. implementation: formulating rules that embody knowledge, and
5. testing: validating rules that embody knowledge.

DSS is popularly used in many areas, one among them being the education domain. This system is used to understand out the growth of learners such as students' learning capability, performance analysis, and prediction of future performance. The DSS is used in many more education applications, where the primary purpose is to achieve educational goals.

2.4.2.2 Machine learning

ML is an intelligent algorithm that learns from experience to make predictions for a specific predetermined objective. This algorithm is acknowledged as a game-changer in many sectors like healthcare, manufacturing, transportation, education, etc. In education, it plays a vital role in all stages such as primary, middle, and higher education both in the offline and online modes of education. ML not only contributed to ITSs, predicting student dropout, predicting student performance, understanding the (adaptive and predictive) learning style and group-based learning but also automated the entire teaching, learning, and assessment models and performance analysis (Munir, Vogel, & Jacobsson, 2022). ML algorithms are proving that it is capable of providing extensive support to tutors, students, education institutions, and policymakers.

2.4.2.3 Reinforcement learning

RL is a type of algorithm that helps to develop the learning policies in real time as a model that can learn the relation between activity, action, and outcome of any educational course to increase the learning gains. A reinforcement scheduling algorithm (Bassen et al., 2020) is introduced to improve learning, reduce the work of learners, instructors, and course designers. In this algorithm, an RL agent assigns activities in an online course. Over time, this method learns latent relationships between actions (assignments), states (learner traces), and rewards (outcomes) to schedule better and fewer activities for these learners. This method helps the instructor to frame assignment strategy, number and nature of assignments, student dropout, and finally design the course without the intervention of the course instructor.

2.4.2.4 Deep learning

DL is a type of algorithm based on neural networks that train the computer to think and act like a human. DL is the subset of ML which is inspired by the function of the human brain to perform real-time complex tasks. In education, these algorithms are used to support teachers to identify the slow and weak learners, predict students' performance, provide customized teaching, and organize content effectively to improve retention. A case study conducted to predict the probability of students dropping out of universities in Taiwan revealed that the reasons for dropout are students' academic performance, study/educational loans, and irregularity in attending class (Tsai, Chen, Shiao, Ciou, & Wu, 2020). The finding of this study can help universities to strategize and suggest courses based on their interests and capability to avoid future dropouts.

2.5 Role of artificial intelligence in education

The application of AI enables an interdisciplinary approach to face challenges in all sectors. In the same way, the role of AI in education may enhance the whole teaching, learning, and evaluation process. All the stakeholders of the education sectors, namely, the government, regulatory authorities, management, teachers, and students understand the requirements, the effectiveness of the teaching pedagogy, and so on. However, the advantage of AI can be enjoyed if an appropriate plan with AI governance is developed.

2.5.1 Intelligent assistance for education

To understand the role of AI in education from the perspective of teaching, learning, and assessment, six objectives are stated for data analysis. The mapping of the dataset with examples, along with their focus and study objectives are mentioned in Table 2.1. The six datasets are retrieved from a public domain Kaggle—a subsidiary of Google LLC which is a repository of the volume of data for research purposes.

Table 2.1 Intelligence assistance in teaching, learning, and assessment.

Perspective	Example and dataset	Focus	Study objective
Teaching	Example 1: Data from Das (2022)	Learning analytics	To analyze the effect of different teaching styles on student's math scores
	Example 2: Data from Alshiekh (2021)	Knowledge dissemination	To understand the responses to different levels of course in Udemy
Learning	Example 3: Data from Kiwelekar (2020)	Adaptive learning	To predict end-semester exam performance
	Example 4: Data from Seshapanpu (2018)	Personalized learning	To understand the influence of test preparation on student's performance
Assessment	Example 5: Data from Ferrari (2019)	Feedback assessment	To understand student's online behavior and their grading for classroom participation
	Example 6: Data from Caellwyn (2021)	Course assessment	To predict student success in online courses using a virtual learning environment

The following examples demonstrate the benefits of using AI in teaching, learning, and assessment as discussed in Fig. 2.1.

2.5.1.1 Artificial intelligence in teaching

Example 1: Learning analytics.

Data from Das (2022) explain the three teaching methods, the traditional method and the standards-based method in problem-solving used by three different teachers who teach math to 8th-grade students. Ms. Wesson's approach to teaching math would be defined as the traditional method, whereas Ms. Ruger and Ms. Smith's approach to teaching math is defined as the standards-based method. Teachers are very confident and comfortable in their methods of teaching. School management wishes to know whether they must adopt different methods for different sections or one best method for all the students. Hence, they have investigated the past three years' data to understand the effectiveness of the teaching methods followed by three math teachers. Fig. 2.2 reveals that there is an impact of the method of teaching adopted by the teachers on the math scores obtained by students. This is an opt example to prove that, using appropriate statistical tools and techniques, the effectiveness of teaching can be assessed and enhanced (Fig. 2.2).

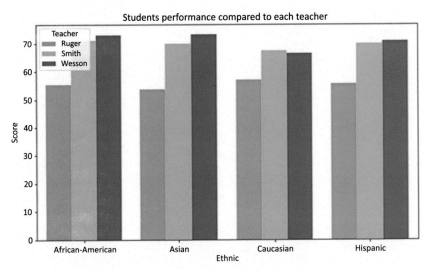

Figure 2.2 Student's math scores for different teaching styles.

Example 2: Knowledge dissemination.

Another interesting piece of data from Alshiekh (2021) collected by Udemy online education platform on various levels of courses offered is to understand the effectiveness of the courses and the acceptance level of the learners.

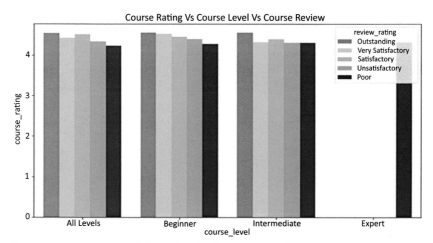

Figure 2.3 Responses to different levels of courses in Udemy.

Fig. 2.3 shows that the expert-level courses are not rated well by the learners. Based on this finding, Udemy can plan the new courses to be introduced and the modifications required in the existing courses offered. This also proves the need for and importance of using advanced tools and techniques to analyze the student's response for a better learning experience.

2.5.1.2 Artificial intelligence in learning

Example 3: Adaptive learning.

AI can be used to assess the factors influencing students' learning. Data from Kiwelekar (2020) were made to predict the performance of students in the end-semester exam (ESE). The various parameters considered are the number of hours of study, attendance of students, and the marks obtained in the mid-semester exam (MSE).

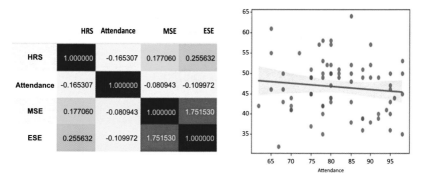

Figure 2.4 ESE performance. *ESE*, End-semester exam.

Based on Fig. 2.4, attendance has a very low negative relation with all the three independent variables, HRS (hours spent), MSE, and ESE. MSE exam scores can be used to predict ESE exam scores since both are correlated to each other. Hence it is proven that advanced tools like AI, ML, DL, and RL can be used to predict the factors influencing the dependent variable (knowledge acquisition, learning styles, student performance in ESE, etc.).

Example 4: Personalized learning.

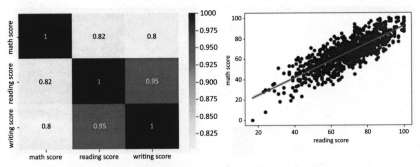

Figure 2.5 Influence of test preparation on students' performance.

Data from Seshapanpu (2018) were used to understand students' performance in math exams based on the relationship between reading and writing scores, results presented in Fig. 2.5. Teachers can show these results and motivate the students to improve their reading and writing skill to improve their performance in the exam. Hence it can be recommended that AI as an advanced tool can help in understanding the learning styles of the students and its effect on their performance through different types of data, namely, structured and unstructured. Personalized learning is an emerging area which can be applied to the available data and modifications in the learning styles can be recommended authentically.

2.5.1.3 Artificial intelligence in assessment

Example 5: Feedback assessment.

AI can help in assessing the student feedback on the sessions conducted for different courses in different dimensions. An example using data from

Ferrari (2019) demonstrates that in addition to the traditional grading system, the faculty can take instant feedback on the students. Even feedback from the students on their peers' postings is encouraged in the form of reactions. This innovative assessment of the teacher can be evaluated to understand the effectiveness of this method as well as students' response and participation with the available data through AI tools.

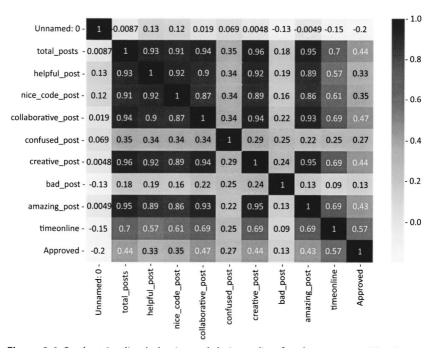

Figure 2.6 Students' online behavior and their grading for classroom participation.

Fig. 2.6 depicts the correlation between online behavior and their grading for classroom participation. It is clear that with the help of AI not only the results but also the approaches to get the results can be evaluated. This will help in improving the quality of the data, methods, and assessments.

Example 6: Course assessment.

With the help of AI, the teacher can plan an intervention to make the course more effective.

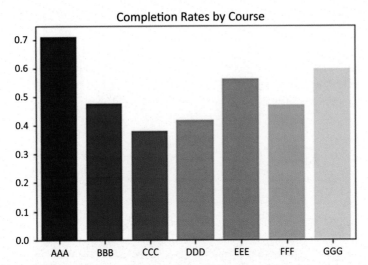

Figure 2.7 Student success in online courses using a virtual learning environment.

Using data from Caellwyn (2021), the assessment scores were captured and analyzed on seven online courses (coded as AAA, BBB, CCC, DDD, EEE, FFF, and GGG). The main objective is to understand students' performance and its effect on their successful completion of the courses to predict whether they will ultimately pass or fail a course. This model captured the underlying patterns of students' behavior which can predict the success of students in any self-paced online learning environment. Fig. 2.7 exhibits the comparative distribution and outcome of the efforts. This will help the tutor to plan and execute future courses accordingly.

The rationale for using the above datasets is to demonstrate the role of AI techniques to investigate the effectiveness of teaching, learning, and assessment as shown in Fig. 2.1. Based on the results and discussion presented in this section, it is evident that the collection of data about various methods used for teaching, learning, and assessment support the study objectives and the examples help to understand the effectiveness of the same. To be specific, Figs. 2.2 and 2.3 indicate to the management the teaching method to be used to meet the requirements of the learner, whereas Figs. 2.4 and 2.5 demonstrate the effect of learners' effort and its impact on their academic performance. In the same way, Fig. 2.6 indicates the teachers about the behavior of students and their feedback patterns to understand their involvement in providing feedback on peers' performance. Fig. 2.7 demonstrates the factors to be considered to make a course successful in self-paced learning courses.

2.5.2 Applications of artificial intelligence

AI applications are considered game-changing technological innovations in the education sector. AI, including ML and DL, techniques can be used to facilitate effective learning systems by customizing the content, delivery, and assessment based on the requirement of students. AI-powered predictive models can be applied to predict the student's performance in terms of their involvement, engagement, dropouts, and learning rates. AI application improves the overall efficiency of the education system by including all the stakeholders such as students, management, teachers, parents, and society. Some of the important applications of AI are discussed next.

2.5.2.1 Artificial intelligence–powered chatbots

The various applications of chatbots in education include teaching, learning, assessment research and development, administration, and other advisory services (Okonkwo & Ade-Ibijola, 2021). AI-powered chatbots can interact with students' questions automatically and improve the learning experience. Chatbots focus on personalized learning of each student based on their skills, needs, aptitudes, and academic and personal data. These interactive AI platforms can make the learning process interesting and fun. This AI technology encourages students to participate actively and engage students more effectively (Aivo, 2019). AI chatbots create innovative learning platforms, allowing the students to have a series of interactive conversations that are available 24/7. Chatbots understand the student's shortcomings and improve the student's academic performance by providing intelligent and genuine feedback. AI chatbots are digital learning assistants and can store a massive amount of information, questions, and summary points related to the subject concepts. Further, students can access these insights instantly. The monotonousness and fatigue of teaching the same concepts and clarifying the same doubts can be done by the chatbot. Finally, based on the student's feedback, AI chatbots can help to design smart subject content for a better learning process and experience (Soni, 2022).

2.5.2.2 Artificial intelligence–assisted tutor

ITSs use advanced computer systems such as AI-based DL algorithms to provide personalized learning to users based on their requirements, namely, preferred learning methods, timing, the pace of learning, and so on. Personalized learning emphasizes face-to-face learning and tries to customize unique content, learning methods, and teaching strategies for each student. ITS can be implemented through four main interactive components (Akyuz, 2020).

1. The knowledge base is the central component of the learning process which contains the domain knowledge.
2. The student model analyses the student's current learning state and finds out the level of training required.
3. The pedagogical module contains unique and suitable training methods.
4. Finally, the user interfaces to effectively communicate between the students and instructors.

Designing the AI-powered intelligent tutoring robots (ITR) process starts with understanding the environment and suggesting interactive models for students, the social milieu, and the curriculum (Yang & Zhang, 2019). The ITR model teaches the learning process achieved through three phases, perception–planning–action.

1. Perception—It uses a multimodel communication channel to gather sufficient information about the student and analyze the student's current state in terms of knowledge and learning style.
2. Plan—Develop a model for each student or group of students that predict short- and long-term teaching strategies.
3. Action—Delivering and transmitting the teaching content to students and receiving feedback.

2.5.2.3 Artificial intelligence–assisted teaching plan and evaluation

Assessment and feedback outcomes are very critical elements in the educational system. Post-COVID-19, its role has changed significantly. Due to the pandemic, there is a rise in online learning. AI technology made assessment and feedback processes more effective, reliable, and valid. Finally, learning need and outcome decides the right type of assessment method. The roles of AI in different types of assessments in higher education are as follows:

1. Summative assessment—Students' performances are assessed at the end of the course through tests, grades, and projects.
2. Formative assessment—Students' performances are assessed throughout the course and continuous feedback is given to students on their learning performance.

3. E-Assessment—It is a technology-enabled assessment that uses advanced technology in the assessment and feedback process. It provides a flexible learning system using innovative and collaborative methods.
4. Self and peer assessment—Self-assessment encourages students to involve actively in their evaluation process and makes them independent learners. Peer assessment involves fellow students assessing and assigning grades. Generally, quizzes, presentations, and test performances are assessed using peer assessment. It encourages students' learning and effective feedback system. It supports collaborative learning and encourages independent learning (Hooda, Rana, Dahiya, Rizwan, & Hossain, 2022).

The AI technology is to enhance the quality of continuous assessment mainly to have personalized feedback from students and assess their performance with different types of information. Samarakou et al. (2016) studied detailed reviews on AI-based assessment and found that most of the literature supports AI technology is mostly used for automating the grading of students based on the task performed (González-Calatayud, Prendes-Espinosa, & Roig-Vila, 2021). Perhaps AI and ML models place a significant role in the formative and summative educational assessment process (Gardner, O'Leary, & Yuan, 2021). Computerized adaptive test is a vital ML-based assessment mainly used in summative assessment processes like a large number of employee selection processes, a large number of applicants' selection for business schools through the entrance test for Graduate Management Admission Test, and their assessment.

2.5.2.4 Virtual reality and augmented reality in education

AR and VR are immersive technologies where users can learn digital content and physical elements through visualization. It is a blend of virtual and real-world learning. VR turns out more of a virtual environment wherein AR augments more of the real-world scenes. AR/VR can create innovative and interactive learning platforms for all educators. These include the creation of low-risk virtual simulations for higher education courses like medical, science, and technical courses. Further, it can extend to libraries of virtual content and learning tools for disabled students (Martin, 2022).

Some of the courses which use AR/VR applications are as follows:
1. STEM education—provides immersive learning which offers hands-on experiences that would be practically difficult in the real world.

For example, a team of researchers from the University of Arizona (Dick, 2021) developed a VR teaching tool named polar explorer. This VR tool teaches students the effect of climate change on polar environments. It provides students with an interactive virtual field trip experience to the Arctic.

2. Medical training—AR/VR tools provide in-person training to medical students for interacting with patients, handling complex situations, and providing virtual solutions with low risk and cost. For example, a team of researchers of Case Western Reserve University developed a program named "HoloAnatomy" which assists the students to learn with 3D anatomical models and can get instant feedback.

3. Arts and humanities—university of arts initiated a VR program named "immersive media" which provides innovative instruction methods based on immersive technologies.

4. Soft skills and career development—digital soft skills training institute developed a platform known as Bodyswaps which designs a 15-min training model and trains workplace communication skills and instant feedback system for new employees (Dick, 2021)

2.6 Strengths, weaknesses, opportunities, and challenges of digital education

Fig. 2.8 shows SWOC analysis of digital education from the point of view of teaching (T), learning (L), and assessment (A) as per the framework in explained in Fig. 2.1.

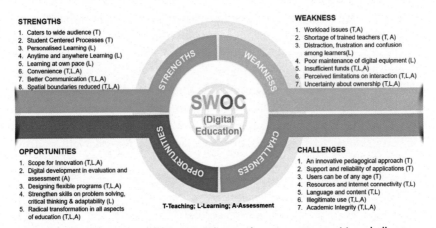

Figure 2.8 SWOC analysis. *SWOC*, Strengths, weaknesses, opportunities, challenges.

2.6.1 Strength

Digital education facilitates anytime and anywhere learning. Across the globe disturbances and delay in learning was avoided during COVID-19 due to the shift from traditional or campus-based teaching to remote teaching. Most of the courses are self-paced. So, learners can schedule their convenient time to learn. Recorded sessions can be played several times to get more clarity. This motivated more adults to participate in digital learning. Learning happens in the learners' location. This has reduced the time of travel to a greater extent, leading to more productive hours of learning. Digital education is student centered. They can choose the course, mode of learning, time of learning, required pattern of assessment, institution as well the tutor from whom they want to learn which broadens the horizon. This led to students reaching out to expert faculty across the globe. Unlike the campus-based classes, there is no restriction on the audience for the session. Depending on the technology and platform used, digital education caters to a wide audience. Digital education overcomes two important barriers (strict timetable and physical presence) leading to the inclusion of more learners. AI-powered chatbots focus on personalized learning for each student and provide intelligent and genuine feedback. AI models use the outcome of the assessment mainly the grades obtained by the students to capture the underlying patterns of students' behavior to predict students' success in an online learning environment. The immersive technologies of AR and VR are used to learn digital content and physical elements through visualization and simulation.

2.6.2 Weakness

Most of the repeated tasks like attendance monitoring, learning styles assessment, assignment tracking, assessment, and eligibility for the final exam take a maximum workload on the faculty. It is always perceived that online education lacks a personal touch. Since tutors and students lack personal touch in digital education, they are uncertain about ownership of teaching and learning. Teachers are very new to the digital educational environment, so trained teachers are relatively few. Investment in digital infrastructure is huge; most of HEI's management is in a dilemma. Learning setup in digital learning results in distractions, frustration, anxiety, and confusion.

2.6.3 Opportunities

The digital shift in the education sector has paved the way for innovation in evaluation and assessment. Need-based flexible programs can be designed to cater to the new trends and demands in the education environment. Industry 4.0 requirements can be embedded in the curriculum to develop problem-solving and critical thinking among digital native students. Earning while learning is possible by taking up a part-time job or even courses for career growth that can be undertaken simultaneously while on the job.

2.6.4 Challenges

Digital resources, accessibility, the openness of technology, and Internet connectivity in all places are still a dream. In an ongoing 2017—18 study, the Ministry of Rural Development found that about 47% of Indian family units get about 12 h of electricity and over 36% of schools in India work without power, which demonstrates the present condition of digital space (Bhuvaneswari & Sahayam, 2022). The Government of India (GoI), Ministry of Human Resource Development, All India Council for Technical Education, and University Grants Commission have initiated the translation of course content into regional languages, but still, it has not reached an appreciable rate. The legitimate use of AR-, VR-, ML-, AI-based teaching tools and authorized software is another challenge which is to be addressed seriously to make digital education a successful outcome. An important advantage of online learning, age relaxation is becoming a challenge to design the course content, pedagogy, and assessment. Currently, Academic integrity and research misconduct are the major challenges raised by AI-based tools. Students, authors, and researchers are using AI-based Automatic Article Generators (AAGs) which generate writings such as research articles, theses, written assignments, and books for their academic work. Further, the process of detecting the originality and genuineness of work is very difficult for teachers as well as anti-plagiarism tools (Abd-Elaal, Gamage, & Mills, 2019).

2.7 Digital education—the way forward

With the advent of the internet, the teaching and learning processes have become more sophisticated, smart, and advanced. This has led to the development of new platforms for educational learning. Further, the

COVID-19 pandemic has necessitated digital agility which demands technology in every sphere of daily activities. Digital literacy is a must to enjoy a hassle-free day-to-day life. At the same time, the concept of tech for community development needs to be looked at seriously since it has to address the problems of underprivileged sections of society. There is a need to fasten the initiatives to bridge the digital divide to facilitate digital education. Once the digital infrastructure is set, teachers might develop the best method to stimulate the learners' learning process through effective ICT infrastructure. This paradigm shift also paves a new look for the employability quotient of the learner. The government's digital initiative in attracting the young population toward various digital platforms, tools, and the digital repository is to be strengthened. The educational authorities must set the benchmark for digital infrastructure in the institutional premises to establish new standards. Perhaps management should provide training incentives for teachers to equip themselves for the new digital infrastructure. The virtual lab can be established to make digital learning full-fledged.

2.8 Conclusion

This chapter has presented the various aspects of digital education namely teaching, learning, and assessment as described in Fig. 2.1. The application of AI and its relevance are well presented in the subsections considering six datasets. Equitable use of digital technology can be ensured via digital education which aims to reach out to the maximum number of stakeholders in the educational sector especially students. There are hindrances to the management, teachers, students, and policymakers, foreseeing the benefits like connecting the students and teachers across the globe at affordable cost, making use of the Internet penetration everywhere, students' attraction toward technology, and digital education will become the order of the day. This will make the educators incorporate digital components in all courses at school, undergraduate, and postgraduate levels. There are many initiatives by the GoI to strengthen the digital infrastructure, namely, virtual labs, national digital educational architecture (NDEAR) 2021−22, PM eVIDYA Programme: 2020, DIKSHA: Digital Infrastructure for Knowledge Sharing, SWAYAM: Study Webs of Active Learning for Young Aspiring Minds, and ePathshala Portal. Also, it is important to understand and take measures to adopt digital education in such a way that it nullifies the adverse impact of excessive dependence on electronic mediums of learning as youth should be protected and kept away from behavioral or psychological imbalances. Adoption of AI will not substitute teachers in the classroom, but it will provide teachers with vital tools to ensure successful teaching, learning, and assessment. AI can enhance digital education. Both teachers and students require to have adequate training to implement AI in digital education and maximize the benefits. Hence it is the need of the hour that policymakers bring in a digital education system that combines traditional and modern methods of teaching along with the application of AI to develop strong relationships between teachers and students in the new normal. Though there is an increase in the application of AI for better student learning experiences and teaching, it mandates proper alignment between the technology and curriculum to achieve the intended learning outcomes.

References

Abd-Elaal, E. S., Gamage, S. H., & Mills, J. E. (2019, January). Artificial intelligence is a tool for cheating academic integrity. In: *30th annual conference for the Australasian association for engineering education (AAEE 2019): Educators becoming agents of change: Innovate, integrate, motivate* (pp. 397—403). Queensland: Engineers Australia.

Aivo. (2019, September 11). *AI and chatbots in the education sector: The future of learning.* Available from https://www.aivo.co/blog/ai-and-chatbots-in-education.

Akyuz, Y. (2020). Effects of intelligent tutoring systems (ITS) on personalized learning (PL). *Creative Education, 11*(6), 953—978.

Alshiekh, M. (2021). *Udemy course (academy-teaching)* [Data set]. Kaggle. Available from https://www.kaggle.com/mariahalshiekh/udemy-course-academy-teaching.

Banerjee, A., Lamrani, I., Hossain, S., Paudyal, P., & Gupta, S. K. (2020). *AI enabled tutors for accessible training.* International Conference on Artificial Intelligence in Education (pp. 29—42). Springer, July.

Bassen, J., Balaji, B., Schaarschmidt, M., Thille, C., Painter, J., Zimmaro, D., . . . Mitchell, J.C. (2020, April). Reinforcement learning for the adaptive scheduling of educational activities. In: *Proceedings of the 2020 CHI conference on human factors in computing systems* (pp. 1—12).

Bhuvaneswari, G., & Sahayam, B. D. (2022). A Study on the impact of COVID-19 pandemic: Gendered digital divide and sustainable development goals. *ECS Transactions, 107*(1), 10603.

Caellwyn. (2021). The model predicts student success in online courses using virtual learning environment interaction statistics [Data set]. GitHub. Available from https://github.com/Caellwyn/ou_student_predictions.

Chaudhry, M. A., & Kazim, E. (2021). Artificial intelligence in education (AIEd): A high-level academic and industry note 2021. *AI and Ethics,* 1—9.

Das, S. (2022). *Student's math score for different teaching styles* [Data set]. Kaggle. Available from https://www.kaggle.com/soumyadiptadas/students-math-score-for-different-teaching-style.

Dick, E. (2021). The promise of immersive learning: Augmented and virtual reality's potential in education. *Information Technology and Innovation Foundation.* Available from https://itif.org/publications/2021/08/30/promise-immersive-learning-augmented-and-virtual-reality-potential/.

Ferrari, M. (2019). *E-learning student reactions* [Data set]. Available from https://www.kaggle.com/marlonferrari/elearning-student-reactions.

Gardner, J., O'Leary, M., & Yuan, L. (2021). Artificial intelligence in educational assessment: "Breakthrough? Or buncombe and ballyhoo?". *Journal of Computer Assisted Learning, 37,* 1207−1216.

González-Calatayud, V., Prendes-Espinosa, P., & Roig-Vila, R. (2021). Artificial intelligence for student assessment: A systematic review. *Applied Sciences, 11*(5467), 1−15.

Kaur, A., Singh, S., Chandan, J. S., Robbins, T., & Patel, V. (2021). Qualitative exploration of digital chatbot use in medical education: A pilot study. *Digital Health, 7,* 1−11.

Kiwelekar, A. (2020). *Predicting end semester performance − Are mid-semester marks and classroom attendance good predictors?* [Data set]. Kaggle. Available from https://kaggle.com/code/akiwelekar/predicting-end-semester-performance.

Law, N., Niederhauser, D. S., Christensen, R., & Shear, L. (2016). A multilevel system of quality technology-enhanced learning and teaching indicators. *Journal of Educational Technology & Society, 19*(3), 72−83.

Hooda, M., Rana, C., Dahiya, O., Rizwan, A., & Hossain, M. S. (2022). Artificial intelligence for assessment and feedback to enhance student success in higher education. *Mathematical Problems in Engineering, 2022,* 1−19.

Martin, M. (2022, July 16). *AR Vs VR: Difference between Augmented reality & Virtual reality.* Guru99. Available from https://www.guru99.com/difference-between-ar-vr.html.

Munir, H., Vogel, B., & Jacobsson, A. (2022). Artificial intelligence and machine learning approaches in digital education : A systematic revision. *Information, 13*(203), 1−26.

Mustapha, Thuy, Van, N., Shahverdi, M., Qureshi, M. I., & Khan, N. (2021). Effectiveness of digital technology in education during COVID-19 pandemic. A bibliometric analysis. *International Journal of Interactive Mobile Technologies, 15*(8), 136−154.

Okonkwo, C. W., & Ade-Ibijola, A. (2021). Chatbots applications in education: A systematic review. *Computers and Education: Artificial Intelligence Journal, 2*(100033), 1−10.

Ozga, J. (2016). Trust in numbers? Digital education governance and the inspection process. *European Educational Research Journal, 15*(1), 69−81.

Paul, P. K. (2021). *Digital education: From the discipline to academic opportunities and possible academic innovations—International context and Indian strategies. Digital education for the 21st century* (pp. 255−281). Apple Academic Press.

Popenici, S., & Kerr, S. (2017). Exploring the impact of artificial intelligence on teaching and learning in higher education. *Research and Practice in Technology Enhanced Learning, 12*(1), 22.

Ragan, S. W., & McFarland, T. D. (1987). Applications of expert systems in education: A technology for decision-makers. *Educational Technology, 27*(5), 33−36.

Samarakou, M., Fylladitakis, E. D., Karolidis, D., Wolf-Gerrit, F., Hatziapostolou, A., Athinaios, S. S., & Grigoriadou, M. (2016). Evaluation of an intelligent open learning system for engineering education. *Knowledge Management & e-Learning, 8*(3), 496−513.

Seshapanpu, J. (2018). *Students' performance in exams* [Data set]. Available from https://www.kaggle.com/spscientist/students-performance-in-exams.

Sharma. (July−August 2021). Applications of artificial intelligence in education. *EducationMatters@ETMA,* 1−8.

Silander, C., & Stigmar, M. (2019). Individual growth or institutional development? Ideological perspectives on motives behind Swedish higher education teacher training. *Higher Education: The International Journal of Higher Education Research, 77,* 265−281.

Soni, A. (2022, March 24). *Importance of AI chatbot in the education industry.* Auxano Global Services. Available from https://www.auxanoglobalservices.com/importance-of-ai-chatbot-in-the-education-industry/.

Tsai, C. C. (2017). Conceptions of learning in technology-enhanced learning environments: A review of case studies in Taiwan. *Asian Association of Open Universities Journal, 12*(2), 184−205.

Tsai, S., Chen, C., Shiao, Y., Ciou, J., & Wu, T. (2020). Precision education with statistical learning and deep learning: A case study in Taiwan. *International Journal of Educational Technology in Higher Education, 17*(12), 1−13.

Yang, S. J. H. (2021). Guest editorial: Precision education − A new challenge for AI in education. *Educational Technology & Society, 24*(1), 105−108.

Yang., & Zhang, B. (2019). Artificial intelligence in intelligent tutoring robots: A systematic review and design guidelines. *Applied Sciences, 9*(2078), 1−18.

Vorst, T. V. D. & Jelicic, N. (2019, June 16−19). Artificial Intelligence in education: Can AI bring the full potential of personalized learning to education? In: *30th European conference of the International Telecommunications Society (ITS): Towards a connected and automated society.* Helsinki, Finland: International Telecommunications Society.

CHAPTER 3

Endured understanding of learning in online assessments: COVID-19 pandemic and beyond

Fay Patel

Independent International Higher Education Consultant, Sydney, NSW, Australia

3.1 Endured understanding of learning in online assessments: enabling learning and learners

International higher education institutions (IHEIs) around the world were divided about online learning however several IHEIs embraced online learning as innovators and early adopters (Frei-Landau, Muchnik-Rozanov, & Avidov-Ungar, 2022; Sydle.com, 2022; Rogers, 1995). Frei-Landau et al. (2022) and the Sydle.com team which builds and integrates digital platforms value Rogers' diffusion innovation, as noted on their blog that Rogers' diffusion of innovation concept "has been around for over 50 years, nowadays it seems more relevant than ever."

The stages of innovation adoption are relevant for the unprecedented growth in the number of online learning platforms that emerged among IHEIs between 2020 and 2022. Morris (2020) asserts that several IHEI administrations are investment focused and regard online programs as a solution to student retention and higher enrollment however they remain unconcerned with the "pedagogy of digital teaching and learning." Other IHEIs (laggards and late adopters) had reservations about the potential of online learning as a catalyst for change and lagged for a variety of reasons, including financial cost, insufficient technology infrastructure, education policy development challenges, online technology development programs for learners, instructors, and professional staff, and the availability and reliability of nonfoolproof plagiarism software.

Following the pandemic, more sophisticated, innovative future-oriented online learning design options, including hybrid models, may become available. Alternative paradigms have the potential to be introduced into online learning design.

3.2 Alternative paradigms in online learning design

Alternative paradigms in online learning design with unconventional approaches to previous applications of learning design provide opportunities to use creative energies and pursue innovative context-based solutions for learner engagement, transforming the online learning design into a living, breathing curriculum (on demand), the expansive curriculum (open to all possibilities), and the untaught curriculum (collaborative learner–instructor dialog about learning design). The author advocates for a multidimensional curriculum and instructional design that is responsive to the glocal community's ongoing diverse digital learning needs.

Unconventional learning design incorporates multiple dimensions into a living, breathing, expansive, and untaught curriculum design. Curriculum design is encouraged to be co-created by stakeholder groups (academics, professional staff, learners, and communities). This multidimensional learning design is not concerned with outcomes-based learning, traditional end-of-term and/or year assessments, or teacher-student-learning objectives and graduate characteristics. It is not based on an evaluation of the curriculum taught. In the alternative paradigm, multidimensional learning design incorporates either one or more of the multi-dimensions as a stepped progression, or it fully incorporates all the multi-dimensions (living, breathing, expansive, and untaught curricula).

The trauma of the historic COVID-19 pandemic will give birth to an alternate paradigm that will embrace humanity with a new zeal. It may guide glocal higher education institutions' commitment in the post-COVID-19 period to refine and expand their online learning design options to include sustained understanding of learning as a key indicator of learning and learner success. Through a collective humane movement, it may also encourage IHEIs to adopt and achieve UNESCO's 2030 Sustainable Development Goals (SDGs).

3.3 The United Nations Educational, Scientific, and Cultural Organization

3.3.1 (UNESCO) 2030 Sustainability Development Goals

"UNESCO's mission is to contribute to the building of a culture of peace, the eradication of poverty, sustainable development and intercultural dialog through education, the sciences, culture, communication and information." (UNESCO website). UNESCO aided in the development of the Millennium Development Goals (MDGs) in September 2000 and announced the Sustainable Development Goals (SDGs) on September 15, 2015. IHEIs, as educational providers, have an advantage in developing mutually respectful stakeholder-driven inter-institutional SDG plans. The plans are supported through negotiated partnership engagement, the exchange of Indigenous and other knowledges, and the inclusion of the seventeen UNESCO SDGs, which are attainable through the design of essential questions, referred to as problem questions by Klyukanov (2021). IHEIs can use Klyukanov's relevant intercultural communication principles in collaboration with global communities to meet mutually agreed-upon 2030 SDGs.

Embedding critical questions around the UNESCO SDGs will necessitate altruistic, respectful collaboration. The developing world has embraced the UNESCO 2030 Sustainable Development Goals as a humanitarian endeavor. Sawahel (2021) reports on the Times Higher Impact Rankings of African universities that among them "a total of 70 African universities located in 11 countries have been ranked in at least one of the United Nations' 17 Sustainable Development Goals (SDGs)." Akwala (2020a, b) and Patel (2020) note that developing countries in Africa have embraced the 2030 SDGs with the same dedication they had adopted with the MDGs. The UNESCO 2030 SDGs have been adopted as national priorities by developing countries in order to improve the quality of life in their communities, including various forms, levels, and categories of health care, among other sustainability goals. Akwala (2020a, b, Chapter 55 p. 977 and Chapter 59 p. 1063) maintains that among a range of health care advancements, maternal health care and the use of mobile phones to enhance rural health care are two examples of commitment to health care sustainability programs. Sawahel (2021) reports that "The 11 African countries—which represents 20% or a fifth of the 55 African countries—included Egypt, with 32 universities listed for their progress on SDGs, Morocco with seven, Algeria, Tunisia and South Africa with six universities each, Nigeria with five, Ghana with three, Kenya with two and Sudan, Tanzania, and Gambia with one university each." and that "South Africa's University of Johannesburg has been placed in the top 100 list in six SDGs. It is the best in the world for SDG 8 (Decent work and economic growth), fourth for SDG 1 (No poverty), 24th for SDG 4 (Quality education), 43rd for SDG 5 (Gender equality), 60th for SDG 10 (Reduced inequalities), and 79th for SDG 12 (Responsible consumption and production)."

Several world communities successfully and naturally gravitate toward "building a global community" (Patel, Li, & Sooknanan, 2011). Malaysia and the Asia Pacific region have demonstrated that their regional partnerships and commitment to innovative context-based solutions, such as the Asia-Pacific University Community Engagement Network (APUCEN) regional partner network and the CEO Faculty program (which maintains close liaison between industry and higher education institutions), improve the quality of life of glocal (local and global) communities (Patel, 2020; Chapter 26, p. 513). The APUCEN regional collective partner network, which aids in the achievement of the 2030 SDGs, is a shining example of the potential of community partnership building models.

The following section clarifies relevant terms of reference and theoretical perspectives on curriculum and instructional design of sustained understanding of learning in higher education, the diffusion of innovation trends in the adoption of education communication technologies (ECTs), and the diverse impact of the COVID-19 pandemic on online learning design and implementation, propelling its' educational communication technological advancement to new heights. According to the author, authentic assessments via simulated games and virtual reality remain superficial and cliched because online learning platforms provide numerous opportunities to engage learners in sustained understanding of learning through direct connectivity with world events as they occur.

3.4 Literature review

Through the cognitive processing of life events, online learning provides an alternative medium for engaging learners at the deep learning level. The expansive quality of online learning for creative thought and innovation will encourage stakeholder communities to co-construct online learning design as a catalyst for reshaping the notion of online assessments into critical dialog about long-term understanding of learning. This will result in the transformation of IHEIs from competitive corporate greed to benevolent glocal (local and global) communities. The preceding discussion of Malaysian and Asia Pacific willingness to collaborate and commit to improving national and regional quality of life is evidence of the successful implementation of innovative programs through community network partnerships.

Collaboration among glocal communities attracts a wide range of worldviews, perspectives, and interactions, including indigenous knowledge forms and cultural perspectives. The expansive nature of online learning is reflected in its respectful embrace of alternative ways of being and knowing, as well as its acceptance of alternative worldviews. Klyukanov (2021) presents complex case studies with deep level problem solving (essential?) questions based on real-life in real-time as a useful guide to navigating challenging intercultural encounters that lead to collaborative engagement. Embedding life events as they happen rather than simulations, games, and other virtual replicas of life will encourage learners to respond from the heart, bringing a human-centered perspective to online learning. It would also facilitate a "development from below" (Grameen Bank Noble Prize, 2006) community perspective to seek mutually acceptable solutions within the "glocal development for sustainable social change" paradigm (Patel, 2020, p. 501).

Using Klyukanov's approach, we can transform the online learning environment into meaningful learning opportunities by incorporating real-life, real-time essential questions for learners' cognitive processing, interrogation, critical analysis, and sustained understanding. The following life events may prompt important questions. The essential questions surrounding these real-world events should be coconstructed by online learning instructional designers and discipline experts. This section includes examples of real-world events that provide opportunities to frame critical essential questions. The following media news refers: *Voices of the Palestinian diaspora: Nakba is an open wound*. Nakba (Soussi, 2018); Foxconn's lost iPhone tragedy, (Foxconn's lost iphone tragedy, 2009; July 22); Foxconns' 2011 suicide of 17 workers; the World Bank and world refugee crisis (UNHCR Database, 2018); and the IMF (2020, 2022) debt recovery among poor nations. Chabert, Cerisola, and Hakura (2022) assert that "Low-income countries face fewer debt challenges today than they did 25 years ago, thanks in particular to the Heavily Indebted Poor Countries initiative, which slashed unmanageable debt burdens across sub-Saharan Africa and other regions. But although debt ratios are lower than in the mid-1990s, debt has been creeping up for the past decade and the changing composition of creditors will make restructurings more complex." How can this assertion be converted into an essential question?

The author believes that critical questions should be posed to raise critical awareness about rogue democracies and oppressive regimes in the west, east, north, and south. Furthermore, it should investigate "bonded development" (Patel et al., 2011) and the International Monetary Fund's (IMF) political economic establishment to keep certain world nations indebted and impoverished. The key questions should be framed around the reimagined corporate racist agendas of color, now known as the Equity, Diversity, and Inclusivity (EDI) portfolios (Patel, 2021). The EDI agendas evolved over time from overt racism and color lines in earlier centuries in the United States, from which millions had to withdraw. These EDI agendas were reintroduced under different terminology and imposed through policies of cultural assimilation, multiculturalism, and cultural diversity, resulting in multiple versions of HEI and corporate EDI/DIE/DEI initiatives. The EDI agendas are a manufactured distraction designed to further disempower poor world communities and annihilate their critical consciousness and fearless spirit as they protest the wealthy's affluence while they go hungry. According to Feagin (2006), cited in Patel (2021, p. 30), the United States manufactured systemic racism as early as the seventeenth century to "perpetuate the cycle of socioeconomic inequities based on skin color."

Next, the framework for the diffusion of innovations and the relevant terms of reference are clarified and applied. The author encourages the framing of key questions to demonstrate the opportunities presented in the media to elicit long-term understanding of learning. Finally, recommendations are made to allow the reader to consider how the psyche can be activated to improve our long-term understanding of learning.

3.5 Diffusing online learning

Frei-Landau et al. (2022) claim that Everett Rogers research on diffusion of innovations is a "well-established empirical framework" to investigate the diffusion innovation of mobile learning during the COVID-19 pandemic. More specifically, Frei-Landau et al. (2022) further contend that "Rogers' DIT (2003) …. conceptualizes the process of innovation diffusion and can likewise be applied to the process of innovation adoption, specifically, to the adoption of educational technology in the field of education" (Al-Mothana & Gasaymeh, 2013). This lends credence to the authors' contention that Rogers' seminal studies will continue to influence the spread of education communication technologies (ECTs) in the third decade of the twenty-first century.

Within the context of innovation diffusion, it is certain that the COVID-19 pandemic, which became the primary catalyst for moving learning to the online learning platform across world regions, influenced the IHEIs rate of adoption of online learning innovations. Rogers (1995, p. 204) asserts that "some innovations diffuse from first introduction to widespread use in a few years" however several factors including the individuals' perceived "attributes of innovations" which include "relative advantage, compatibility, complexity, trialability, and observability" (Rogers, 1995, p. 206) affect their rate of adoption. Other significant factors that influence diffusion rates, according to Rogers, include the innovation decision making process, communication process, social group demographics, and the impact of the role and influence of change agents in innovation diffusion. This premise was challenged by the COVID-19 era, because the COVID-19 factor not only accelerated the diffusion of online learning, but it also influenced the rate of diffusion based on necessity. During the pandemic, innovation diffusion merged geographical distance, space, and time zones.

According to Rogers (1995, p. 216), status motivation is less important for the laggards, late adopters and "late majority" than it is for the innovators, early adopters, and early majority. When considering the adoption of online learning media and electronic products (phones, computers, and tablets) based on their brands, the same holds true for modern-day glocal diffusion of innovations (e.g., Apple, Samsung, and Microsoft).

Diffusion of online learning during the twenty-first century modernity decades is impacted by an additional set of factors over and above that which drove innovation during Rogers (1995) period of research. The impact of innovation diffusion is influenced by the political-socio-economic factors affecting developed and developing world communities; those living in both the developing and developed worlds (as residents, citizens, immigrants, refugees, and migrant workers); the outsourcing of innovation product manufacture to sweatshops in other regions; access to high speed internet connections and services including phone line connections using DSL technology and emerging technology alternatives such as cable, satellite, and fiber optic options; and technology wars between the 5 G networks and those struggling to reach 5 G status.

The emphasis on technology access and online learning is frequently misconstrued as pedagogy, or the design and approach to learning across disciplines. There is a significant difference between taking learning online and using a specific approach in the design and delivery of online learning. The first is merely adopting technology as medium to teach and expecting the technology "to do the teaching" (Morris, 2020), and the second is pedagogy focused, examining, and implementing an effective learning approach for successful cognitive processing of information and knowledge exchange (Morris, 2020; Patel, 2014). Because of a misunderstanding of the reach of pedagogy and the potential of technology among digitally savvy instructional designers and educators as instructional designers of learning, there are ongoing tensions between the pedagogy versus technology teams.

3.6 Online learning: pedagogy before technology

Based on the premise that technology is not pedagogy (Morris, 2020) and that pedagogy comes before technology (Patel, 2014), this section focuses on curriculum and instructional design approaches. Online learning design focuses on the learning experience whereas the technology is the tool that facilitates learning and the cognitive processing of learning (Gosper & Ifenthaler, 2014; Patel, 2014). Gosper and Ifenthaler (2014) contend that it is important to match the "cognitive processing requirements" of the learning goal with suitable capabilities of appropriate technology tools (p. 8). They assert that "the significance of this for curriculum design is that it refocuses the choice of technologies back on the learner and the learning process."

According to Morris (2020), "We can plug our students into the VLE [virtual learning environment], we can mandate that they turn their cameras on in Zoom, we can use remote proctoring services to ensure they're not cheating on their exams... But does that constitute teaching? Does that help us develop a sustainable, equitable digital pedagogy?"

Morris raises pertinent questions about the growing concerns in IHEIs about plagiarism, contract cheating and the remote proctoring saga, and finding alternate solutions in authentic assessments (Collins, 2013; Alexander, 2014; Bretag, 2017; Asher–Shapiro, 2020; Dadashzadeh, 2021; Dhawan, 2020) in online learning which unfolded worldwide during the COVID-19 period of online education obfuscation among IHEIs. During the COVID-19 pandemic, Dhawan (2020) refers to online learning as a panacea noting that HEIS that resisted the shift to online modes were now pushed by the pandemic to embrace it. The remote proctoring decisions at IHEIs caused dissatisfaction among learners stemming from concerns with "privacy, student performance on the exams, implementation, challenges in administering the e-proctoring tool along with related psychological factors," according to Kharbat and Daabes (2021). Another e-proctoring tool Examplify raised further issues related to "data collection, face recognition bias, invasive and unfair surveillance" (Asher–Shapiro, 2020). In light of the numerous challenges, IHEIs have refocused their efforts on developing authentic assessments in online learning platforms, a topic that has been debated for over a decade. The author suggests using assessments that go beyond the authentic assessment level of design, requiring learners to demonstrate a deep level of endured understanding of learning, and for instructional designers and instructors to develop essential questions that require learners to pass the McTighe and Wiggins (2004) test, which is discussed in the endured understanding of learning section below.

The implementation of these alternative curriculum design approaches necessitates a shift in assessment practices in online learning. The discussion of endured understanding of learning in the following section focuses on the requirement for demonstration of endured understanding of learning.

3.7 Authentic assessment

Although authentic assessment design is not the primary subject of discussion in this paper, it is apparent that authentic assessment is not adequate to combat plagiarism. The literature (Wiggins, 1990; Gulikers, Bastiaens, & Kirschner, 2004; Groves, 2012; Collins, 2013; Mueller, 2016) on authentic assessment, plagiarism and contract cheating has grown as rapidly as the increasing availability of plagiarized material on the internet. According to Mueller, the objective of authentic assessment (AA) versus traditional assessment (TA) differs: TA focuses on the demonstration of knowledge development within an outcome-based taught curriculum model, whereas AA encourages the demonstration of the ability to cognitively process and apply knowledge to simulated and real-life situations.

3.8 Endured understanding of learning

McTighe and Wiggins (2004) speak of authentic assessment of long-term understandings. The preferred terminology in this paper is endured understanding of learning. The primary focus of the discussion is to establish learning as a meaningful and sustainable quality long after the learning has occurred. Enduring understanding of learning transcends curriculum coverage and goes beyond the outcomes-based curriculum's identified "learning outcomes" and "graduate attributes." Long-term learning comprehension promotes immediate and long-term rapid response to life events.

Enduring comprehension of learning frames and embeds critical questions within the online learning design on current life events such as the COVID-19 pandemic, glocal refugee crises, volcanic eruptions, drought, war, famine, and collaborative sustainable development humanitarian initiatives among glocal communities. The essential questions are intended to challenge and expand critical thought processes across visible and invisible boundaries, to require learners to consider their response from the perspective of the "other," to engage in inclusive practices through consultation with stakeholder communities, to give stakeholders a voice, and to explore multiple mutually acceptable solutions. Essential questions may not yield correct or incorrect answers, however they necessitate a thorough and thoughtful response. The cognitive processing of endured understanding of learning is relevant to Klyukanov's (2021) demonstration of cognitive processing components in the problem questions he develops around the ten principles of intercultural communication. Klyukanov's problem questions (essential questions) initiate a cognitive journey that necessitates learner engagement from multiple perspectives, negotiation, and consensus building abilities. Participants consider parameters (beliefs and values, transparency, respect, voice, truth, and justice) for respectful dialog about individual and collective responsibility and accountability during negotiated discussion.

In developing and answering *essential* questions, learners and educators will uncover learning (Sample, 2011) through an interrogation of their collective moral consciousness. Sample's (2011) assertion that a curriculum is to be "uncovered" conflicts with the decades old practice of covering the curriculum, teaching to the curriculum, and assessment of curriculum-focused learning outcomes. Sample (2011) is an advocate of "teaching for endured understanding." Uncoverage of the curriculum should be the foremost objective in all curricula and learning design, regardless of the media utilized to deliver and/or inspire endured understanding of learning. According to Bowen (2017) and McTighe and Wiggins' (2004), commitment to backwards design creates a space for learners, learning, and understanding of learning. Beginning with the purpose in mind, one must design sustained understanding of learning opportunities with the purpose in mind. The learning design for long-term understanding should include essential questions that activate cognitive processing and lead to curriculum discovery.

3.9 McTighe and Wiggins test to confirm essential question

The guidelines and test developed by McTighe and Wiggins (2004) are used to determine whether the assessment design of the essential question will elicit a long-term understanding of the learning response. They assert that the answer to two key questions will guide educators in establishing the quality of the essential question:

1. Would the learner pass the test or achieve the desired performance outcome "without an in-depth understanding"?
2. Would the learner understand the key concepts although the performance outcome is poor?

If educators answer *yes* to these two questions, confirming that learners can pass the test without in-depth understanding or understanding of the key conceptual framework, the assessment question design does not meet the requirements for "essential questions."

If educators answer *no* to the two questions, validating that learners cannot pass the test unless they *demonstrate in-depth understanding* and unless they *demonstrate understanding of the key concepts*, then the assessment question design may be classified as essential questions. The author focuses on the formulation of essential questions for cognitive processing.

3.10 Essential questions should inspire endured understanding of learning

What essential questions should be developed in an endured understanding approach in online learning environments? In this section, the COVID-19 pandemic (2019−21) and the two life event case studies from Torres, Garcia-French, Hordijk, Nguyen, and Olup (2012) are reviewed as opportunities to develop essential questions. Educators and learners can co-construct essential questions that elicit meaningful connections, collaborations and sustainable glocal development among glocal communities.

Concerning the previously discussed alternate curriculum design, the COVID-19 pandemic is an example of an opportunity to promote a living, breathing curriculum that raises critical questions as it spreads through developed and developing communities worldwide. The Torres et al (2012) case studies may contribute to the expansive curriculum design approach. The varied curriculum approaches will together and independently constitute the *"untaught curriculum."* So, in essence, it is a curriculum design of critical consciousness and interrogation. To raise critical consciousness and to facilitate cognitive processes towards context-based solutions, committed educators are encouraged to embed alternate curriculum design. The author posits the *living, breathing curriculum* (on demand), the *expansive curriculum* (open to every possibility), and the "untaught *curriculum*" (adopted independently or as a holistic framework) as alternative curriculum approaches.

3.11 COVID-19 pandemic—essential questions

Essential questions about the COVID-19 pandemic provide endless possibilities to integrate interdisciplinary perspectives in both framing the questions and in assessing the unique responses. This means that the educator is expected to be open-minded and accepting of unique learner perspectives and designs the rubric or grading guide to include spaces for creativity and unique perspectives and other worldviews.

The curriculum is alive and breathing, allowing for interdisciplinary teaching, partnerships and collaborations in teaching, learning, grading, and research on a global scale. The following general and specific questions about the COVID-19 pandemic may be important. Responses necessitate collaborative engagement with glocal communities as one humanity, negotiating challenges and quandaries, and recommending context-based solutions to effect change and improve the condition of those who have been negatively impacted.

General and specific essential questions related to discipline content, COVID-19 pandemic, ethical leadership, remote work environments and to the Coca Cola and Apple Inc case studies (Torres et al, 2012) are presented in the next section.

3.11.1 General

- Critically assess the "first world" community (such as the United States, Australia, Canada, France, Italy, and the United Kingdom) reactions if one of them had been the first epicenter of the COVID-19 pandemic (Patel, 2020).
- Discuss how and why the COVID-19 factor may force "first world" communities to rethink, reshape, and reframe internationalization into a glocalization of learning framework. (Patel, 2020)

3.11.2 Health

- Develop a comparative analysis report of the spread and containment of COVID-19 for the year 2020–21 in a selected region and provide context-based solutions, as relevant.

3.11.3 Education

- Humanizing international higher education in a COVID-19 and post-COVID-19 world is a challenge. Discuss how this can be pursued in a specific region? (Patel, 2020)

3.11.4 Management and leadership

- Ethical leadership is a challenge in a COVID-19 and post-COVID-19 world. Critically review, assess, and provide context-based solutions to meet the challenge.

3.11.5 Employment and labor law

- Examine the COVID-19 pandemic's employment and labor law challenges, such as the emerging remote working environments that include child–care, elderly–care, and family responsibilities for both men and women. Present a report with recommendations for revising and improving employment and labor law regulations in the pandemic present and postpandemic period.

3.12 Apple Inc and Coca Cola—essential questions

International higher education has a moral obligation to demonstrate its role as a catalyst for social change (Patel, 2017), and it can do so significantly within the endured understanding discourse (Torres et al, 2012).

From a political economy of communication theoretical perspective (Mosco, 2009, p. 2), there has been an immense impact of two companies (Apple Inc and Coca Cola) on the quality of life of individuals and their communities. Mosco (2009) contends that in the narrow view of the political economy of communication "political economy is the study of the social relations, particularly the power relations, that mutually constitute the production, distribution, and consumption of resources, including communication resources" (p. 2), and which can be viewed in a broader context "by focusing on a set of central qualities that characterize the approach." In the broader context, "political economy places emphasis on social change, historical transformation, and totality of social relations, moral philosophy (with a focus on moral values) and social praxis (thinking and doing to action social change)" (pp. 3—4). The author claims in the following brief reference to two company case studies (Torres et al.), that such life events should form an integral component of endured understanding. Raising important questions will have an impact on deep learning through cognitive processing, revealing critical life learning opportunities.

Brief historical context is presented about the Apple Inc and Coca Cola companies.

3.13 Apple Incorporated

The Apple technology products manufacturing company, an American company based in California, United States, manufactures a wide range of electronic products, including the iPhone smartphone, which was first released in 2007 and has fourteen generations to date (2022). Consumers, in general, are unconcerned and unaware of the socioeconomic and political impact of products such as the iPhone, and are enthralled by the product and its features as a technologically advanced icon and status symbol. Torres et al (2012) highlight the company's transgressions at the Apple manufacturer Foxconn in China; violations of labor, human rights, and health and safety regulation in manufacturing different generations of iPhones are noted in the identified suicide rates (2009—3rd generation 3 GS and 2010—4th generation iPhone 4), an explosion (2010) and child labor (2011—5th generation iPhone 4 S).

From Foxconn's single suicide in 2009 to its seventeenth suicide in 2011, several essential questions can be raised; among them the question of moral values and ethics of consumers who rush out to buy their next iPhone should be framed into essential questions. Perhaps the essential question may be taken from Joel Johnsons (2011), "1 Million Workers. 90 Million iPhones. 17 Suicides. Who's to Blame?"

3.14 Apple Inc—essential questions

1. Assess the human cost of the 3rd generation Apple phone in 2009 and critically analyze its impact on the community that provided labor.
2. Responsibility for the suicidal consequences at Foxconn in China— Apple or Foxconn and accountability should be placed on the United States and not China. Investigate incidents of labor violations in off-shore, outsourced locations and identify key corporate violations.
3. Identify an Apple or another preferred brand product that you use and examine the production of the product in relation to the profit to the company and loss of human life.

3.15 Coca Cola company

Coca Cola, an American company, was introduced to India in the 1950s, exited the project in the 1970s and returned in the 1990s. Products in the region included Coca Cola, Sprite, Fanta with local brands Limca and Thums Up. Although the company appeared to support sustainable development, the Torres et al (2012) study highlighted conflicts that arose in relation to water pollution and pesticides demonstrating that the company reneged on sustainability and social responsibility commitment and promises.

3.16 Coca Cola

1. Review the local community impact of Coca Cola manufacturing in India between 2015 and 2021 and compare the socioeconomic and political impact on the community with the Torres et al study of 2012.
2. Coca Cola is committed to sustainability and has adopted relevant UNESCO 2030 sustainability development goals.

3.17 Recommendations, dilemmas, and challenges

Dilemmas and challenges will present themselves because the design of essential questions in online assessment is a confrontational alternative to former assessment design. Essential questions place real life in real time events under scrutiny; these are *not* virtual reality nor computer games. Recommendations are offered in the next section.

3.18 Recommendations

Recommendations are made to develop a vibrant online learning presence through partnerships and collaborations.
1. The online learning platform should be utilized to its potential within and across disciplines.
2. Educators and learners can form partnerships to coconstruct essential questions, design effective rubric guides for grading purposes and reflect as a global community of research scholars.
3. Adopting real-life in real-time events as endured understanding of learning opportunities is an imperative.

4. Online learning design should adopt endured understanding of learning *as a continuous assessment practice.*
5. Essential questions become the primary assessment design, ensuring academic integrity and challenging contract cheating. In recent decades, increased efforts accelerated the use of multimedia to make learning more accessible; however, the same multimedia is also home to *contract cheating* (Bretag, 2017), which is defined as the availability of purchase options to cheat in examinations, tests, and assignments. Attempting to maintain academic integrity through Turnitin and SafeAssign software to detect cheating is no longer a viable option in the face of such challenges.
6. Utilizing essential questions for online learning design might reduce the contract cheating trend in IHEIs.
7. Assessment design components should require disciplinary and interdisciplinary context-based solutions, creativity, innovative alternatives, and action for change agendas to be integrated in the learner response.
8. IHEIs should align online assessments with their strategic and social responsibility commitments to the UNESCO 2030 Sustainability Development Goals.
9. Embed endured understanding of learning within the glocal (local and global) higher education curriculum through enhanced instructional design; develop essential questions to guide cognitive processing; and explore interdisciplinary assessments.

The capacity and resources of online learning design enable educators and learners to contribute to the long-term social development of their communities. Adopting the UNESCO 2030 SDGs allows communities in all world regions to assess their glocal footprint in terms of meaningful change to quality of life. Endured understanding is an important component of authentic assessment because learners must be able to respond intuitively, quickly, and compassionately to life (and death) situations during natural and man-made disasters. Morris (2020) asserts that the question "what happens when learning goes online?—is not a question technology can answer. It's one we need to answer. Teachers, librarians, learning designers, students. Good online education comes not from the purchase of another platform, but out of dialog, out of the will to empower everyone involved in teaching and learning to create together a digital learning that isn't just instrumental, that isn't just performative, but that's authentic, meaningful, and just."

Educators and learners will respond as responsible glocal citizens as they intuitively draw on their collective learning experience. When they demonstrate compassion and a duty of care for all humans, their humanity will transcend all boundaries. Daily life events and crises include natural disasters (for example, the Kilauea volcanic eruption in Hawaii on 3rd May 2018, CNN—June 2018) and human strife such as the Al Nakba or catastrophe and displacement of Palestinians on 15 May 1967 and their ongoing struggle to reclaim their home until 2022; the war against Islamic terrorism (ISIS) in Syria, 2018; and the plight of refugees across Europe, Australia and North America (UNHCR Database, 2018). These life events cross the glocal sphere and affect all humanity. Morris (2021) contends that in "humanizing digital pedagogy" one has to acknowledge the "role of imagination in distance teaching." In this paper, the alternate paradigm of the living, breathing curriculum, the expansive curriculum, and the untaught curriculum is the point of departure for the imagination that Morris advocates as an essential component of distance learning. He asserts that "We have to begin to imagine better digital learning than one which is operational. We have to begin to imagine better digital pedagogies, more critical digital pedagogies, which go farther than the mere implementation of design. And we need to remind ourselves that if our best practices for online learning are leaning too much on unquestioned tradition, we are at risk of losing our "might be," and of slipping drowsily into the little world someone else invented for us to occupy."

3.19 Limitations of the study

Limitations of the study are noted below.

1. Reference to the diffusion of innovations theoretical framework is limited to Roger's specific relevance to Education Communication Technology (ECT) adoption and utilization within IHEIs in recent decades.

2. Brief commentary is provided about the alignment of the curriculum development objectives and outcomes approaches as these were espoused by "experts" from the United Kingdom, Australia, and Canada (in that order) and recycled over decades among developed and developing countries.

3. Plagiarism and contract cheating are acknowledged although this is not the focus of the paper; and are considered a significant area of concern in online learning environments in IHEIs. However, framing essential questions is an important step in mitigating plagiarism, contract cheating and e-proctoring dilemmas.

3.20 Conclusion

The paper emphasized sustained understanding of learning as an important component of learning design. The author identified key questions to consider when assessing the impact of COVID-19 and other life events. More importantly, sustained understanding through the use of essential questions necessitates educators and learners working together as partners in the co-construction of learning, as open-minded educators, creative thinkers, and courageous innovators.

Enduring understanding of learning necessitates learners' exploration of possibilities, responses to challenges, confrontation of the truth, investigation of socioeconomic and political inequities, assessment of the extent of harm and affliction to individuals and communities, and actioned change. Critical life events should be integrated into continuous assessment practices to impact endured understanding.

In order for endured understanding of learning to be the core priority in online learning design, it will require a partnership of instructional designers (learner, online educator, discipline expert, educational developer and instructional designer) to "bridge the pedagogical divide" (Patel, 2014, pp. 32-33). Furthermore, Siragusa's twenty-four instructional design guidelines (Patel, 2014, p. 42) and pedagogical dimensions (p. 98) for effective online learning are part of the "essential dialog" on pedagogy and quality assurance that should remain a fundamental starting and departure point in online learning design.

Dhawan (2020) asserts that the pandemic situation demanded "humanity and unity," that "efforts should be made to humanize the learning process" and that "quality enhancement of online teaching -learning was crucial." These sentiments were expressed collectively in all regions at the onset of the COVID-19 pandemic in 2019–20, and which continue to be of highest importance in the postpandemic period. Learning and learner empowerment to succeed is critical beyond the COVID -19 era.

Learners and IHEIS are struggling to balance their corporate and vocational needs with their promise to serve humanity.

References

Akwala, A.O. (2020a). Millennium development goals and maternal health in Africa.

Akwala, A.O. (2020b). New media: The changing dynamics in mobile phone application in accelerating health care among the rural populations in Kenya.

Alexander, S. (2014, November 11). Buying essays: How to make sure assessment is authentic. The conversation. https://theconversation.com/buying-essays-how-to-make-sure-assessment-is-authentic-34125.

Al-Mothana, M. J. and Gasaymeh, M. (2013). Using the diffusion of innovation theory to explain the degree of English Teachers' Adoption of Interactive Whiteboards in the Modern Systems School in Jordan: A Case Study June 2013 Contemporary Educational Technology 4(2):138-149. https://doi.org/10.30935/cedtech/6098.

Asher-Shapiro, A. (2020). 'Unfair surveillance'? Online exam software sparks global student revolt Thomson Reuters Foundation November 10, 202011:25 pm Updated 2 years ago https://www.reuters.com/article/us-global-tech-education-feature-trfn-idUSKBN27Q1Q1.

Bowen, R. S. (2017). Understanding by design teaching guide.

Bretag, T. (2017). Six percent of uni students cheat on their studies, research shows April 19, 2017 News.com.au – Australia's leading news site https://www.news.com.au/technology/gadgets/six-percent-of-uni-students-cheat-on-their-studies-research-shows/news-story/78918253fb9af5c775c7bc556427a5d8.

Chabert, G., Cerisola, M., & Hakura, D. (2022). Debt sustainability restructuring debt of poorer nations requires more efficient coordination. April 7, 2022 https://www.imf.org/en/Blogs/Articles/2022/04/07/restructuring-debt-of-poorer-nations-requires-more-efficient-coordination.

Collins, R. (2013, May 24). Authentic assessment: assessment for learning. *Curriculum & Leadership Journal.* http://www.curriculum.edu.au/leader/authentic_assessment_%20assessment_for_learning,36251.html?issueID = 12745.

Curriculum models for the 21st century. In M. Gosper, & D. Ifenthaler (Eds.), *Using learning technologies in higher education.* Verlag New York: Springer.

Dadashzadeh, Mohammad (2021). The online examination dilemma: To proctor or not to proctor? *Journal of Instructional Pedagogies*, *25*, Jan 2021. Available from https://eric.ed.gov/?id = EJ1294386.

Dhawan, S. (2020). Online learning: A Panacea in the time of COVID-19 crisis. *Journal of Educational Technology Systems*, *49*(1), 5−22. Available from https://doi.org/10.1177/0047239520934018.

Foxconn's lost iphone tragedy. (2009, July 22). Forbes. https://www.forbes.com/2009/07/22/apple-iphone-foxconn-markets-technology-china.html?sh = 2a700f7723a8.

Frei-Landau, R., Muchnik-Rozanov, Y., Avidov-Ungar, O. (2022). Using Rogers' diffusion of innovation theory to conceptualize the mobile-learning adoption process in teacher education in the COVID-19 era Education and Information Technologies https://doi.org/10.1007/s10639-022-11148-8.

Feagin, J. R. (2006). *Systemic racism: A theory of oppression.* Routledge/Taylor & Francis Group.

Grameen Bank Noble Prize. (2006). Nobel Prize - Grameen Bank and Muhammed Yunus - Prize motivation: For their efforts to create economic and social development from below Microcredit as a Means of Fighting Poverty https://www.nobelprize.org/prizes/peace/2006/grameen/facts/.

Groves, N. (2012, October 24). Authentic assessment: What does it mean for students, staff, and sector? The Guardian. https://www.theguardian.com/higher-education-network/blog/2012/oct/24/authentic-assessment-university-teaching-learning.

Gulikers, J. T., Bastiaens, T. J., & Kirschner, P. A. (2004). A five-dimensional framework for authentic assessment. *Educational Technology Research and Development*, *52*(3), 67−86. Available from https://doi.org/10.1007/bf02504676.

IMF (2020). Enhancing Access to Opportunities Prepared by a team of staff of the International Monetary Fund (IMF) and the World Bank Group (WB) led by Lone Christiansen (IMF) and Ambar Narayan (WB) https://www.imf.org/external/np/g20/pdf/2020/061120.pdf.

Johnson, J. (2011). 1 million Workers. 90 million iPhones. 17 Suicides. Who's to Blame? https://www.wired.com/2011/02/ff_joelinchina/2011.

Kharbat, F., & Daabes, A. S. A. (2021). E-proctored exams during the COVID-19 pandemic. *A close understanding Educ Inf Technol (Dordr) 2021, 26*(6), 6589−6605. Available from http://doi.org/10.1007/s10639-021-10458-7. Epub 2021 Feb 15. https://pubmed.ncbi.nlm.nih.gov/33613081/.

Klyukanov, I. E. (2021). *Principles of intercultural communication (2nd ed.). Routledge.*

McTighe, J. & Wiggins, G. (2004). Understanding by design: Professional development workbook association for supervision and curriculum development (ASCD) Alexandria, VA, USA.

Morris, S. M. (2020, June 10). Technology is not pedagogy. Sean Michael Morris. https://www.seanmichaelmorris.com/technology-is-not-pedagogy/.

Morris, S. M. (2021). *On silence: Humanising Digital Pedagogy.* Sean Michael Morris. Retrieved October 9, 2021, from https://www.seanmichaelmorris.com/on-silence-humanising-digital-pedagogy.

Mosco, V. (2009). The political economy of communication (2nd ed.). Sage Publications.

Mueller, J. (2016). Authentic Assessment Toolbox North Central College, Naperville, IL. http://jfmueller.faculty.noctrl.edu/toolbox/whatisit.htm, 2016.

Patel, F. (Ed.). (2014). Online learning: An educational development perspective. Nova Science Publishers, Inc. https://novapublishers.com/shop/online-learning-an-educational-development-perspective/.

Patel, F. (2017). International higher education as catalyst for social change. *Journal of Educational Leadership in Action*, 4(2), Article 4. https://digitalcommons.lindenwood.edu/ela/vol4/iss2/4.

Patel, F. (2020). Glocal development for sustainable social change. In J. In, & Servaes (Eds.), *Handbook of communication for development and social change.* Singapore: Springer, Vol. 1, pp. 501−518. Available from https://doi.org/10.1007/978-981-15-2014-3_77.

Patel, F. (2021). *Power imbalance, bullying and harassment in Academia and the glocal (local and global) workplace.* Nova Science Publishers, Inc. Available from https://novapublishers.com/shop/power-imbalance-bullying-and-harassment-in-academia-and-the-glocal-local-and-global-workplace/.

Patel, F., Li, M. & Sooknanan, P. (2011). Intercultural communication: Building a global community, Sage India.

Rogers, E. M. (1995). Diffusion of innovations *(4th ed.).* Free Press.

Sample, M. (2011, August 10). Teaching for enduring understanding. Chronicle of Higher Education. https://www.chronicle.com/blogs/profhacker/teaching-for-enduring-understanding.

Sawahel, W. (2021, April 29). Growing number of universities in Africa ranked for SDGs. University World News: African Edition. https://www.universityworldnews.com/post.php?story = 20210427165907124.

Soussi, A. (2018, May 8). Voices of the Palestinian diaspora: Nakba is an open wound. Al Jazeera. https://www.aljazeera.com/news/2018/5/8/voices-of-the-palestinian-diaspora-nakba-is-an-open-wound.

Sydle.com (2022). Innovation and technology diffusion of innovations. What is it? How does it work? https://www.sydle.com/blog/diffusion-of-innovation-61829eca3885651fa294b9e6/.

Torres, C. A., Garcia-French, M., Hordijk, R., Nguyen, K., & Olup, L. (2012). Four case studies on corporate social responsibility: Do conflicts affect a company's corporate social responsibility policy. *Utrecht Law Review, 8*(3), 51−73. Available from https://doi.org/10.18352/ulr.2052012.

United Nations High Commissioner for Refugees (UNHCR) Database (2018). More information. https://data.worldbank.org/indicator/SM.POP.REFG, The World Bank Group.

Wiggins, G. (1990). The case for authentic assessment. *Practical Assessment, Research, and Evaluation, 2*(2). Available from https://doi.org/10.7275/ffb1-mm19.

CHAPTER 4

Transformative course design practices to develop inclusive online world language teacher education environments from a critical digital pedagogy perspective

Giovanna Carloni
University of Urbino, Urbino, Italy

4.1 Introduction

In today's higher education contexts, digital educational practices are being reshaped worldwide. The Covid-19 outbreak has triggered a fast digitization process at tertiary level (Decuypere, Grimaldi, & Landri, 2021); as a result, teacher education programs have had to rethink their course design for online delivery (Assunção Flores & Gago, 2020; Assunção Flores & Swennen, 2020; Kidd & Murray, 2020; König, Jäger-Biela, & Glutsch, 2020; Moorhouse, 2020; Quezada, Talbot, & Quezada-Parker, 2020). In this light, online world language teacher education courses, where language teachers learn how to teach world languages effectively, need to be redesigned to fit the increasingly diverse language teachers' needs. Likewise, world language pedagogy tenets need to be reconfigured to cater to diverse learners' educational and emotional needs (Cao et al., 2020; Friedland, 2016; Jackson, 2021; Motta & Bennett, 2018). In this ever-changing context, world language education instructors need to "build [...] sustainable transformative organizational cultures [,] [...] [aware that] the new learning ecology is complex and entangled in competing images of the future" (Brown, 2022). In this perspective, university instructors require new digital design and pedagogical skills suitable for developing online environments catering to classes of increasingly diverse world language teachers. Likewise, world language teachers

Digital Teaching, Learning and Assessment
DOI: https://doi.org/10.1016/B978-0-323-95500-3.00007-9

need to develop the competencies necessary to design online and face-to-face language classes for increasingly diverse learners.

This essay outlines a transformative course design pedagogy suited to devising inclusive online world language teacher education environments from a critical digital pedagogy perspective. In this context, the term "transformative" refers to the adoption of both a problem- and creativity-based approach (Graham & Longchamps, 2022) and innovative design practices suitable for developing courses catering to diverse learners' needs and characteristics. Diversity and inclusion play in fact a key role in the course design pedagogy outlined. Diversity is conceived from an intersectionality perspective: "Intersectionality [. . .] refers to the ways that structural oppression is not based only on race or gender identity, but on the intersection of race, gender identity, sexual orientation, class, immigration status, disability, age, and other axes of identity" (Costanza-Chock, 2020, p. 240).

The course design pedagogy outlined entails the application of Design Justice (Costanza-Chock, 2020) to Design Thinking (DT) (Brown, 2009, 2020; d.school, 2010). Combining Design Justice and DT can lead to the development of a course design pedagogy suited to devising online world language teacher education courses catering to diverse end users' needs from a critical digital perspective.

The design pedagogy devised aims to foster equity, inclusion, access, social justice, and pedagogical innovation in keeping with the United Nations Sustainable Development Goals 4 (SDG4) for education of the 2030 Agenda (UNESCO, 2016).

4.2 Developing a course design pedagogy

Due to the Covid-19 disruption, online learning has become mainstream and new digital models of education have emerged. However, new digital models are facing some critique because of the increasing partnerships between higher education institutions and edtech companies, such as commercial digital education platform providers (Brown, 2021; Morris, Ivancheva, Coop, Mogliacci, & Swinnerton, 2020; Williamson, Macgilchrist, & Potter, 2021). Digital education platforms seem in fact to affect pedagogical practices to various extents, leading to platformized education (Perrotta, Gulson, Williamson, & Witzenberger, 2021). Concerns about platform pedagogies have been recently voiced (Decuypere et al., 2021). To counteract the platformization of education, the implementation of a critical approach focusing on the use of education platforms is advocated for (Decuypere et al., 2021). In this light, planning online future-forward learning pathways, course designers need to be wide aware of how digital education platforms' infrastructures can affect pedagogical practices (Perrotta et al., 2021). The course design pedagogy outlined in this essay is also targeted at preventing course designers from being limited or pedagogically guided by the architecture of digital educational platforms (Perrotta et al., 2021).

4.2.1 Open educational resource–enabled pedagogy

Open educational resources (OERs) are openly licensed materials (UNESCO, 2020). OER-enabled pedagogy, informed by the use of OERs, is conceptualized "as the set of teaching and learning practices that are only possible or practical in the context of the 5 R permissions which are characteristic of OER" (Wiley & Hilton, 2018, p. 135). OER-enabled pedagogy adopts a learner-centered approach which values learners' active learning and knowledge coconstruction through collaborative activities within a socio-constructivist framework (Lantolf, 2000; Lantolf, Thorne, & Poehner, 2015; Shiqing, 2014; Vygotsky, 1978; Werth & Williams, 2022). Learners' knowledge coconstruction is pivotal in assessing students' degree of understanding. As a result, renewable assessment, which expects learners to cocreate artifacts made available as OERs, is pivotal (Wiley, 2015, 2016).

OER-enabled pedagogy can be instrumental in fostering equitable education. In line with the United Nations SDG4 for education (UNESCO, 2016), the UNESCO recommendation on OERs identifies access, inclusion, equity, and pedagogical innovation as the main goals of open educational practices (UNESCO, 2020).

4.2.2 Critical digital pedagogy

Freire's critical pedagogy challenged the banking education system, which conceives instructors as knowledge owners who deliver knowledge to students acting as passive knowledge receivers (1970). To free learners' creative and critical thinking, instructors need to engage learners in critical knowledge coconstruction, through problem- and inquiry-based learning, in order for them to become knowledge coinvestigators through dialogical engagement (Freire, 1970). To break down the traditional classroom power matrix, students need to engage in critical dialogical interactions targeted at uncovering underpinning power dynamics (Freire, 1970): "Critical Pedagogy is an approach to teaching and learning predicated on fostering agency and empowering learners (implicitly and explicitly critiquing oppressive power structures)" (Morris & Stommel, 2018).

In recent years, especially due to the Covid-19 disruption, education has moved online globally. As a result, critical pedagogy has developed to include also the digital component of education. In critical digital pedagogy, learners bring their whole experience and engage in dialogical exchanges targeted at analyzing the ideologically loaded elements underpinning the digital aspect of learning processes (Morris & Stommel, 2018). In this light, critical digital pedagogy focuses on the challenges related to access, inclusion, social justice, and pedagogical innovation in digitally enhanced educational contexts. From a power dynamics perspective, critical digital pedagogy thus investigates the digital components of course design, such as the use of digital technologies, educational technologies, and platform pedagogies (Morris & Stommel, 2018). Critical digital pedagogy also examines how more powerful cultures shape digital and educational technologies which implicitly inform pedagogical practices that are adopted in less powerful cultures or communities (Morris & Stommel, 2018).

4.2.3 Design Justice

Design Justice is a contemporary critical multifocal approach to traditional design approaches: "Design justice focuses on the ways that race, class, gender, and disability structure both information asymmetries and variance in user product needs" (Costanza-Chock, 2020, p. 78). Designing courses targeted to the needs of diverse marginalized and/or underrepresented groups informs Design Justice, which uses diverse end user groups in the design process (Costanza-Chock, 2020, pp. 6–23).

Design Justice is especially suitable for designing transformative online learning environments in higher education since it tries to move beyond a system of technology design largely organized around the reproduction of the matrix of domination. In its place, we need to imagine how all aspects of design can be reorganized around human capabilities, collective liberation, and ecological sustainability (Costanza-Chock, 2020, p. 72).

Design Justice challenges inequality, starting from the conceptualization of design processes (Costanza-Chock, 2020, p. 76). In Design Justice, diverse end users, who are representatives of the marginalized and/or underrepresented communities targeted in the design procedure, engage in all design practices actively since they have the experiential knowledge necessary to voice the needs and identify the affordances, disaffordances, and dysaffordances of the digital artefacts being developed (Costanza-Chock, 2020, pp. 36–85).

4.2.3.1 Design Thinking and Design Justice

DT is a "human-centered design [that] emphasizes better understanding of everyday user needs and experiences in professional technology design and development" (Costanza-Chock, 2020, pp. 88). DT has five phases, also called modes (d.school, 2010). The five-phase design process is suitable for educational practices; DT has in fact been implemented in various educational contexts (Koh, Chai, Wong, & Hong, 2015; Meinel & Krohn, 2022; Panke, 2019; Scott & Lock, 2021). In this essay, we suggest the adoption of DT in connection with Design Justice.

Our proposal to combine DT and Design Justice to develop inclusive online language teacher education courses aims to meet Wrigley and Mosely's call for "reshaping the boundaries of design education" (2022). To foster critical pedagogy, social justice, and didactic innovation, Freire advocated the adoption of a problem-posing approach enhancing knowledge, coinvestigation and cocreation (1970) that Morris and Stommel define as "a space of cognition not information" (2018). A course design pedagogy featuring DT and Design Justice can promote inclusion by challenging ableism through the use of diverse design teams, including representatives of the diverse communities for whom a new artefact is designed (Costanza-Chock, 2020, p. 100). Abled designers typically focus on an ableist approach to technologically modifying or augmenting the individual bodies of disabled people to approximate normative mobility styles; on the other hand, disabled people may be more interested in architectural and infrastructural changes that fit their own mobility needs (Costanza-Chock, 2020, pp. 83–84).

In this light, combining problem-based DT (Brown, 2009, 2020; d. school, 2010) with Design Justice, to challenge ableism, may be suitable for designing online world language teacher education courses promoting inclusion, social justice, and pedagogical innovation from a critical digital pedagogy perspective.

In DT, the design teams engage in five phases (empathize, define, ideate, prototype, and test) targeted at generating new ideas, solutions, or artefacts tailored to end users' needs (d.school, 2010). DT design teams develop artefacts catering to end users' needs, features, and expectations, using "unmarked user[s]" (Costanza-Chock, 2020, p. 77). End users' participation in design processes is limited to some design stages in human-centered approaches; on the other hand, in participatory design and code-sign, diverse end users are involved in the whole design process (Costanza-Chock, 2020, p. 100). In the new design pedagogy, diverse end users, representatives of the targeted communities, are involved throughout the five phases of DT to various degrees.

A description of how DT and Design Justice may be combined in course design follows. In DT, team members empathize with end users to research and understand their needs; empathy plays a key role in human-centered DT since the final artefact needs to cater to end users' needs (d.school, 2010). To understand end users' expectations and preferences, DT design teams usually interview end users, watch them while engaged in specific tasks, ask them to keep a diary, collect data through surveys, or use a mix of these strategies (Brown, 2009, 2020; d.school, 2010). In the new course design pedagogy, combining DT and Design Justice, diverse end users become active members of the DT design team for the whole design process.

In the define phase, the DT design team analyzes the data collected to identify end users' features and state end users' problems or challenges (d.school, 2010). To this purpose, the DT design team usually creates user personas outlining users' main features (such as needs, preferences, beliefs, expectations, and motivation) (Brown, 2009, 2020; d.school, 2010). In the newly framed course design pedagogy, instead of using personas who, as Costanza-Chock suggests, may perpetrate false assumptions and stereo-types (2020), the diverse DT design team interacts directly with the diverse team members involved in the design process.

In the ideate phase, the DT design team generates ideas to find possible solutions catering to the end user group's needs previously identified (d.school, 2010). At the beginning of the idea generation session, participants brainstorm ideas and pin them all on a shared space, like a digital noticeboard; all ideas are accepted and valued (Brown, 2009, 2020; d.school, 2010). Here, divergent thinking is fostered; participants are encouraged to think big and challenge their assumptions; everything is possible at this stage (Brown, 2009, 2020; d.school, 2010). Then, participants narrow down the ideas generated and select those to develop; while shortlisting ideas, team members also decide the ideas to archive for future projects (Brown, 2009, 2020; d.school, 2010). At the end of the process, just one idea is selected among those shortlisted. In keeping with the newly framed course design pedagogy, diverse end users take part in the generation idea and shortlisting decision-making processes, thereby making diverse end users accountable for their decisions in the selection phase.

In the prototype phase, the DT design team creates a prototype, that is a visual and possibly interactive representation of the idea selected in the ideate phase, for end users to test (d.school, 2010). In line with Design Justice, diverse end users, who can be those already part of the DT design team or others belonging to the targeted communities, can test the prototype to identify its affordances, disaffordances, and dysaffordances. The prototype can then be modified on the basis of diverse end users' feedback.

In the test phase, the solution devised is tested out in a social context (d.school, 2010). In the new course design pedagogy, a group of diverse end users, different from the diverse design members involved in the previous design stages, tests the product developed and provides feedback through surveys or interviews. The artefact can then be improved and developed in its final form on the basis of the feedback collected.

The new course design pedagogy, combining DT and Design Justice, can be used to design inclusive online world language teacher education courses fostering access, inclusion, social justice, and didactic innovation. The new course design pedagogy is developed through iterative processes of piloting and revisioning. The design pedagogy is thus conceived as research-based and adaptable to fit ever-changing diverse learning ecologies at tertiary level.

4.2.3.2 Diverse design teams at work

In our reimaged higher education ecology, diverse DT design teams engage in the development of online language teacher education courses fostering access, inclusion, and equity through pedagogical innovation. Online language teacher education design needs to account for the development of pedagogical language teaching skills, digital teaching skillsets, soft skills (such as critical thinking, problem-solving skills, creativity, collaborative skills, and interdisciplinary skills), and course design skills, including the ability to cater to diverse language students' backgrounds and needs from a critical digital pedagogy perspective. Interdisciplinarity, suited to tackling contemporary complex educational ecologies, is also pivotal in future-forward online language teacher education course design. In this context, it is noteworthy that both DT and Design Justice require an interdisciplinary approach to design. As a result, in diverse DT design teams, featuring members with various competencies and knowledge, diverse end users' needs drive an interdisciplinary course design approach (Costanza-Chock, 2020, p. 95). Diverse DT design teams, engaged in language teacher education design, include: digital instructional designers; university language education instructors and special needs education instructors; middle/high school language teacher representatives, middle/high school special education teachers, and middle/high school language teachers with specific learning disabilities; middle/high school language learner representatives (with various language repertoires and backgrounds), middle/high school students with special educational needs and middle/high school students with specific learning disabilities.

Adopting the new course design pedagogy, which combines DT and Design Justice, diverse DT design teams outline first the professional profile, including pedagogical skills and subject-specific knowledge, of future world language teachers collaboratively. Then, diverse DT design teams decide how to design the various components of inclusive online language teacher education courses. Diverse DT teams thus select: the approaches and methods to be adopted to foster active learning, engagement, problem-solving skills, critical thinking, creative thinking, and inclusion in online learning environments; course objectives and course content; the pedagogical skills and subject-specific knowledge to be fostered; the kind and degree of student—student, student—content, and student—instructor engagement to be implemented to achieve the course objectives; activity and assessment types (including renewable assessment); the digital/educational technologies and digital educational platforms suited to enhancing inclusive and active learning.

OER-enabled pedagogy, fostering the use of OERs and active learning, is especially suitable for empowering learners and fostering active learning in online language teacher education courses. OER-enabled pedagogy (Wiley & Hilton, 2018) and a culturally responsive pedagogical approach (Diaz, Suarez, & Valencia, 2019; Ladson-Billings, 2014; Samy Alim & Paris, 2017; Ladson-Billings, 2020) are instrumental in the development of online course design promoting equity, inclusion, access, social justice, and student agency.

Within a Design Justice framework, online language teacher education courses need to enable language teachers to engage critically with concepts such as course design principles, power dynamics, ownership, and diversity (Costanza-Chock, 2020, p. 187). From a critical digital pedagogy and Design Justice perspective, diverse DT design teams can thus develop a language teacher education course syllabus featuring social justice objectives targeted at fostering language teachers' critical thinking and pedagogical skills, suited to creating inclusive learning environments for increasingly diverse world language learners (Tarnawska Senel, 2020; Wassell, Wesely, & Glynn, 2019; Wesely, Glynn, & Wassell, 2018). As a result, the activities devised are targeted at teaching world language teachers how to integrate social justice-focused tasks in their language classes (Florian & Pantic, 2016; Pantić & Florian, 2015; Pantić, 2015; Pantić, 2017). For example, from an intersectionality perspective, language teachers can engage in tasks fostering the development of the skills necessary to implement social justice education through students' critical engagement with texts focusing on cutting-edge social justice issues, including power dynamics and diversity (Wassell et al., 2018, 2019). To rethink world language instruction from a critical perspective, it is pivotal to train world language teachers to design ecologies fostering the development of engaged members of global and local communities; the course design pedagogy illustrated in this essay seems to meet these needs.

From a critical pedagogy and Design Justice perspective, for language teachers to be empowered, they need to be critically and inductively introduced to the theoretical tenets of DT and Design Justice after experiencing the new design pedagogy as learners. Furthermore, language teachers need to learn how to implement the new design pedagogy while devising their future language classes.

4.3 Conclusion

Reimaging online, equitable, inclusive world language teacher education courses, we need to account for the complexity of communities' diverse needs and put them at the center of our course design processes. From an intersectionality perspective, we need to tackle inequalities, including those emerging from the interaction between learning and technology, and foster equity and inclusion in online world language teacher education course design. To promote inclusion, diversity, and social justice in institutional cultures, diverse DT course design teams can adopt a design pedagogy combining DT and Design Justice, targeted at enhancing student agency and empowerment from a critical digital pedagogy perspective: "In universities, a design justice approach can shift the way design is taught [. . .] and help develop a generation of designers who practice community leadership, accountability, and control" (Costanza-Chock, 2020, p. 101). In this light, it is noteworthy that the new course design pedagogy is combined with critical pedagogy and critical digital pedagogy (Crookes, 2021; Freire, 1970, 1974, 1998; Masood & Haque, 2021; McLaren & Jandric, 2020; Mclaren, 2020), which conceive social justice as deeply connected to educational goals (Bali, Cronin, & Jhangiani, 2020; Bali, Cronin, Czerniewicz, DeRosa, & Jhangiani, 2020; Shank Lauwo, Accurso, & Rajagopal, 2022).

References

Assunção Flores, M., & Gago, M. (2020). Teacher education in times of COVID-19 pandemic in Portugal: National, institutional and pedagogical responses. *Journal of Education for Teaching*, *46*(4), 507–516. Available from https://doi.org/10.1080/02607476.2020.1799709.

Assunção Flores, M., & Swennen, A. (2020). The COVID-19 pandemic and its effects on teacher education. *European Journal of Teacher Education*, *43*(4), 453–456. Available from https://doi.org/10.1080/02619768.2020.1824253.

Bali, M., Cronin, C., & Jhangiani, R. S. (2020). Framing open educational practices from a social justice perspective. *Journal of Interactive Media in Education*, *1*, 10. Available from https://doi.org/10.5334/jime.565.

Bali, M., Cronin, C., Czerniewicz, L., DeRosa, R., & Jhangiani, R. S. (Eds.), (2020). *Open at the margins: Critical perspectives on open education*. Pressbooks/Rebus Community.

Brown, M. (2021). What are the main trends in online learning? A helicopter view of possible futures. *Asian Journal of Distance Education*, *16*(2), 118–143.

Brown, M. (2022). Leading in changing times. In O. Zawacki-Richter, & I. Jung (Eds.), *Handbook of open, distance and digital education*. Singapore: Springer. Available from https://doi.org/10.1007/978-981-19-0351-9_28-1.

Brown, T. (2009). *Change by design: How design thinking transforms organizations and inspires innovation*. New York: HarperBusiness.

Brown, T. (2020). *Design thinking*. *HBR's 10 must reads on design thinking*. Boston: Harvard Business Review Press.

Cao, W., Fang, Z., Hou, G., Han, M., Xu, X., Dong, J., & Zheng, J. (2020). The psychological impact of the COVID-19 epidemic on college students in China. *National Library of Medicine*, 112934. Available from https://doi.org/10.1016/j.psychres.2020.112934.

Costanza-Chock, S. (2020). *Design justice: Community-led practices to build the worlds we need*. Boston: The MIT Press.

Crookes, G. V. (2021). Introduction to the special issue on critical language pedagogy. *Education Sciences*, *11*, 694. Available from https://doi.org/10.3390/educsci11110694.

Decuypere, M., Grimaldi, E., & Landri, P. (2021). Introduction: Critical studies of digital education platforms. *Critical Studies in Education*, *62*(1), 1–16. Available from https://doi.org/10.1080/17508487.2020.1866050.

Diaz, J., Suarez, C., & Valencia, L. (2019). Culturally responsive teaching: A framework for educating diverse audiences: AEC678/WC341, 10/2019. *EDIS 2019*, *5*(5). Available from https://doi.org/10.32473/edis-wc341-2019.

d.school. (2010). *An introduction to design thinking*. *Process guide*. Available from https://s3-eu-west-1.amazonaws.com/ih-materials/uploads/Introduction-to-design-thinking.pdf.

Florian, L., & Pantic, N. (2016). *Teacher education for the changing demographics of schooling: Inclusive learning and educational equity* (Vol 2). Cham: Springer.

Freire, P. (1970). *Pedagogy of the oppressed*. New York: Continuum International Publishing Group.

Freire, P. (1974). *Education for critical consciousness*. New York: Continuum International Publishing Group.

Freire, P. (1998). *Pedagogy of freedom: Ethics, democracy, and civic courage*. New York: Continuum International Publishing Group.

Friedland, D. (2016). *Leading well from within: A neuroscience and mindfulness-based framework for conscious leadership*. San Diego, CA: SuperSmart Health Publishing.

Graham, C., & Longchamps, P. (2022). *Transformative education: A showcase of sustainable and integrative active learning*. Abington, Oxon: Routledge.

Jackson, L. (2021). *Beyond virtue: The politics of educating emotions*. Cambridge: Cambridge University Press.

Kidd, W., & Murray, J. (2020). The Covid-19 pandemic and its effects on teacher education in England: How teacher educators moved practicum learning online. *European Journal of Teacher Education, 43*(4), 542−558. Available from https://doi.org/10.1080/02619768.2020.1820480.

Koh, J. H. L., Chai, C. S., Wong, B., & Hong, H. Y. (2015). *Design thinking for education: Conceptions and applications in teaching and learning*. Singapore: Springer.

König, J., Jäger-Biela, D. J., & Glutsch, N. (2020). Adapting to online teaching during COVID-19 school closure: Teacher education and teacher competence effects among early career teachers in Germany. *European Journal of Teacher Education, 43*(4), 608−622. Available from https://doi.org/10.1080/02619768.2020.1809650.

Ladson-Billings, G. (2014). Culturally relevant pedagogy 2.0: a.k.a. the remix. *Harvard Educational Review, Spring, 84*(1), 74−84.

Ladson-Billings, G. (2020). Toward a theory of culturally relevant pedagogy. *American Educational Research Journal, 32*(3).

Lantolf, J. (2000). Introducing sociocultural theory. In J. Lantolf (Ed.), *Sociocultural theory and second language learning* (pp. 1−26). Oxford: Oxford University Press.

Lantolf, J., Thorne, S. L., & Poehner, M. (2015). Sociocultural theory and second language development. In B. van Patten, & J. Williams (Eds.), *Theories in second language acquisition* (pp. 207−226). New York: Routledge.

Masood, M. M., & Haque, M. M. (2021). From critical pedagogy to critical digital pedagogy: A prospective model for the EFL classrooms. *Saudi Journal of Language Studies, 1*(1), 67−80. Available from https://doi.org/10.1108/SJLS-03-2021-0005.

Mclaren, P. (2020). The future of critical pedagogy. *Educational philosophy and theory, 52*(12), 1243−1248. Available from https://doi.org/10.1080/00131857.2019.1686963.

McLaren, P., & Jandric, P. (2020). *Postdigital dialogues on critical pedagogy, liberation theology and information technology*. London and New York: Bloomsbury.

Meinel, C., & Krohn, T. (2022). *Design thinking in education: Innovation can be learned*. Cham, Switzerland: Springer.

Moorhouse, B. L. (2020). Adaptations to a face-to-face initial teacher education course 'forced' online due to the COVID-19 pandemic. *Journal of Education for Teaching, 46*(4), 609−611. Available from https://doi.org/10.1080/02607476.2020.1755205.

Morris, N., Ivancheva, M., Coop, T., Mogliacci, R., & Swinnerton, B. (2020). Negotiating growth of online education in higher education. *International Journal of Educational Technology in Higher Education, 17*(48), 1−16. Available from https://doi.org/10.1186/s41239-020-00227-w.

Morris, S. M., & Stommel, J. (2018). Critical digital pedagogy: A definition. In S. M. Morris, & J. Stommel (Eds.), *An urgency of teachers: The work of critical digital pedagogy*. Hybrid Pedagogy Inc.

Motta, S. C., & Bennett, A. (2018). Pedagogies of care, care-full epistemological practice and 'other' caring subjectivities in enabling education. *Teaching in Higher Education, 23*(5), 631−646. Available from https://doi.org/10.1080/13562517.2018.1465911.

Panke, S. (2019). Design thinking in education: Perspectives, opportunities and challenges. *Open Education Studies, 1,* 281–306.

Pantić, N. (2015). A model for study of teacher agency for social justice. *Teachers and Teaching, 21*(6), 759–778.

Pantić, N. (2017). An exploratory study of teacher agency for social justice. *Teaching and Teacher Education, 66,* 219–230.

Pantić, N., & Florian, L. (2015). Developing teachers as agents of inclusion and social justice. *Education Inquiry, 6*(3), 333–351.

Perrotta, C., Gulson, K., Williamson, B., & Witzenberger, K. (2021). Automation, APIs and the distributed labour of platform pedagogies in Google Classroom. *Critical Studies in Education, 62*(1), 97–113. Available from https://doi.org/10.1080/17508487.2020.1855597.

Quezada, R. L., Talbot, C., & Quezada-Parker, K. B. (2020). From bricks and mortar to remote teaching: A teacher education program's response to COVID-19. *Journal of Education for Teaching, 46*(4), 472–483. Available from https://doi.org/10.1080/02607476.2020.1801330.

Samy Alim, H., & Paris, D. (Eds.), (2017). *Culturally sustaining pedagogies: Teaching and learning for justice in a changing world.* Teachers College Press.

Scott, D., & Lock, J. (2021). *Teacher as designer: Design thinking for educational change.* Singapore: Springer.

Shank Lauwo, M., Accurso, K., & Rajagopal, H. (2022). Plurilingualism, equity, and preservice teacher identity: Centring (linguistic) diversity in teacher education. *TESL Canada Journal, 38*(2), 114–139. Available from https://doi.org/10.18806/tesl.v38i2.1359.

Shiqing, Y. (2014). Systemic linguistic interpretation of constructivism. In F. Yan, & J. Webster (Eds.), *Developing systemic functional linguistics — Theory and application* (pp. 68–84). Equinox eBooks Publishing.

Tarnawska Senel, M. (2020). Social justice in the language curriculum: Interrogating the goals and outcomes of language education in college. In R. Criser, & E. Malakaj (Eds.), *Diversity and decolonization in German studies.* Cham: Palgrave Macmillan. Available from https://doi.org/10.1007/978-3-030-34342-2_4.

UNESCO. (2016). *Education 2030: Incheon declaration and framework for action for the implementation of sustainable development goal 4: Ensure inclusive and equitable quality education and promote lifelong learning opportunities for all.* <https://unesdoc.unesco.org/ark:/48223/pf0000245656>.

UNESCO. (2020). *Recommendation on Open Educational Resources (OER).* Ref: CL/4319. <http://portal.unesco.org/en/ev.php-URL_ID = 49556&URL_DO = DO_TOPIC&URL_SECTION = 201.html>.

Vygotsky, L. S. (1978). *Mind in society: The development of higher psychological processes.* Cambridge, MA: Harvard University Press.

Wassell, B. A., Wesely, P., & Glynn, C. (2019). Agents of change: Reimagining curriculum and instruction in world language classrooms through social justice education. *Journal of Curriculum and Pedagogy, 16*(3), 263–284. Available from https://doi.org/10.1080/15505170.2019.1570399.

Werth, E., & Williams, K. (2022). The why of open pedagogy: A value-first conceptualization for enhancing instructor praxis. *Smart Learning Environments, 9,* 10. Available from https://doi.org/10.1186/s40561-022-00191-0.

Wesely, P. M., Glynn, C., & Wassell, B. A. (2018). *Words and actions: Teaching languages through the lens of social justice.* Alexandria: ACTFL American Council on the Teaching of Foreign Languages.

Wiley, D. (2015). *An obstacle to the ubiquitous adoption of OER in US higher education.* Available from https://opencontent.org/blog/archives/3941.

Wiley, D. (2016). *Toward renewable assessment.* Available from https://opencontent.org/blog/archives/4691.

Wiley, D., & Hilton, J. L. (2018). Defining OER-enabled pedagogy. *International Review of Research in Open and Distance Learning, 19*(4), 133–146.

Williamson, B., Macgilchrist, F., & Potter, J. (2021). Covid-19 controversies and critical research in digital education. *Learning, Media and Technology, 46*(2), 117–127. Available from https://doi.org/10.1080/17439884.2021.1922437.

Wrigley, C., & Mosely, G. (2022). *Design thinking pedagogy facilitating innovation and impact in tertiary education.* London: Routledge.

CHAPTER 5

New teaching and learning strategies during the COVID-19 pandemic: implications for the new normal

Hanoku Bathula, Patricia Hubbard and Tae Hee Lee
University of Auckland, Auckland, New Zealand

5.1 Introduction

The COVID-19 pandemic has transformed higher education delivery globally. Regular face-to-face interactions and classroom teaching could not occur due to new restrictions such as lockdowns, border controls, face masks, and social distancing imposed to deal with the pandemic. Such pervasive challenges across the globe simultaneously are unique in modern times as they impact all sectors of society (Hussein, Daoud, Alrabaiah, & Badawi, 2020). In general, teachers and students could not meet physically in one place. Like other sectors in society that addressed the COVID-19 pandemic challenges, the higher education sector responded to the emergency with innovative ideas to continue delivering courses to tertiary students (Katz, Jordan, & Ognyanova, 2021). Fortuitously, various information and communication technology (ICT) tools were readily available to take advantage of to continue delivering the courses in higher education. These ICT tools include the Zoom conference platform, Microsoft Teams, Google Docs, Mentimeter, Miro, Padlet, Inspera, etc. However, each country, university, or even faculty responded differently based on its context—needs and availability of resources.

When many countries imposed a lockdown in their countries to face the COVID-19 pandemic, it immediately impacted the education sector. The lockdowns continued for nearly two years in New Zealand (NZ), with short and long periods which occurred sporadically. Such disruptions mainly impacted the delivery mode rather than the curriculum content, with the delivery of courses moving totally to online platforms. Even

Digital Teaching, Learning and Assessment
DOI: https://doi.org/10.1016/B978-0-323-95500-3.00006-7

when classes resumed on campus in 2021 and in some countries in 2022, despite lockdowns, the higher education sector continued to deliver programs online or in hybrid form to respond to various needs of both learners and staff, which may be unable to access onsite for the purposes of teaching and learning for a wide range of reasons. The "aftermath" of the rapid changes that had taken place resulted in a discernable shift in the use of online platforms and remote learning tools in higher education by disrupting the primary model of face-to-face learning as had been the norm in the past. While the challenges are well known, the responses continue to evolve to form a coherent set of resilient, flexible, and future-focused changes (Li, Xu, Deifell, & Angus, 2021) at both program and institutional levels. Given the dependence of higher education on online education tools and delivery platforms, their use is expected to be embedded and entrenched in the way higher education will be delivered in the learning and teaching journey beyond the pandemic (Asare, Yap, Ngoc, & Sarpong, 2021).

The authors of this chapter are members of the business faculty of a leading university in NZ. They experienced the sudden transition from face-to-face to remote teaching when the first pandemic wave hit in early 2020. They delivered courses in a professional master's program where students could complete the program using online platforms and other ICT tools while aiming to maintain the same quality and learning outcomes of the courses as intended before the onset of the pandemic. In this chapter, we aim to not only share our experiences but also posit that the use of new ICT tools and online platforms will be embedded in the teaching and learning strategies in higher education, even in the post pandemic era. Such an approach facilitates the smooth delivery of courses and provides contemporary skills necessary for employability in line with the changes the industry and workforce are experiencing. This alignment of the new learning and teaching practices with the industry work practices creates a compelling need to continue them in the journey beyond the pandemic.

In general, it is reasonably clear that there is an irreversible trend toward blended/online delivery as we look to the future; hence there is an urgent need to review educational strategies that best accommodate such future demands in an uncertain environment. We want to present our experience and approaches to managing online delivery and innovative assessment practices at the University of Auckland in NZ. We use an autoethnographic approach to offer our reflections on our authentic experience of experiential learning (Lützhöft, Nyce, & Styhr Petersen, 2010). In recent times, similar studies using autoethnography reflections by teachers were used to gain insights into online teaching (Godber & Atkins, 2021; Jung, Omori, Dawson, Yamaguchi, & Lee, 2021). We intend to evaluate our own pandemic delivery experiences against context and structures aligned with the pre-pandemic environment.

The rest of the chapter is presented in six sections. Section 5.2 provides the context of the courses taught. Section 5.3 focuses on the preparation and delivery challenges. Section 5.4 explores reflections on delivering classes during COVID-19 lockdowns. Section 5.5 examines the reshaping of assessment used during the COVID-19 pandemic that has implications for the future. Section 5.6 presents the implications of the COVID-19 experience on the future of higher education teaching and learning. Finally, Section 5.7 concludes the chapter.

5.2 Context of the programs

The authors teach in a business master's program, primarily composed of international students, that seeks to produce "business-ready" graduates. The program is called professional masters and consists of 180 credits (1.5 years equivalent) and 240 credits (2 years equivalent) types. The difference between the two programs is that the latter program has extra 60 credits focused on industry-based projects addressing the business problems of real companies. The program offers specializations in accounting, marketing, management, international business, and human resources. With an applied focus, all the courses aim to develop students with both business disciplinary knowledge and applied (professional) skills. Students gain industry-based or workforce skills throughout the program to be applied in their careers. The condensed nature of the quarter system, compared to the traditional semester system, allows students to prepare and enter the workforce in an expedited timeframe.

To provide some additional context to our andragogical responses to the pandemic, we draw from our teaching experience in the business master's program. As the program is typically delivered synchronously in person and on campus, we had to pivot to online delivery (with a mix of synchronous and asynchronous methods) suddenly when the country experienced a series of lockdowns. As a result, we now have mixed cohorts of those in NZ and those learning from overseas, operating under a vastly different delivery model than in the past. In addition, the typical format of the courses per week consist of three sessions - a plenary (lecture), tutorial, and team-based learning (TBL). The TBL sessions typically use a flipped classroom approach in which the students complete self-directed learning before the class (Herreid & Schiller, 2013; Milman, 2012). The plenary earlier in the week provides the students with more context on the weekly topic or area of study and the active learning or application occurs in the TBL sessions. The students apply their theoretical understanding from their readings, videos, case studies, and problem-solving exercises in these hands-on sessions.

NZ has experienced the pandemic at a slightly slower pace than elsewhere due to its geographic isolation. This pace has provided valuable time to learn by observing how others addressed the challenges and translating them into practical measures to deal with the pandemic in NZ, including within the higher education setting. Our university provided some support, templates, and webinars but left it to individual teachers to continue teaching in ways they thought were most appropriate for the course.

The unique characteristic of the program is an embedded approach to building critical employability skills even when students focus on their specialization. These include Professional Development (PD) papers and Business Communication courses that run alongside the main disciplinary curriculum. The extensive PD program is unique to this master's delivery and carefully curated to prepare students for their chosen specialization career paths, focusing primarily on soft skills rather than "hard" skills. Soft skills comprise a broad range of skills that focus on communication and working well with others, among other critical professional skills (Goodheart-Willcox, 2018). The PD papers focused on fostering learners' ability to be ready as professionals and equip them with workforce skills. Additionally, students were supported academically by a learning support unit built into the department. Its primary focus was on developing learners' communication skills for academic and business purposes throughout their learning journey.

Beatty, Collins, and Buckingham (2014) explored the benefits of providing contextualized and integrated support and skills development courses within a program, through which learners in the academic context could access professional practice communities within the program. Hocking and Fieldhouse (2011) define an embedded approach as "incorporating skills as an integral part of the program of study," which requires collaboration between those who teach such skills and the wider program academics whose focus may be primarily disciplinary. An embedded approach to supplement the core curriculum is, therefore, a practical and forward-thinking measure. It will help learners become aware of the demands and discourse of their subjects (McWilliams & Allan, 2014). It will also help learners build important soft/hard skills in a carefully guided and discipline-aligned manner to improve employability for learners after graduation.

5.3 Preparation and delivery challenges

While the news about COVID-19 spread fast at the beginning of 2020, the closing of international borders by the NZ government was sudden and pervasive. The initial lockdown was enforced through a state of emergency from 25 March 2020 to 13 May 2020. The announcement came in the third week of the semester on a Monday, and only two days were given for the whole country to prepare for a complete lockdown to organize their life in isolation by gathering necessary food and other resources. When the lockdown was announced, no one knew how long it would last or how strictly it would be implemented. There was no prior experience or knowledge of dealing with such a situation. The government's approach was guided by "Go hard, go early" to stop the spread of the virus and flatten the curve of COVID-19 infections (Ardern, 2020).

All the higher education stakeholders — students, teachers, university administrators, and support services — scrambled to prepare for the lockdown. Preparation was required in three areas. First, like other members of society, the stakeholders in higher education had to make preparation to live in isolation for an extended period. Second, both students and teachers needed to get ready with computers and laptops for online teaching and learning. For teaching staff, their laptops had to be quickly installed with a Virtual Private Network (VPN) connection to access their individual folders on the university server. The Zoom video conference software was downloaded on students' and staff's computers/laptops as the main course delivery platform. For this purpose, the university's Information Technology (IT) support teams of different departments coordinated and arranged technical support staff to help download software and deal with other technical issues. Third, the teaching staff had to learn the functionalities of the Zoom software such as creating groups and using breakout rooms along with other supporting online teaching tools such as Mentimeter and Padlets. Based on their newly acquired knowledge, the teaching staff had to provide essential guidelines for online learning to the learners. Table 5.1 shows a list of online tools with a brief description of their usage.

The multimodal nature of Zoom came with textual chats, closed captions, transcriptions, video, and voices occurring synchronously, which fundamentally shifted the communication landscape (Thorne & Hellermann, 2022). So, both staff and students had to quickly learn how to use these tools and establish "cultures-of-use" (Thorne, 2016), a concept defined as to how individuals or groups implicitly create an acceptable set of communicative behaviors, quickly coming to a consensus on new teaching and learning behaviors. The staff then had to send specific instructions to students on using these new pedagogical tools. Being new to these technological tools, challenges such as freezing, delays, and weak Wi-Fi connections became recurring challenges in the early days before the Zoom interactions became better. The director of the programs arranged a half-an-hour catch-up meeting where staff could share their experiences daily. This time allowed staff to exchange notes and support each other collegially. Many other issues were dealt with as the staff encountered them regularly.

A serious pastoral care issue was related to unequal access to digital resources. Some students did not have suitable hardware — desktops or laptops appropriate for online learning — and/or lacked financial resources to buy them. For such students, the university management arranged laptops for their use and couriered them. Some other students did not have suitable space to study at their homes. They either had smaller houses with many members to share, which made it difficult to have a dedicated space for their study, or lacked adequate Internet and Wi-Fi facilities. For all such students, a common university space was offered in two major locations in the city. Naseer and Rafique (2021) find how support from teachers and other university managers made a difference in students' learning during the COVID-19 period. Katz et al. (2021) identify that those at the unfavorable end of the "digital divide" experienced negative outcomes under these conditions, where affected learners lacked the resources tended to have access to lower quality digital information as well as lower levels of digital literacy to engage in class activities meaningfully and assessments. The flow-on effect is that they were significantly disadvantaged in the pandemic learning environment. Additionally, those with language challenges, such as English as a Second Language (ESL) speakers, experienced greater marginalization. Communication with the

Table 5.1 Information and communication technology educational tools.

Tool	Purpose	Engagement benefits	URL links
Zoom	Video communication platform that allows connecting with others face-to-face virtually	Allows flexibility for face-to-face simulated contact, recording features for viewing later and breakout rooms for more student engagement.	https://zoom.us/
Padlet	Real-time collaborative web platform in which users can upload, organize, and share content to virtual bulletin boards	A creative way for students to display ideas and brainstorm. An open collaboration tool that students can use in their teams as well.	https://padlet.com/
Mentimeter	Web-based software that develops and maintains an eponymous app used to create presentations with real-time feedback	Allows for polling and voting options as well as presentations. Students can use their own devices and create a fun and engaging environment.	https://www.mentimeter.com/
Google Jamboard	A digital interactive whiteboard	For various delivery modes, boards can be configured ahead of time to give students a space to work during class. This enables live feedback and presentation capabilities during class time.	https://jamboard.google.com/
Google Docs	An online word processor and real-time collaboration by participants	Ease of collaboration and sharing features allow teachers to provide group access to the same documents, which can serve as at-home study guides.	https://docs.google.com/document/u/0/
Miro	A digital interactive whiteboard	Ease of collaboration and sharing ideas as a class group or team.	https://miro.com/

(Continued)

Table 5.1 (Continued)

Tool	Purpose	Engagement benefits	URL links
Kahoot	Game-based learning platform	Gamification can be used in all delivery modes to enhance learning engagement and fun with the content topics. This tool can also be used in a team setting to increase collaboration.	https://kahoot.it/
YouTube	Online video sharing	Students can use this platform to gather information, form content and work to create a different kind of submission.	https://www.youtube.com/
Piazza	An intuitive platform for instructors to efficiently manage class Q&A	Students can post questions and collaborate to edit responses to these questions. Instructors can also answer questions, endorse student answers, and edit or delete any posted content.	https://piazza.com/
Microsoft Teams	Offering workspace chat and videoconferencing, file storage, and application integration	Ability to use a live chat function, host team meetings, and record. It enables students to maximize collaborative space by sharing documents too.	https://www.microsoft.com/en-nz/microsoft-teams/log-in
Canvas LMS discussion forum	Canvas provides an integrated system for class discussions, allowing both instructors and students to start and contribute	Discussions allow for interactive communication between two or more people; users can participate in a conversation with an entire class or group.	https://canvas.com/

LMS, Learning management system; Q&A, question & answer.

instructors during remote learning was hampered considerably due to limited language abilities and lack of confidence. In our context, the communication challenges could be mitigated with the support of an learning support unit within the department, as well as experienced instructors that understand international learner needs. They took a compassionate approach to emerging challenges and provided additional support to help students in learning and assessments; such support was continued throughout the pandemic period.

Undoubtedly, the impact of the pandemic on education has been enormous. The preparation and delivery had challenges that needed to be addressed urgently by teachers and students alike. Many of the changes and strategies deployed to respond to the crisis were through delivery and assessment. The new online delivery methods will carry on beyond the pandemic era based on demand and necessitate flexible modes. The assessments that were innovated for online teaching will continue based on the positive experiences and outcomes. When classes resumed on campus, students voiced their opinions on things they wanted to see continued in the classroom and online. Upon reflection, the challenges of the lockdowns and pandemic presented new, creative ways to deliver content to students.

5.4 Reflections on delivering classes during COVID-19 lockdowns

After the challenges relating to the initial preparation were addressed, regular classes were held online. Before this, the authors taught many courses in the program. But delivering classes completely online was a new experience. As mentioned, the program uses a TBL approach, so students do their reading before coming to interactive class sessions. When they attend the TBL sessions, students undertake various learning activities using case studies and other problem-solving exercises relevant to the week's topic. When we moved to online teaching, we tried to maintain the same TBL approach to delivering the course to the best of our ability. For this purpose, we used a range of IT-based tools, as seen in Table 5.1. The key features of our teaching during the lockdown are highlighted in three ways.

First, we aimed to preserve the quality and integrity of the courses. All the topics that were part of the course remained as previously, along with relevant exercises, where the plenary (or lecture) was delivered either online or prerecorded. In either case, the full lecture recording and the lecture slides were made available to students for their review later.

To manage the heightened risks of academic integrity issues due to the inability to invigilate, the university introduced an institution-wide software called Inspera, which enables the auditing of learner input and behavior during tests and examinations. Additionally, specific Academic Integrity Officers were appointed for each department to frequently audit and review suspicious behavior, resulting in the identification of dishonest behavior. These approaches successfully ensured that the course's integrity was maintained. However, research shows that the transition to digital learning and assessments has resulted in increasing violations that necessitated swift measures to mitigate such risks (Davies & Sharefeen, 2022). However, after the initial spike of such cases of integrity, the number of violations dropped to pre-COVID-19 levels.

Second, like in face-to-face sessions during normal times, the TBL sessions during the lockdown were also conducted using small groups (or teams) of four to six students. Practically, these small teams (groups) are the actual units of learning for students as they interact and challenge each other with novel ideas and solutions. Organizing students into teams in online teaching was made possible using Zoom's "Breakout Rooms" option. Students were either preselected or allocated to their respective rooms, or they were allowed to self-select to join those rooms depending on the exercises. In addition, there was an additional benefit of timer for the breakout room discussions - students could see the countdown of time allocated for the discussions. Students were then brought to the main forum to share the main points identified in the breakout rooms.

Third, there were other ways in which engagement and interaction were ensured. The options of Chat and Polls on Zoom were frequently used to let students give feedback or ask questions, or even take a poll on their preferences. To provide a variety, sometimes, the authors used Mentimeter, a web-based engagement tool. Students could interact with Mentimeter using their smartphones to indicate their choice out of multiple options. Similarly, online "whiteboards" like Padlet, Miro, and Google Jamboard allowed students to collaborate and share ideas on common problems or themes.

Collaboration in the classroom can come in many forms, a popular model being a hyflex approach (Liu & Rodriguez, 2019). Hyflex combines the terms "hybrid" and "flexible" to create a new learning mode that gives a wider choice. This delivery method gives a choice to students to attend learning sessions either face-to-face or synchronously, or asynchronously. This model allows maximum flexibility for the instructor and students in the mode of delivery. In contrast to a traditional classroom, the hyflex model will enable students to select their preferred method while also allowing the instructor to identify the most suitable options for delivery. This model proves helpful in times of pivoting and a need for flexibility. However, the last few years of classroom delivery have shown that all stakeholders desire flexibility. Flexibility has come in many forms and utilizes various ICT educational tools (Kanuka, 2010); see Table 5.1 for a list of online tools and their features.

While online teaching during the COVID-19 lockdown delivered the content with good engagement options, we faced three unanticipated challenges as teachers.

First, it is nonengagement by a section of students by not switching on their cameras and hiding behind "tiles" on the Zoom platform. Despite repeated requests by the teaching team, these students did not switch on their cameras. Some students informally mentioned that they were reluctant to switch on the cameras. They do not want to show their residential rooms (as they work from home) or not comfortable with their personal presentability, which they would otherwise be ready with when coming to a university campus in person. Such challenges were also identified by Barror, Llenares, and del Rosario (2021). Clearly, this is related to personal and cultural issues. So, we did not push such students in the initial period. However, in 2021 and 2022, we made it clear to students that online conference platforms have evolved as industry practice, so students should learn to switch on their cameras and participate actively. But our experience shows that students, particularly international students from non-Western countries, were slow to actively immerse in the new learning environment.

Second, some students did not actively participate in the breakout rooms. They were passively present in their breakout rooms on the Zoom platform. Only one or two students were active, and others were not. The teaching team members had to drop by each breakout room to motivate the students to talk and to encourage them to take notes collaboratively. We used class representatives to seek feedback and informal Zoom polls to gauge class participation. In addition, some courses added participation marks to contribute to the overall course grade. The change introduced led to other challenges of rubrics being crafted to reflect class participation and equity in a virtual classroom. However, it was not immediately clear if this was an effective approach, as we noticed many students still struggling to be active participants in class discussions even after many months of online learning.

Third, the complete lockdown meant that students could not meet each other in person outside their homes or flats to undertake studies in small groups. Lack of opportunity to meet other students adversely affected international students more than domestic ones. The international students who were away from their homes interacted more with their classmates and other students as part of their social network, which happens to be the closest to what family is to them in NZ. As a result, many students, particularly international students, lost motivation to study and could not actively participate in the discussions, which is consistent with the findings by Adara and Najmudin (2020). The teachers had to keep an eye on them and reach out to them to encourage them during this time.

5.5 Reshaping assessments

An important part of the course delivery is assessments. Traditionally, in business programs, assessments take various forms, such as writing essays, reports, oral presentations, tests, and examinations. While essays or reports were given a couple of weeks to write, tests and examinations were conducted under close supervision to protect their integrity. Oral presentations were held in class sessions either as a group or individually. However, when the COVID-19 lockdown started, the delivery of the assessments had to be quickly reconfigured.

While the assignments' content and quality continued as envisaged originally the actual requirements were designed keeping the online delivery challenges in mind. For example, the requirements and guidelines for each assignment are explained more clearly. No assignment required the collection of primary data. Students were required to submit their assignments on the Canvas (our learning management system) page, and the submission dates were extended by a few days when new lockdowns were imposed or students were infected by COVID-19. However, the initial cautious approach was largely replaced by the pre-pandemic practices. The changes in assessments are shown in Table 5.2.

Multiple-choice (MC) questions presented a challenge without the ability to proctor in class. This challenge meant that instructors needed to be more creative in providing MC answer options or shuffling questions from a bank of questions. As the test environment is not adequately secure, this type of assessments were removed or sparingly used. In the future, it is necessary to limit their use or build in fail-safes for academic integrity.

Table 5.2 Adapting assessments.

	Assessments	Changes for the first lockdown in 2020	Changes to later semesters and terms
1	Multiple-choice questions	Removed or offered multiple versions with shuffled questions to maintain the integrity	Used sparingly and carefully curated for student needs to maintain the integrity
2	Essay or report	Extra time and being kind in marking	Regular requirements
3	Oral presentations	Oral presentations were shifted to Zoom online	Many oral presentations use Zoom online platform along with traditional classroom presentations
4	Tests	Open book and 24 h to submit through Canvas	Open book but only 30 min extra time to submit on Canvas
5	Exam	Open book and 24 h to submit through Canvas	Open book but only 30 min extra time to submit on Canvas

Oral presentations were done both individually and in groups as per the course requirements on the Zoom platform. In fact, for large classes of around 100 students, the individual presentations were organized in two concurrent panels to save time. During the group presentations, other students provided feedback comments on the Chat option of the Zoom platform. To ensure, the robustness of the presentation assessments, the same rubric used in traditional classroom presentations was used after making minor changes.

Compared to other types of assessments, significant changes were made in tests and exams. In the first lockdown, the usual test/exam hall supervised tests were converted to open-book tests and given a 24-h window to complete the tests/exams. The semester impacted all the stakeholders in the university, and students were in isolation for an extended period. So, a 24-hour window was considered appropriate to allow all students to take tests in this format and upload the answered documents on Canvas. However, in the semesters and terms that followed the first long lockdown, the 24-hour window was removed and only an extra 30-minutes was given to allow for any technical issues relating to their computer/laptop or Wi-Fi. As the COVID-19 lockdowns kept repeating later, sometimes with only half-day notice, many courses in the business school started using Inspera, an online assessment platform. Inspera is also used by top universities such as the University of Oxford, Lund University, and the University of New South Wales. Using Inspera allowed the university to make the big transition to digital assessments. Students could write their answers in the space provided on the Inspera page for the relevant questions of the test/examination. The university administration established a separate team to support staff and students using Inspera, which slowly has become a default assessment option for tests and examinations of most courses.

5.6 Implications for future delivery of higher education programs

Online learning opportunities existed previously, but the pandemic gave a new sense of urgency to understand the needs and potential of an integrated approach. Broadly, it is anticipated that there is an irreversible trend toward blended/online delivery as we look to the future. Hence, there is an urgent need to review educational strategies which would best address the future demands. We point out significant implications for stakeholders in higher education.

There is a an urgent need for reframing of e-learning approaches. The disruptive effect of the pandemic meant that andragogical interaction opportunities with learners were dramatically reduced, requiring steps to mitigate the situation. The online transition did create continuity to a certain extent, where educators found creative methods to alleviate educational difficulties using old and novel tools. However, the pace of transition was fast, leaving limited time to explore the potential benefits and challenges of new methods applied under implicit duress. While teachers and learners faced some limitations, the wide range of online educational tools helped to overcome them. Also, the real potential of online integration into courses could be realized by gaining experience in the use of online platforms for a strengthened online/hybrid practice moving forward.

As we explore the generative potential of online tools and instruments, looking at the ways in which interaction determines learning experience and success is essential. Using self-governing online forums built into online delivery platforms provided authentic learning opportunities and empowered students to self-direct their learning with instructor guidance. Over time, it became evident that such resources provided opportunities for learners to engage in problem-solving discussions confidently. Therefore, even with minimal teacher steering in an online environment, learners can find ways to benefit and augment their learning (Kanuka, 2005).

The contact and a sense of immediacy with learners were increased via digital tools to make the learning experience seem more personal despite the limitations posed by the disruptions. Ladyshewsky (2013) argued that "teacher immediacy in providing feedback is also an important factor in student satisfaction" and that instructor presence positively affected student satisfaction in an online environment. We addressed the initial lack of personal interaction and instructor presence using humor, relatable media, and casual language. This shift created a sense of empathy and reduced the power distance between instructors and learners. It allowed learners to feel that there is still a real person "interacting" with everyone to overcome the risk of impersonal and mechanistic approaches to teaching in an online environment. Digital tools also enabled frequent formative analysis of learner needs to better understand learner perspectives and circumstances and utilize built-in metrics to determine engagement levels. These approaches enabled reflection on what was successful and what needed improvement for the smooth delivery of the course.

Facilitating class interactions rather than traditional one-way lecturing could improve participation and maximize the learning outcomes. Through carefully managing and scaffolding interactions with the unique functions of available educational tools, a teacher can help shape the sense of self-efficacy (Bandura, Freeman, & Lightsey, 1999; Shortridge-Baggett, 2000) of learners as effective and independent learners. In this instance, professionals in their chosen fields of business studies increase their confidence to engage with the discourse communities. An important contributing aspect to learner immersion into online professional/business cultures is consistent with Thorne's (2016) view that people's online activity is mediated by "cultures-of-use" that was explored earlier. This concept creates a learner-generated values system when participating in online communicative activities as afforded by specific tools, which are moderated and enforced through peer influence and expectations in their natural online settings. As a learner, one can see how others behave in this environment and gauge what would be appropriate and what should be avoided through observation and reflection, supported by a formal or informal code of conduct. Peer and instructor involvement in this process results in social collaboration and validation to strengthen learner identities to engage in their target communities confidently.

There is also a need to consider how program design processes can play a significant role in delivery, emphasizing how design should be considered to support and empower learners in a hybrid environment. In our delivery, adopting a systems-based approach (Sork, 2000) to program design when integrating support for students was necessary. This approach places learner experience and feedback at the center of the program design process to overcome a distinctly "learning objective"— dominated perspective created by traditional linear-technical/rational program design concepts (Wilson, 2005). Contemporary understandings of the pandemic's impact on learner experience reveal that instruction has become more transmissive with reduced interactions (Katz et al., 2021). This change is owing to the limitations of the online environment and "Zoom fatigue," heightening the learning objective-dominated andragogy over ones that recognize individual learner needs and agency.

As many international learners were geographically distributed across countries and possessed specific needs, the pandemic experience revealed that learners themselves could achieve the best outcomes. Learners can play a leading role and have a say in determining what support they wish to receive through negotiating with lecturers and support staff via formal and informal feedback mechanisms. Ensuring that learners feel comfortable voicing their needs was achieved by reducing the perception of professional distance, as alluded to earlier (within reason), which allowed learners to be active agents in determining what kind of support they wish to receive (Allaudin & Ashman, 2014) rather than being prescribed a course of instruction or support that they may not actually require nor benefit from (McWilliams & Allan, 2014). This approach is distinctly different from the traditional models of designing and delivering courses that enhance responsiveness to uncertainties and learner circumstances beyond instructor control. Therefore, to enhance learner experience in the new ways forward, a more frequent formative evaluation-driven design scheme needs to be adopted, a design that closely observes learner contexts and needs and offer a more responsive and learner-centered experience.

More broadly, professional programs can benefit from exploring the wider benefits of learning beyond acquiring mere degrees. All forms of education provide benefits measured in terms of outcomes, whether explicitly intended or otherwise. In management and professional education, there is a strong need to closely examine what outcomes and benefits are provided to learners, as many participants in postgraduate studies are seeking a second chance to advance their qualifications and subsequent employment opportunities. The pandemic clearly highlighted the challenges of international students compared to domestic students in coping with the lockdowns and other constraints. Having charged higher tuition fees from international students, institutions need to take an empathetic approach to enable fair participation and success in their learning journey.

For example, during the pandemic, focusing on learners' resilience during times of uncertainty provided significant employability and identity development opportunities. Motivation, self-esteem, a sense of purpose, and critical thinking abilities as a by-product of learning (Schuller, 2004) can strengthen the capacity to deal with life's challenges and negotiate obstacles on their own, thus creating independent learners and professionals. Thus identity capital could be seen to heavily influence the acquisition of human and social capital that typically frame the design of professional/business courses. An interesting question arising from the experiences of the pandemic is about one's outlook and self-image as a person and as a learner. A professional program can help with identity development for employability and resilience in the workplace.

5.7 Conclusion

We acknowledge that the effects of COVID-19 are not over yet and it will continue to have an impact globally on education with varying levels of disruption. Emerging variants of the COVID-19 virus will continue to place new demands on higher education to prepare for ongoing uncertainty. However, the COVID-19 pandemic has brought about some dynamic and new challenges to higher education globally. While the challenges are well known and have been experienced by many, they continue to evolve with ongoing and sometimes unpredictable developments, which require a resilient, flexible, and future-focused response from educators at both program and institutional levels. As the use of digital technologies increases worldwide, many regular teaching and learning activities are likely to shift to the digital platform making the class a blended learning experience. Many face-to-face meetings that moved to the Zoom platform are likely to continue in the post-COVID-19 era. There is, thus, a strong alignment of the current workforce practices in the industry and the teaching and learning methods of existing programs.

Integration of online tools in the traditional delivery systems has been a highly productive and effective approach in our program delivery that helped to overcome the pandemic restrictions. Despite being physically disconnected, our experiences have shown that digital tools carry significant potential for enhancing learner-centered program design and delivery beyond the pandemic. These tools can serve as an elegant solution to engaging learners outside of a physical or face-to-face class setting while maintaining the integrity of andragogical interactions. Additionally, student-led online learning activities suit constructivist/progressive principles as they can genuinely experience the personal meaning-making of disciplinary discourses in the context of their shared experiences. This context enhances not only disciplinary learning but also other personal capabilities relating to cultures, professionalism, communication, and digital citizenship. This holistic development of students prepares them for confident and seamless entry into the industry.

References

Ardern, J. (2020). *Major steps taken to protect New Zealanders from COVID-19*. Available from http://www.beehive.govt.nz/release/major-steps-taken-protect-new-zealanders-covid-19.

Adara, R. A., & Najmudin, O. (2020). Analysis on the differences in EFL learners' demotivating factors after COVID 19 Pandemic. *Ta'dib: Jurnal Pendidikan Islam, 23*(2), 1–12.

Allaudin, M., & Ashman, A. (2014). The changing academic environment and diversity in students' study philosophy, beliefs and attitudes in higher education. *Higher Education Research & Development, 33*(5), 857–870.

Asare, A. O., Yap, R., Ngoc, T., & Sarpong, E. O. (2021). The pandemic semesters: Examining public opinion regarding online learning amidst COVID-19. *Journal of Computer Assisted Learning, 37*(6), 1591–1605.

Bandura, A., Freeman, W. H., & Lightsey, R. (1999). Self-efficacy: The exercise of control. *Journal of Cognitive Psychotherapy, 13*(2), 158–166.

Barror, J. S., Llenares, I., & del Rosario, L. S. (2021). Students' online learning challenges during the pandemic and how they cope with them: The case of the Philippines. *Education and Information Technologies, 26*(6), 7321–7338.

Beatty, S., Collins, A., & Buckingham, M. (2014). Embedding academic socialisation within a language support program: An Australian case study. *The International Journal of the First Year in Higher Education, 5*(1), 9–18.

Davies, A., & Shareefen, Al (2022). Enhancing academic integrity in a UAE safety, security defence emergency management academy—The Covid-19 response and beyond. *International Journal for Educational Integrity, 18*(1), 1–18.

Godber, K. A., & Atkins, D. R. (2021). COVID-19 impacts on teaching and learning: a collaborative autoethnography by two higher education lecturers, In *Frontiers in Education, 6*, 647524.

Goodheart-Willcox. (2018). *Soft skills for the workplace*. IL, United States: The Goodheart-Willcox Company Inc.

Jung, I., Omori, S., Dawson, W. P., Yamaguchi, T., & Lee, S. J. (2021). Faculty as reflective practitioners in emergency online teaching: An autoethnography. *International Journal of Educational Technology in Higher Education, 18*(1), 1−17.

Herreid, C. F., & Schiller, N. A. (2013). Case studies and the flipped classroom. *Journal of College Science Teaching, 42*(5), 62−66.

Hocking, D., & Fieldhouse, W. (2011). Implementing academic literacies in practice [online]. *New Zealand Journal of Educational Studies, 46*(1), 35−47.

Hussein, E., Daoud, S., Alrabaiah, H., & Badawi, R. (2020). Exploring undergraduate students' attitudes towards emergency online learning during COVID-19: A case from the UAE. *Children and Youth Services Review, 119*, 1−7.

Kanuka, H. (2010). Cultural diversity, technologically-mediated learning and instructional design: Implications for choosing and using communication tools. *Asia-Pacific Collaborative education Journal, 6*(1), 1−16.

Kanuka, H. (2005). An exploration into facilitating higher levels of learning in a text-based internet learning environment using diverse instructional strategies. *Journal of Computer-Mediated Communication, 10*(3), JCMC1032.

Katz, V. S., Jordan, A. B., & Ognyanova, K. (2021). Digital inequality, faculty communication, and remote learning experiences during the COVID-19 pandemic: A survey of U.S. undergraduates. *Public Library of Science, 16*(2), 1−16.

Ladyshewsky, R. (2013). Instructor presence in online courses and student satisfaction. *The International Journal for the Scholarship of Teaching and Learning, 7*(1), 1−23.

Li, J., Xu, Y., Deifell, E., & Angus, K. (2021). Emergency remote language teaching and U.S.-based college-level world language educator's intention to adopt online teaching in postpandemic times. *The Modern language journal (Boulder, Colo.), 105*(2), 412−434.

Liu, C.-Y. A., & Rodriguez, R. C. (2019). Evaluation of the impact of the Hyflex learning model. *International Journal of Innovation and Learning, 25*(4), 393−411.

Lützhöft, M., Nyce, J. M., & Styhr Petersen, E. (2010). Epistemology in ethnography: assessing the quality of knowledge in human factors research. *Theoretical Issues in Ergonomics Science, 11*(6), 532−545.

McWilliams, R., & Allan, Q. (2014). Embedding academic literacy skills: Towards a best practice model. *Journal of University Teaching & Learning Practice, 11*(3), Art. 8.

Milman, N. B. (2012). The flipped classroom strategy: What is it and how can it best be used? *Distance Learning, 9*(3), 85.

Naseer, S., & Rafique, S. (2021). Moderating role of teachers' academic support between students' satisfaction with online learning and academic motivation in undergraduate students during COVID-19. *Education Research International*. Available from https://doi.org/10.1155/2021/7345579.

Schuller, T. (2004). Three capitals: A framework. In T. Schuller, et al. (Eds.), *The benefits of learning: The impact of education on health, family life and social capital*. New York, NY: Routledge Falmer.

Shortridge-Baggett, L. M. (2000). The theory and measurement of the self-efficacy construct. *Self-efficacy in nursing: Research and measurement perspectives*, 9−28.

Sork, T. J. (2000). Planning educational programs. *Handbook of adult and continuing education*, 2.

Thorne, S. L. (2016). Cultures-of-use and morphologies of communicative action. *Language Learning & Technology, 20*(2), 185−191.

Thorne, S. L., & Hellermann, J. (2022). Coda: the interactional affordances and constraints of technology-rich teaching and learning environments. *Classroom Discourse*, 2.

Wilson, A. L. (2005). Programme planning. In L. M. English (Ed.), *Encyclopaedia of adult education* (pp. 524−529). Basinstoke, England: Palgrave Macmillan.

CHAPTER 6

Birley Place: a digital community to enhance student learning

Kirsten Jack[1], Ryan Wilkinson[2], Eleanor Hannan[1] and Claire Hamshire[3]
[1]Faculty of Health and Education, Manchester Metropolitan University, Manchester, United Kingdom
[2]Lifelong Learning Centre, University of Leeds, Leeds, United Kingdom
[3]University of Salford, Salford, United Kingdom

6.1 Introduction

Over the last 20 years, advances in digital technologies have had the potential to expand our learning community spaces in ways that are unbounded by location, time, or physical presence (Klappa et al., 2019). These technologies range from the basic use of managed learning environments to provide easy access to learning materials through to immersive reality in which education revolves primarily around the digital platform (Benavides et al., 2020; Bowen, 2015; Crawford et al., 2020; Sormunen et al., 2020). Learning is both a social and spatial experience (Bilham et al., 2019) and as learning technologies continue to develop, our higher education (HE) environments can be easily transferred across a range of technological communities (Klappa et al., 2019).

Much has been written about the potential of digital education to transform student learning, and digital technologies remain a topical issue across the sector as institutions consider how these methods can extend, expand, or replace physical learning spaces (Klappa et al., 2019). While the utilization of digital technologies had already been found to enhance learning for students (Arkorful & Abaidoo, 2015; Kattoua, Al-Lozi, & Alrowwad, 2016), technologies became invaluable during the recent COVID-19 pandemic as universities utilized them to facilitate remote-only learning (Cesco et al., 2021; Crawford et al., 2020). To maintain placement opportunities at a time of remote working, health- and social care—related disciplines quickly utilized digital technologies for simulated placement opportunities for students (Burki, 2020; Haslam, 2021; Salter et al., 2020; Torda, 2020; Twogood et al., 2020). The increased reliance on digital technologies throughout the pandemic has resulted in

Digital Teaching, Learning and Assessment
DOI: https://doi.org/10.1016/B978-0-323-95500-3.00004-3
99

considerable changes across the HE sector, particularly with an increased move toward blended learning opportunities for students (Guppy et al., 2022).

This chapter presents an overview of an online digital community called "Birley Place" named after the site on which our Faculty of Health and Education is situated, Birley Fields, an inner-city area of Hulme in Manchester, United Kingdom. The digital community is utilized to enhance the learning experiences of students studying on health and social care programs, with a focus on personal and professional skill development in a collaborative space. Using publicly available health and population data of the large metropolitan city in which our institution is based, we created a virtual map populated with people, places, and scenarios matched with the real-world areas based on health and lifestyle data to provide digital place-based learning opportunities. This process ensured that the homes, businesses, and services in the community are representative of distinct socioeconomic areas of our city (Wright et al., 2021) and learners get a real-world simulation experience. Learners get to meet the digital residents in their own homes and gain an understanding of the importance of their family and community networks for their emotional and physical well-being.

6.2 Background

The move toward the provision of digital learning within HE is motivated by both institutional and learner requirements (Flavin & Quintero, 2018; Harasim, 2017; JISC, 2011; Sharpe, Benfield, & Francis, 2006) with health-related subjects responding to this changing landscape (Regmi & Jones, 2020). At an institutional level, the driving forces are the changing economic market and future workforce needs as we continue to develop graduates with the skills employers require (Bridgstock & Tippett, 2019; Pucciarelli & Kaplan, 2016). Universities need to continue to develop and deliver programs that meet the needs of both national and international students within a competitive market, with a view to accessibility and extending the philosophy of flexible learning. Student expectations also have a key influence as they assume universities will offer digital learning resources allowing flexibility and collaborative learning (Arkorful & Abaidoo, 2015; Guppy et al., 2022). Many students also wish to study at times and in surroundings that suit their individual needs (Sormunen et al., 2020).

Digital technologies afford possibilities of more flexible ways of interacting and enable learners to work without the constraints of time and place, providing opportunities for them to work outside the normal working day or in places other than in formal education settings (Castro & Tumibay, 2021). For many students, a flexible approach to their studies is important, as the demands on their time are increasingly varied and complex. For these students, as well as for others who simply prefer a digitally enhanced learning model, online and simulated learning experiences can be a huge advantage to them. Accessibility can easily be provided for individuals with disabilities or additional learning needs, via design features such as ALT-text and screen readers (Burgstahler, 2000).

As technology evolves, resulting in changing workplace expectations, communicating and collaborating effectively with others, while respecting their values and beliefs, are skills that all graduates need to develop (Bridgstock & Tippett, 2019; Kornelakis & Petrakaki, 2020). This is particularly important in health and social care professions although all graduates need to develop effective communication and collaboration skills and can simulate these experiences in a digital setting. Rosen (2008) details the history of digital medical simulation and its growth in the late 1980s and early 1990s, with the first meeting of *Medicine Meets Virtual Reality* taking place in 1991. As the capabilities of new technologies developed, health-care professionals used these technologies in their simulation work, including in virtual worlds (Walia, Zahedi, & Jain, 2017; Wiecha et al., 2010) and other computer-based systems (Bradley, 2006). There has been recent development to both digital and physical simulation throughout health-care programs internationally (Chernikova et al., 2020; Health Education England, 2018; Jeffries, 2020; Nursing & Midwifery Council, 2019) to offer high quality, immersive learning opportunities to replicate real-world experiences, through innovative and engaging activities (Gaba, 2004). Simulated learning adds an extra dimension to the curriculum, providing a space in which learners can interact and make decisions as they would in real life, but in safe spaces without real-life consequences (Wright et al., 2021). The emergence of social media as a tool to create virtual communities in healthcare has been researched in professional settings (Rolls et al., 2016; Sibbald et al., 2022; Thoma et al., 2018), but this approach can lack the support, control, engagement, and scaffolding needed for undergraduate collaborative learning (Chugh & Ruhi, 2018).

Institutional virtual learning environments often lack the functionality and flexibility for subject-specific pedagogies (Laurillard, 2013) so, a tailored resource was developed to address these concerns.

6.2.1 Building Birley Place—digital community development

Birley Place is a bespoke online digital community built on a WordPress site enabling it to be sustainable and easily accessible to internal and external stakeholders at a local and global level. Learners can explore the community map, visit residents at home, and gain an understanding of the socioeconomic factors that can impact on their lives, by interacting with people, places, and scenarios (Figs. 6.1 and 6.2). Developing a learning resource which focuses on communities is important, due to the influence of the socioeconomic influences on health and well-being. Health does not only relate to the standard and funding of health services, it is inextricably linked to the conditions in which people live, work, and age and the inequity in resources and money that they have (The Health Foundation, 2019). Birley Place enables students to understand these factors by contextualizing all scenarios in an authentic setting.

Scenarios, which might require the development of new resident profiles, are developed in relation to curriculum needs across the different

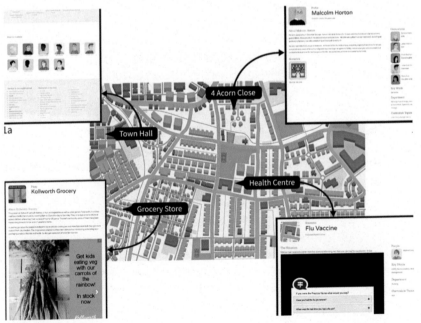

Figure 6.1 The Birley Place community.

Profile

Joseph Quinn

Flat 3, 6 Cotton Road / 17 years old

About Joseph Quinn

Joseph Quinn (Joey) is a white teenager who lives in a flat in Kollworth, which he rents through a social renting scheme with his girlfriend Laila and their 6 month-old baby, Jake. Joey and Lailas' parents were disappointed when they announced she was pregnant as they were still 'kids' in their eyes.

Joey is determined to prove to them that he has what it takes to be a good dad and partner. He left school with four GCSEs and has secured a full-time apprenticeship in the construction industry, which he is enjoying so far. Leila can't work at the moment as she is looking after baby Jake at home, so their household income is below average. She often takes Jake to the Sure Start Centre on Jack Road to attend baby groups and meet with other young mums.

Figure 6.2 Example of a resident profile.

health and social care courses. Scenarios might be based on real-life experiences, developed by the academic teams although care is taken to ensure that anonymity of service users is maintained. All scenarios that are included relate to specific learning aims and objectives of the various programs and this ensures that students have a set of distinct experiences, without repetition. Scenarios can vary in length and therefore will take more or less time to develop within Birley Place. Academic teams and e-learning developers work in collaboration to develop profiles ensuring that both subject knowledge and digital skills development are combined effectively, to provide an effective resource for our students. Scenarios and tasks are updated when required, to reflect changes in policy and practice and developed in line with student evaluation. Site analytics are helpful to support academic staff in understanding student usage of the resources, and to assess time spent on each element, to inform developments. Formative assessments are built into Birley Place and there is an option to ensure that an assessment is completed before students can move onto the next learning task.

The development of Birley Place commenced in 2016 using a basic website with a map, a small number of residents and associated case studies. Over the following four years, it was gradually expanded as we included activities for additional groups, followed by rapid expansion in

2020 and 2021. The cost for the initial setup of Birley Place was approximately 10000 GBP (including web development and software licenses) and 3500 GBP to maintain annually (for web domain, hosting, and maintenance). In addition, our faculty employs an e-learning developer to manage and develop the Birley Place platform, and this accounts for ~50% of their workload. There are additional costs associated with staff time for the planning and development of the teaching, learning, and assessment activities used within Birley Place and this forms part of academic workload.

A WordPress site is advantageous for both technical and nontechnical site administration. Harnessing the power of WordPress user management and role permissions has enabled multiple universities to simultaneously interact with the platform, upload their own students and tutors, and manage content assignment. From a nontechnical point of view, as WordPress has easy-to-use content management system functionality, it empowers project staff to update and add to the site without the requirement for specialist technical assistance. WordPress also enables users across organizations to sign in without needing an institutional identification. This removes the technical and organizational barriers that can often be found when working across multiple sectors with varying degrees of technological firewalls and policies. Working in this way enabled an inclusive learning experience since the site can be accessed from mobile phones, laptops, and a range of electronic devices.

WordPress as a content management system enabled the creation of custom post types (a technical term to describe specific types of content, e.g., a "profile," "place," and "scenario") built to contain each instance's specific information such as, among others, a profile required an age field, and a place required an address field. During the planning phase, it became clear that supporting a large volume of linked posts could become problematic and confusing if not built to be dynamically linked. This led to the incorporation of a bidirectional postrelationship workflow which allowed for multiple posts to be dynamically linked, enabling an update in one area to be cascaded to the relevant associated posts. An example of this being a profile that was associated to a place, or a scenario involving multiple profiles and places. When creating a virtual "real-world" platform that catered for a user's progression through the university life cycle, there was a need for the profiles to mature and for their background story to develop. This profile progression of age and history needed to be linked to the specific level of the logged-in user to ensure that a Year 1 student did not see the profile journey of what was visible to a Year 3 student. Providing specific profile fields for this content enabled dynamic coding on the front-end of the website to show only the relevant content for the user. The ability to assign certain scenarios and learning packages—custom-built content, including links to scenarios, profiles, and places, is a key piece of functionality. This required user group management to be developed, enabling a tutor-level user to manage multiple different groups of students and the ability to assign to these groups. Following the assignment of scenarios or learning packages, it was then necessary to build in appropriate timeframes and reporting mechanisms to provide vital insights into user behavior and engagement.

Utilizing flexible, customizable technology in this way in the development of Birley Place enabled a bespoke online community to be created to help students achieve the required learning outcomes across several different pathways. Birley Place aims to enhance our students' understanding of lived experience through a community setting along with the key aspects of interprofessional working, including collaboration, communication, and respect for others. The significant change and disruption due to the pandemic fast-tracked development of Birley Place out of necessity and we reconfigured the community to be a replacement for physical placements. The two examples below detail how we have used the digital community to develop innovative pedagogy with a focus on accessibility and convenience by creating a social space for learning.

6.2.2 Case study one—interactive digital placements

During the COVID-19 pandemic in 2020—22, when a significant number of our students were unable to attend physical work placements, the digital community was used to develop online clinical placements. During the academic year 2020—21, many of our students completed the virtual placements, including 100 nursing students, 325 physiotherapy, and 74 speech and language therapy students. Interactive simulated placements have become more prevalent across health- and social care—related disciplines with the COVID-19 pandemic prompting institutions to pivot toward different modes of delivery using digital tools (Gordon et al., 2020).

Working within the constraints of professional body stipulations, we developed an interactive digital placement across acute, primary, and intermediate care settings for preregistration physiotherapy, speech and language therapy, and nursing students. Students were central to the development of the digital resources within Birley Place and were able to explain their priorities and ensure that any resources focused on their needs. Several of our student partners shared clinical experiences with us to inform the development of digital stories for the placement. Although this development was in response to the pandemic, the simulated placement will continue beyond this era, not only as a response to the ongoing clinical placement pressure but because it provides an effective and sustainable learning opportunity for our students.

Using Birley Place enabled us to situate the students' clinical learning within specific socioeconomic contexts to gain an understanding of health and social inequalities. The community enables students to understand the complex issues that contribute to ill health and the importance of effective collaboration required to support well-being. The prevalence of long-term conditions is influenced by an array of social, economic, political, and environmental conditions (The Health Foundation, 2019). Birley Place supports understanding of these factors and the knowledge gained can subsequently be applied in practice to support quality of care provision. For example, learners can click on the map to visit buildings to access information about the people who live or work there. There is a minimum amount of background information provided for each person in the form of a role profile, containing details such as their age, occupation, hobbies, and lifestyle. Scenarios related to the person bring a narrative context related to their health status. These might include text-based descriptions or audiovisual case-based interactive media that bring describe events from the person's life or interactions they had with health or social care professionals. Several of the scenarios are interactive and include reflective activities, which support the students to think critically about their beliefs and responses. Birley Place has advantages over traditional online learning platforms as learners are encouraged to interact socially to explore outcomes of their individual and joint decisions about the issues. Students begin to think about their role in the placement and where they fit within the wider team, underlining the need for respect for other values, beliefs, and difference.

Recording student engagement with Birley Place placement was important to ensure that the statutory amount of practice hours was completed by each student. Measuring engagement in digital spaces is vital in helping to track student progress and help shape future iterations of the Birley Place platform (El Alfy, Marx Gómez, & Dani, 2019). This was achieved by the requirement to complete a piece of reflection on the digital placement, which was informed by the scenarios within it. Noncompletion of the digital placement hours would have meant that students would not be able to complete the reflection and could therefore lose practice hours, which would need to be completed elsewhere.

6.2.3 Case study two—interprofessional education

Being able to work effectively with others is essential for future employability across all disciplines and recent high-profile cases in the public domain have highlighted critical failures in interprofessional communication within health and social care (Francis, 2013). Facilitating student cross-disciplinary working in our digital community was essential, within health and social care, this is known as interprofessional education (IPE). IPE involves learners from a minimum of two different professions learning with, from, and about each other, to improve collaboration and health and social care provision (Centre for the Advancement of Interprofessional Education, 2016), and has been at the core of several innovations which have been facilitated using Birley Place. IPE has been linked to positive outcomes to support an agile workforce, including improved attitudes to other professional groups and development of knowledge and skills needed to work collaboratively, leading to enhanced employability prospects (Reeves et al., 2016). However, the facilitation of IPE can be challenging due to the logistics of bringing together student groups from different disciplines at the same time. University structures tend to promote uniprofessional approaches and there can be confusion over definitions about what IPE means (Donnelly, 2019; Xyrichis, Reeves, & Zwarenstein, 2018). These challenges can lead to short-term solutions which leave students feeling like IPE is an additional extra rather than an integral aspect of their education, leading to lack of engagement and ultimately, negative implications for quality-of-care provision.

Using Birley Place we were able to bring together students from nursing, physiotherapy, social work, social care, and speech and language therapy to explore tasks housed in the digital community, in this example 825 first-year students and 698 second-year students. Students were required to explore how their own disciplinary expertise would inform care for a resident within the digital community and consider the skills of others, for example, working together to develop a care plan for a resident with specific health needs. These collaborative activities enabled each professional discipline to consider their own role while learning more about others (Jack et al., 2022). Rehearsing such skills is helpful, to inform future interprofessional practice in the clinical area and thereby enhancing care provision (Brock et al., 2013).

6.3 Evaluating Birley Place—methodology

Exploring our students' perceptions and experiences of using the digital community was central to inform ongoing developments of the platform; therefore we utilized an action research design (Cohen, Manion, & Morrison, 2017), taking data from both case studies (the digital placements project and IPE project). This multimethod approach allowed the researchers to utilize a variety of different data collection methods and data analysis methods to explore staff and student experiences of using Birley Place in different contexts (Greene, 2015; Johnson, Onwuegbuzie, & Turner, 2007). Data collection methods included online surveys, listening events, workshops, and one-to-one interviews, combining quantitative and qualitative data for comprehensive analysis (Hesse-Biber & Johnson, 2015). The iterative approach embedded in action research (Clark et al., 2020) has meant that Birley Place is constantly being developed to meet the needs of the users. Multimethod approaches allow multiple viewpoints, perspectives, and positions (Ivankova & Wingo, 2018) and were the most appropriate for evaluating Birley Place as the use of more than one method allowed a more complete picture of the students' experiences to be assembled.

Involvement in both the staff and student evaluations was voluntary and ethical committee approval was given by the institution. In total, 276 students completed at least one of the quantitative surveys, which represents 11.6% of the eligible cohort. A total of 13 students and 7 members of staff have taken part in either an interview, workshop, or listening event. The survey data were collected using an online survey tool consisting of both open and closed items. The closed items were analyzed using descriptive statistics and a thematic analysis of the open responses was undertaken. The interviews, listening events, and workshops were digitally recorded and transcribed verbatim, with each transcript reviewed with the recording to ensure accuracy. A thematic analysis was undertaken by two members of the research team, with the analysis leading to emergent themes agreed across the team (Clarke & Braun, 2014).

6.4 Evaluation findings

Overall, both academic staff, involved in the design and delivery of the learning resources, and students, were positive about the digital community. The students reported that Birley Place assisted them with their personal and professional skill development, prompted them to reflect on their learning, and provided a safe space to collaborate with their peers. Most students also reported that they enjoyed using the interactive resources on Birley Place, often requesting more of these when considering what could be improved. Furthermore, students noted that the online community supported "real-life" practices and interactions which "open our eyes to see the reality of work in the future." Staff also highlighted the flexibility it offers students in being self-directed and reflective in their learning.

The thematic analysis of the data identified four key themes, which supported students' personal and professional development:
1. authentic learning experiences
2. digital place-based learning
3. opportunities for collaboration
4. flexibility and convenience

6.4.1 Theme 1—authentic learning experiences

Student feedback demonstrated that using Birley Place to develop authentic characters, scenarios, and settings enabled students to imagine they were attending a real placement. This helped them to situate their learning within a work-based context, enabling them to prepare for future physical placements:

I liked the videos of patients which allowed me to feel I was on a real placement. I liked the links and resources that were provided as they allowed me to develop my understanding (First Year Undergraduate Physiotherapy Student)

Even though it's not in real life, I was able to relate the scenarios to real life and when I'm on placement I could reflect on it. (First Year Undergraduate Speech and Language Therapy Student)

Students also valued the opportunities that Birley Place offered to prepare for future physical placements, which helped reduce their anxiety and increase their insight into potential future issues:

(Birley Place) gives a sense of what to expect when I have my first placement which reduces the anxiety around placement for me. For this reason, I think Birley Place should be accessible for all especially those who are anxious or

have disabilities because this may help them to become familiar with how the placement will work (First Year Undergraduate Physiotherapy student)

(Birley Place) gives an insight into the issues we may face while on placement (and) allows us to learn from situations that we are faced with in varied environments. (First Year Undergraduate Physiotherapy student)

The learning experiences offered by Birley Place also provided opportunities for the students to make theory-practice links and relate the work they did in Birley Place to their wider degree, person-centered care provision and future employment. This was also something that staff members felt was an important element of Birley Place. The following excerpts suggest the ways in which the digital resources enabled theory-practice links:

I found Birley Place a good starting point to try and link some of the theory that I was talking about in class to real people, to think about ... some of them were good because they had embedded links in there as well. But I think they're a good teaching aid ... (Staff Member)

Birley Place offers students the opportunity to experience authentic learning experiences that have "real-world" replicability. This helps students consider and reflect on both the competencies that are useful in a placement setting and the knowledge and skills they need as part of their degree.

6.4.2 Theme 2—digital place-based education

Situating students' learning within a digital online community allowed them to explore the influence of place and environmental factors on the virtual service users they encounter. This allows students to consider elements such as inequality and lived experience and explore how these influences health and well-being:

I really enjoyed when you were taken through understanding how a community was evaluated and how their health and social needs were evaluated. I'd not seen these mosaic reports or any other community report, I hadn't understood how they were put together so I've learnt something new from that. And I just I enjoyed that and I can see the relevance to my degree, because I have to have something like that to know what services to put in place with the local population. (First Year Undergraduate Adult Nursing Student)

I just think it was good to have a bit of awareness of how it's not just the patient you're looking at, it's the whole area the patient lives in that comes into play when you're looking at treatment plans, especially, in community settings, yes it's not just the person, it's the three-mile radius around them that you need to consider as well. (First Year Undergraduate Adult Nursing student)

Staff also highlighted how helping students consider a range of factors within a digital community—aided students in their learning, offering realistic learning opportunities:

I think that it's a really useful resource. I think the town hall where you can get all the information about the demographics, about the community profiling stuff, about health, about how many people smoke and drink and about the middle class or whatever, about the unemployment rates, I think it's really quite realistic (Staff member)

It's a really good basis for trying to get students to look at the health needs of a population and try and become a little bit more familiar with some sort of virtual characters or some simulated characters. It's a little bit of a stepping-stone, I think, from looking at stuff on paper which it allows things to come a little bit more to life before they go out into the world and see real patients. So, I think it's a little bit of a stepping-stone for students really if that makes sense for them to have that sort of simulated environment really. (Staff member)

Using Birley Place enabled the replication of a physical place-based project, which students had to undertake by visiting a local community. Birley Place enabled students to experience the place-based learning opportunities in a digital context:

... we were teaching students about community in place; buildings that have been bought up and then turned into shops, gentrification, all that sort of stuff ... getting them to think about how where people lived mattered ... so we got them to go on a bus trip from one part of the city out into a more rural area, and to get off at various stages and to take field notes to bring it back and do a presentation about it ... and in the pandemic we developed loads of content for those students to be able to do it in Birley Place. (Staff member)

This project enabled students to experience the elements of place-based work that had been developed in a safe, flexible digital context.

6.4.3 Theme 3—opportunities for collaboration

Place-based digital working in Birley Place incorporates collaborative practices for students on different degree pathways to work together to reach shared learning goals. Working collaboratively with their colleagues is pivotal skill students are required to develop in preparation for quality care provision and subsequent employment in dynamic, cross-disciplinary settings. This would not have happened physically, due to the logistical challenges of facilitating learning for so many students at the same time:

> I enjoyed working with people from different courses because it allowed be to see things from different viewpoints. Also, we were all able to respect each other and communicate effectively. (First Year Undergraduate Speech and Language Therapy Student)

> I enjoyed working with my groupmates, they are nice and considerate. I'm a shy person, I know I shouldn't be because I'm going to face lots of patients in the future, this course gave me the chance to communicate with other professions, which helped me a lot. I enjoyed working as a team because I'm not alone and I can always seek help from my helpful groupmates. (First Year Adult Nursing Student)

> I think out of having to complete the task, I got more of a sense of how to try and engage with people and check in on people in terms of a bit of a, not leadership activity, but you know what I mean? The driving force of the group type of thing. I think that's a role that I've not really had to step that much into before, so it was good being able to hone those skills and get used to leading those kinds of conversations. (First Year Undergraduate Mental Health Nursing student)

The following participants valued the digital group assignment which enabled students to build information on a weekly basis, involving other disciplines in a collaborative approach:

> And people are being trained to go and work in the same sector, the same kind of sector, so it is really important to have that, kind of, collaborative approach and also to have those kinds of understandings of what skills different people bring. So, I see that as important. (Senior Lecturer, Integrated Health and Social Care)

> It's a collaborative, yes, multidisciplinary group assignment, a group task activity where you get different information each week to inform the picture of a health plan, you need to build for somebody, an awareness of the area and services that need to go out and find, that exist in the real world. (First Year Undergraduate Adult Nursing Student)

6.4.4 Theme 4—flexibility and convenience

As Birley Place is a web-based platform, students and staff both within and external to the institution and external partners can access resources. This makes Birley Place accessible to users without an institutional log-in, meaning that external partners, such as clinical educators, can access the site.

The flexible nature of Birley Place assumed more importance during the facilitation of logistically difficult aspects of the curriculum, such as IPE. This was important not only during the pandemic but is a sustainable way to emulate the realities of clinical practice, as stated by academics in these excerpts:

> *I think being online lends itself quite well to IPE, because I think that's how many of us communicate and collaborate anyway. We don't necessarily all get in a room together; we do things online. And I think it's going to be a skillset that people are going to need to have, and I think we need to start doing that right from the beginning. (Senior Lecturer, Social Work)*

> *I think there are some definite benefits of being online for something like this where you are trying to...I think it's good for students to get together and meet each other but obviously there can be a lot of flexibility to do some delivery online (Lecturer, Integrated Health and Social Care)*

Students valued the sequential nature of the resource delivery, such as the use of service user personal narratives, which unfolded over the weeks of the program. Using this approach enabled important aspects of information to be revealed about the digital residents, which might have altered the care planning or assessment of them. This approach supports the questioning of stereotypes and assumptions students might make about individuals:

> *It's good that it's given to you and developed as a story, rather than given to you (all at once) so you can scan it and read over it. You read the parts, so I think that was done well (First Year Undergraduate Adult Nursing student)*

For the following students, the accessibility of the digital resources meant that they did not have to travel onto campus, which reduced the stresses of access to learning—was conducive to learning. This can be especially helpful for students whose travel time might exceed the length of the lesson itself:

> *It was really good. I think with it all being online it has really helped me because I live in ****, so when we were on campus it was a bit of a just a bit of a stretch for me to go there (university) all the time. (First Year Integrated Health and Social Care Student)*

> *It was great to be able to access it in your own time (First Year Undergraduate Physiotherapy Student)*

> *Flexible learning during a pandemic is a big bonus of Birley Place, and its a great way of dipping your toe in before jumping in the deep end of hospital placements. (First Year Undergraduate Physiotherapy Student)*

This view was supported by staff, who viewed Birley Place as accessible and flexible, in that it was being used with other students and in other areas of the program that it had not originally been designed for:

> I thought Birley Place was really good for that (accessibility of resources) I thought whether we're in a pandemic or not I think Birley Place is a very useful resource. I know that colleagues have used it since then on units with other students, Birley Place has been used to do some community profiling and things. (Senior Lecturer, Social Work)

6.5 Discussion and conclusions

Digital technologies have a key part to play in providing opportunities to extend and enhance physical learning spaces through a virtual ecosystem, facilitating new learning opportunities and collaboration. Birley Place digital community enables students to situate all their learning in the socio-economic context in which people live, helping them to understand the inextricable link between this and a person's health and well-being. The examples provided within this chapter have focused on health and social care programs; however, there is potential for a full spectrum of disciplines to engage in the digital community. The core competencies of communication, collaboration, and respect for another person's values and ethics are essential for all graduates as they proceed into employment. The potential for digital communities such as "Birley Place" to be used to enhance learning, teaching, and assessment is therefore immense.

The multimethod evaluation has clearly highlighted the benefits of using a virtual community as it does not rely on the availability of classroom space, nor does it need students to be available at the same time for them to collaborate. This is helpful when trying to bring together students from several disciplinary programs to facilitate collaborative learning, such as during the IPE project detailed earlier. An additional advantage of the digital community was the opportunity to incorporate a diversity of lived experiences for the fictional residents, without the need for their physical presence within face-to-face teaching sessions on campus. Working with service users and carers in the teaching, learning, and assessment of health and social care students is important to support person-centered care provision, and several reports note the need for the involvement of patients in the training of all health-care professionals (Berwick, 2013). However, involving service users in face-to-face teaching can be problematic as it can be burdensome for people with long-term conditions who may have limited mobility and exercise tolerance, life-limiting conditions, or anxiety to meet with students on campus and staff might be uncomfortable with the idea of coteaching. Further, lack of funding, support, and resources can present barriers to involvement (McSherry & Duggan, 2016). One aspect of this cocreative process was facilitated by the development of short films, made by service users, focusing on the importance of topics such as active listening and teamwork. This enables students to repeat or pause content and learn at a pace that suits them, repeating until they understand what is being said (Bal & Bicen, 2017).

6.6 The future

To date, we have focused on how we can develop Birley Place to address core areas of importance for HE and during the COVID-19 pandemic, the development of Birley Place digital placements was essential in enabling placement hours to be undertaken. There are ongoing challenges in health and social care education, whereby the number of students often exceeds the amount of clinical learning placements available. Consequently, post-COVID-19, Birley Place will change the clinical teaching and learning space by continuing to offer digital placement experiences for students as an alternative to face-to-face teaching and learning or as part of hybrid delivery model. This will relieve pressure on the placement circuit and further, takes advantage of the opportunities explored earlier in terms of preparation of students for the real world of practice and support for their mental health and well-being. If utilized in a hybrid way, benefits can include a more gradual introduction to the practice setting, which can be stressful for students who are unused to this area of work. Plans are underway to develop Birley Place to support student teachers, who are also challenged with learning in practice and who can gain from the digital setting in areas such as interpersonal communication, to prepare them for practice. The Birley Place school and associated scenarios are being developed in collaboration with colleagues in education with a view to implementation during the next academic year.

The digital nature of Birley Place makes it easily accessible on a national and international scale, meaning that involvement of external students and wider stakeholders is achievable. Developing the resources to explore global issues is important and enables students to appreciate the broader contexts which impact on health and social care. Further, due to the accessibility of the digital space, students can learn during different time zones, contexts, and physical spaces.

Developing the ability to track engagement and progression through individual log-in details can enable the tracking of student activity more easily. This is helpful, for example, for the digital placement activity in line with professional, statutory and regulatory body (PSRB) requirements, where a core number of hours need to be completed. Working alongside our web development team, we are looking beyond the measurement of "page views" to a more holistic approach, which shows meaningful data to explore our students' learning journeys. Embedding reflective tasks within the learning resources, important for students' personal and professional development, will also enable us to undertake a more detailed evaluation of the impact of the digital community on learning and development of groups and individual students.

The aim of this chapter was to explore how a digital learning resource enabled undergraduate health and social care students to situate their learning within a socioeconomic context. This was applicable to their interprofessional learning opportunities both on campus and during their clinical placement. The flexibility and accessibility of digital learning spaces is well known. Birley Place provides an additional advantage of bringing context to the learning environment, helping students situate their learning in a realistic community. The possibilities of Birley Place are endless not only for health and social care students but also for all learners who need to develop skills to enable working with others in an authentic context.

Acknowledgment

We acknowledge the contributions of Adam Palin and colleagues at Gas Mark 8.

References

Arkorful, V., & Abaidoo, N. (2015). The role of e-learning, advantages and disadvantages of its adoption in higher education. *International Journal of Instructional Technology and Distance Learning*, *12*(1), 29–42.

Bal, E., & Bicen, H. (2017). The purpose of students' social media use and determining their perspectives on education. *Procedia Computer Science*, *120*, 177–181. Available from https://doi.org/10.1016/j.procs.2017.11.226.

Benavides, L. M. C., et al. (2020). Digital transformation in higher education institutions: A systematic literature review. *Sensors*, *20*(11), 3291.

Berwick, D. (2013). A promise to learn — A commitment to act: Improving the safety of patients in England. London, UK. Retrieved from https://assets.publishing.service.gov.uk/government/uploads/system/uploads/attachment_data/file/226703/Berwick_Report.pdf [Accessed 17 January 2023].

Bilham, T., et al. (2019). *Reframing space for learning: excellence and innovation in university teaching*. London, UK: UCL Institute of Education Press.

Bowen, W. G. (2015). *Higher education in the digital age. Higher education in the digital age*. Princeton University Press.

Bradley, P. (2006). The history of simulation in medical education and possible future directions. *Medical Education*, 40(3), 254−262. Available from https://doi.org/10.1111/j.1365-2929.2006.02394.x.

Bridgstock, R., & Tippett, N. (2019). *Higher education and the future of graduate employability*. Edward Elgar Publishing. Available from https://books.google.co.uk/books?id = SqGdDwAAQBAJ.

Brock, D., et al. (2013). Republished: interprofessional education in team communication: Working together to improve patient safety. *Postgraduate Medical Journal*, 89(1057), 642−651.

Burgstahler, S. (2000). Web-based instruction and people with disabilities. In F. Cole (Ed.), *Issues in web-based pedagogy: A critical primer*. Westport, Connecticut: Greenwood Press.

Burki, T. K. (2020). COVID-19: Consequences for higher education. *The Lancet Oncology*, 21(6), 758.

Castro, M. D. B., & Tumibay, G. M. (2021). A literature review: Efficacy of online learning courses for higher education institution using meta-analysis. *Education and Information Technologies*, 26(2), 1367−1385. Available from https://doi.org/10.1007/s10639-019-10027-z.

Centre for the Advancement of Interprofessional Education. (2016). *Interprofessional education − A definition*. <https://www.caipe.org/about> Accessed 08.05. 22.

Cesco, S., et al. (2021). Higher education in the first year of COVID-19: Thoughts and perspectives for the future. *International Journal of Higher Education*, 10(3), 285−294.

Chernikova, O., et al. (2020). Simulation-based learning in higher education: A meta-analysis. *Review of Educational Research*, 90(4), 499−541.

Chugh, R., & Ruhi, U. (2018). Social media in higher education: A literature review of Facebook. *Education and Information Technologies*, 23(2), 605−616. Available from https://doi.org/10.1007/s10639-017-9621-2.

Clark, J. S., et al. (2020). *Action research*. Manhattan: New Prairie Press.

Clarke, V., & Braun, V. (2014). *Thematic analysis. Encyclopedia of critical psychology* (pp. 1947−1952). Springer.

Cohen, L., Manion, L., & Morrison, K. (2017). *Action research. Research methods in education* (pp. 440−456). Routledge.

Crawford, J., et al. (2020). COVID-19: 20 countries' higher education intra-period digital pedagogy responses. *Journal of Applied Learning & Teaching*, 3(1), 1−20.

Donnelly, P. (2019). *How to succeed at interprofessional education*. Oxford, UK: Wiley.

El Alfy, S., Marx Gómez, J., & Dani, A. (2019). Exploring the benefits and challenges of learning analytics in higher education institutions: A systematic literature review. *Information Discovery and Delivery*, 47(1), 25−34. Available from https://doi.org/10.1108/IDD-06-2018-0018.

Flavin, M., & Quintero, V. (2018). UK higher education institutions' technology-enhanced learning strategies from the perspective of disruptive innovation. *Research in Learning Technology*, 26(1063519), 1−12. Available from https://doi.org/10.25304/rlt.v26.1987.

Francis, R. (2013). *Report of the Mid Staffordshire NHS Foundation Trust public inquiry: Executive summary*. The Stationery Office.

Gaba, D. M. (2004). The future vision of simulation in health care. *BMJ Quality & Safety*, 13(suppl 1), i2−i10.

Gordon, M., et al. (2020). Developments in medical education in response to the COVID-19 pandemic: A rapid BEME systematic review: BEME Guide No. 63. *Medical Teacher*, *42*(11), 1202–1215. Available from https://doi.org/10.1080/0142159X.2020.1807484.

Greene, J. C. (2015). Preserving distinctions within the multimethod and mixed methods research merger. In Hesse-Biber, S.N., & Burke Johnson, R. (Eds.), The Oxford Handbook of Multimethod and Mixed Methods Research Inquiry, Oxford Library of Psychology. https://doi.org/10.1093/oxfordhb/9780199933624.013.37 [Accessed 17 January 2023].

Guppy, N., et al. (2022). The post-COVID-19 future of digital learning in higher education: Views from educators, students, and other professionals in six countries. *British Journal of Educational Technology*, *n/a*(n/a). Available from https://doi.org/10.1111/bjet.13212.

Harasim, L. (2017). *Learning theory and online technologies*. Routledge. Available from https://doi.org/10.4324/9781315716831.

Haslam, M. B. (2021). What might COVID-19 have taught us about the delivery of Nurse Education, in a post-COVID-19 world? *Nurse Education Today*, *97*, 104707. Available from https://doi.org/10.1016/j.nedt.2020.104707.

Health Education England. (2018). *National framework for simulation based education*. Available from https://www.hee.nhs.uk/sites/default/files/documents/National framework for simulation based education.pdf.

Hesse-Biber, S. N., & Johnson, B. T. A.-T. T. (2015). *The Oxford handbook of multimethod and mixed methods research inquiry*. Oxford: Oxford University Press (Oxford library of psychology). Available from http://www.dawsonera.com/depp/reader/protected/external/AbstractView/S9780199933631.

Ivankova, N., & Wingo, N. (2018). Applying mixed methods in action research: Methodological potentials and advantages. *American Behavioral Scientist*, *62*(7), 978–997.

Jack, K., et al. (2022). Using a virtual community to support learning about the complexities of interprofessional working. In S. Norton, & A. Penaluna (Eds.), *3 Es for wicked problems: employability, enterprise, and entrepreneurship: Solving wicked problems* (pp. 97–102). Advance HE. Available from https://www.advance-he.ac.uk/knowledge-hub/3-es-wicked-problems-employability-enterprise-and-entrepreneurship-solving-wicked.

Jeffries, P. (2020). *Simulation in nursing education: From conceptualization to evaluation*. Lippincott Williams & Wilkins.

JISC. (2011). *Emerging practice in a digital age*. Available from http://www.jisc.ac.uk/digiemerge.

Johnson, R. B., Onwuegbuzie, A. J., & Turner, L. A. (2007). Toward a definition of mixed methods research. *Journal of Mixed Methods Research*, *1*(2), 112–133.

Kattoua, T., Al-Lozi, M., & Alrowwad, A. (2016). A review of literature on E-learning systems in higher education. *International Journal of Business Management and Economic Research*, *7*(5), 754–762.

Klappa, P., et al. (2019). Towards a learning landscape — The potential for technologies to create social learning spaces. In C. Hamshire, T. Bilham, & M. Harthog (Eds.), *Reframing space for learning: Empowering excellence and innovation in university teaching and learning*. London, UK: IoE Press.

Kornelakis, A., & Petrakaki, D. (2020). Embedding employability skills in UK higher education: Between digitalization and marketization. *Industry and Higher Education*, *34*(5), 290–297. Available from https://doi.org/10.1177/0950422220902978.

Laurillard, D. (2013). *Rethinking university teaching: A conversational framework for the effective use of learning technologies*. Rethinking university teaching : *[Preprint]*. London: Routledge Falmer.

McSherry, R., & Duggan, S. (2016). 'Involving carers in the teaching, learning and assessment of masters students'. *Nurse Education in Practice*, *16*(1), 156–159.

Nursing and Midwifery Council. (2019). *Standards of student supervision and assessment*. Available from https://www.nmc.org.uk/standards-for-education-and-training/standards-for-student-supervision-and-assessment/.

Pucciarelli, F., & Kaplan, A. (2016). Competition and strategy in higher education: Managing complexity and uncertainty. *Business Horizons*, *59*(3), 311–320. Available from https://doi.org/10.1016/j.bushor.2016.01.003.

Reeves, S., et al. (2016). A BEME systematic review of the effects of interprofessional education: BEME Guide No. 39. *Medical Teacher*, *38*(7), 656–668.

Regmi, K., & Jones, L. (2020). A systematic review of the factors—enablers and barriers—affecting e-learning in health sciences education. *BMC Medical Education*, *20*(1), 1–18.

Rolls, K., et al. (2016). How health care professionals use social media to create virtual communities: an integrative review. *Journal of Medical Internet Research*, *18*(6), e5312.

Rosen, K. R. (2008). The history of medical simulation. *Journal of Critical Care*, *23*(2), 157–166. Available from https://doi.org/10.1016/j.jcrc.2007.12.004.

Salter, C., et al. (2020). Working remotely: Innovative allied health placements in response to COVID-19. *International Journal of Work-Integrated Learning*, *21*(5), 587–600.

Sharpe, R., Benfield, G., & Francis, R. (2006). Implementing a university e-learning strategy: Levers for change within academic schools. *Alt-J*, *14*(2), 135–151. Available from https://doi.org/10.1080/09687760600668503.

Sibbald, S. L., et al. (2022). Building a virtual community of practice: Experience from the Canadian foundation for healthcare improvement's policy circle. *Health Research Policy and Systems*, *20*(1), 95. Available from https://doi.org/10.1186/s12961-022-00897-0.

Sormunen, M., et al. (2020). Digital learning interventions in higher education: A scoping review. *Computers, Informatics, Nursing : CIN*, *38*(12), 613–624. Available from https://doi.org/10.1097/CIN.0000000000000645.

The Health Foundation. (2019). Creating healthy lives. London, UK. Retrieved from https://www.health.org.uk/publications/reports/creating-healthy-lives [Accessed 17 January 2023].

Thoma, B., et al. (2018). Establishing a virtual community of practice in simulation: The value of social media. *Simulation in Healthcare*, *13*(2), 124–130.

Torda, A. (2020). How COVID-19 has pushed us into a medical education revolution. *Internal Medicine Journal*, *50*(9), 1150–1153.

Twogood, R., et al. (2020). Rapid implementation and improvement of a virtual student placement model in response to the COVID-19 pandemic. *BMJ Open Quality*, *9*(4), e001107. Available from https://doi.org/10.1136/bmjoq-2020-001107.

Walia, N., Zahedi, F. M., & Jain, H. (2017). Potential of virtual worlds for nursing care: Lessons and outcomes. *OJIN: the Online Journal of Issues in Nursing*, *23*(1).

Wiecha, J., et al. (2010). Learning in a virtual world: experience with using second life for medical education. *Journal of Medical Internet Research*, *12*(1), e1. Available from https://doi.org/10.2196/jmir.1337.

Wright, D. J., et al. (2021). Birley Place: A virtual community for the delivery of health and social care education. *BMJ Simulation & Technology Enhanced Learning*, *7*(6), 627–630.

Xyrichis, A., Reeves, S., & Zwarenstein, M. (2018). Examining the nature of interprofessional practice: An initial framework validation and creation of the InterProfessional Activity Classification Tool (InterPACT). *Journal of Interprofessional Care*, *32*(4), 416–425.

CHAPTER 7

Assessment: higher education institutions' innovative online assessment methods beyond the era of the COVID-19 pandemic

Mercy Dube[1], Reason Masengu[2], Sinothando Sibanda[3] and Lucia Mandongwe[4]

[1]Department of Information and Marketing Sciences, Faculty of Business Sciences, Midlands State University, Gweru, Zimbabwe
[2]Department of Management Studies, Middle East College, Knowledge Oasis Muscat, Oman
[3]Department of Marketing, Zimbabwe Open University, Harare, Zimbabwe
[4]Department of Accounting, Manicaland State University of Applied Sciences, Mutare, Zimbabwe

7.1 Introduction

Over the past 10 years (2012–22), the incorporation of the digital aspect in teaching and learning proliferated in research and academic discourse. This in turn led to an increased interest in online assessment as a key component of standardized e-learning and teaching. However, there has been mixed reactions toward the aspect of online assessment in higher education by both academics and practitioners. It is against this background that researchers have advocated for a complete overhaul of the traditional assessment system toward innovative online assessment methods. The researchers argue that innovative online assessment can drive change toward modernizing education systems. Introducing innovative online assessment can also affect how teaching and learning takes place in an increasingly digital society and economy (Organisation for Economic Cooperation and Development [OECD], 2020). This new phenomenon has not only been a preserve for discussion in the higher education institution (HEI), but other fields outside the traditional education system such as interest groups, lobbying, and public institutions have also joined the discussion. One major challenge in the implementation of online assessment has been the ambiguity surrounding this modern concept.

Recently, COVID-19 pandemic brought disruptions in the learning and assessment methods. The lockdown regulations and rules prompted academic institutions to increase their awareness and adoption of innovative assessment

Digital Teaching, Learning and Assessment
DOI: https://doi.org/10.1016/B978-0-323-95500-3.00010-9
121

methods. This affected conventional education as most HEIs tried to integrate online teaching and assessments. Several discussions began to center on methods of assessment methods to be adopted during and beyond the pandemic. Educational institutions adopted interactive online learning strategies and the entire learning process became digitalized. Hybrid learning, flipped learning, and blended learning synchronous and asynchronous learning have been adopted by many HEIs. All these modes of learning were meant to improve the learning and assessment methods in most HEIs. Online learning gave students the capabilities to think critically and solve problem while facilitators developed different kinds of assessment to evaluate students' performance. This chapter aims to critically review the pre- and post-COVID-19 pandemic teaching and learning, evaluate the various innovative formative assessment methods adopted during the pandemic, critically analyze summative assessment currently adopted and their future use in the education sector, and proffer solution to teaching, learning, and assessment in times of disruptions.

7.2 Background to the study

According to the United Nations Educational Scientific and Cultural Organization [UNESCO] (2022), the pandemic has disrupted teaching and learning around the globe. This has led to new student teaching, assessment, and evaluation methodologies. Selected HEIs in countries such as South Africa, Cambodia, and Estonia pioneered alternative online solutions to conduct examinations using standardized assessments. In 2019 the United Arab Emirates introduced a smart evaluation system that incorporated artificial intelligence to automatically monitor assessment and prevent cheating without human element. The pandemic invigorated the discourse surrounding innovative formative assessment (Snyder, 2021). While a lot of innovative assessment methods were introduced during the pandemic, prospects are high that new assessment strategies are still needed post-COVID-19 (Khan & Masood, 2020). Despite the phenomenal achievements realized during the COVID-19, debates still exist regarding online assessment. Research conducted by Snyder (2021) and UNESCO (2022) highlighted a need to design, administer, and interpret disparities that exist in different learning environments (urban and rural). Vulnerable and disadvantaged communities' performance on online assessment may be distorted due to disparities in technology diffusion and connectivity.

To ensure the continuity of education despite the lockdown, HEIs sought to use technology and offer online classes and learning experiences as a substitute for on-campus (face-to-face) classes. School closures have necessitated changes and, in some cases, caused serious changes on how students are assessed (Schleicher, 2020; United Nations, 2020). In most countries, examinations were postponed; in a few, they were canceled; and, in others, they were replaced by continuous assessments or alternative modalities, such as online testing for final examinations. The pandemic forced educational institutions to introduce and improve digital learning and teaching systems to the absolute best level as never been before (Iradukunda & Kumar, 2021). Based on the abovementioned literature discussion, this chapter will cover the following areas:

- Online learning and assessment.
- HEIs online assessment: the evolution and the paradigm shift.
- Innovative formative assessment adopted during the COVID-19 pandemic.
- Summative assessment currently adopted and their future use in the education sector.
- Blended learning and blended assessment during and post the COVID-19 era.

7.3 Literature review

Assessment is the systematic collection of information about student learning, using the time, knowledge, expertise, and resources available to inform decisions that affect students learning (Walvoord, 2010 cited by Conrad & Openo, 2018). This section of the chapter will conceptualize literature in line with the innovative online assessment techniques to be implemented by HEI during and post the COVID-19 pandemic.

7.3.1 Online learning and assessment

Different teaching and assessment methods have been initiated to serve specific purposes and situations. COVID-19 disruption to the status quo is not a surprise but a learning curve in HEIs. The students and the lecturers began year 2019 with prospects full of ambiguity and complexity of learning. The uncertainty of the environment was described by Harris and Jones (2021) as if institutions once experienced it (déjà vu feeling). In Huber and Helm (2020), empirical study showed that students were not willing to learn online, and they described the situation as stressful. Masengu, Ruzive, & Mandongwe (2022) highlight that the disruptions caused by COVID-19 gave HEIs and other centers of learning in Oman the opportunity to embrace technology in a much greater speed. Despite the fact that technology is expensive for developing and underdeveloped countries, they are long-term benefits from online teaching and learning (Harris & Jones, 2021; Huber & Helm, 2020). The level of adoption of online teaching and assessment indicates that many institutions will adopt the new paradigm for the benefit of their staff members and students (Masengu, Ruzive, & Mandongwe, 2022). The teaching, learning, and assessment are now based on technology although some HEIs, staff, and students in some spheres have reservations.

Education institution closures and disruption due to COVID-19 pandemic has taken place in diverse conditions. The landscape in the learning environment is not even hence, adoption of technology in an abrupt manner proves the fact that digital deprivation is real and divisive (Glied & Lleras-Muney, 2008). The abrupt adoption of technology puts certain learners at an advantage than others. In the context of the disruption caused by COVID-19 pandemic, it is unequivocal that it widened the gaps of leaners (Harmey & Moss, 2021; Huber & Helm, 2020; UNESCO, 2020). The technological imbalances indicate that the government and learning institution need to introduce support systems and resources to enhance the holistic acceptance of the learning mode (Huber & Helm, 2020).

According to Woolf et al. (2007), the most urbanized tend to benefit from the first-mover advantage as they adopt new technologies first. The UNESCO (2020) report shows that COVID-19 pandemic negatively impacted education in many countries and the impact is unprecedented. This is evident from the spring 2020 statistics that showed that 1.5 million school going children were affected by the COVID-19 pandemic (Huber & Helm, 2020; UNESCO, 2020). Harmey and Moss (2021), concur that schools play a crucial role in educating its students about new emerging technologies. Harmey and Moss (2021) recommend that school management need to educate student and craft appropriate strategies to support response and recovery.

Harmey and Moss (2021) looked at effects of unplanned events to young people's mental health and the study reviewed that after Hurricane Katrina students had difficulty in concentration during learning. Many empirical studies focus on the need for HEIs and other learning institutions to understand how to deal with trauma amongst students (Glied & Lleras-Muney, 2008; Hoffmann et al., 2016; Woolf et al., 2007). The need for psychological support is emphasized by Harris and Jones (2021) empirical study in New Zealand and Japan which revealed that students' responses to disruption may manifest for longer periods after the occurrence, hence affecting their way of learning. In conclusion, Harmey and Moss (2021) recommends that to invigorate learning, schools should:

- develop contingency plans;
- provide school leadership with the time and support to reflect on the experience of the event and to develop a clear contingency plan that would account for communication systems, chains of information, and the needs of the community;
- provide school leadership with the necessary resources to support their own, employees', and children's mental health;
- provide learning materials that will educate children about the facts about COVID-19 and opportunity to reflect on the events; and
- conduct research that goes beyond calculating learning loss and documents to include the reflections of the school community on the experience of educating during the COVID-19 pandemic.

7.3.2 Higher education institutions' online assessment: the evolution and the paradigm shift

Successful HEIs engage student in all aspects of their learning and assessment. The students' engagement in the online learning environment is a critical component of online learning. The engagement is made possible by balancing both formative and summative assessments since they are both integral parts of information gathering (Garrison & Ehringhaus, 2020). The use of effective assessment techniques is an essential part of effective teaching and learning in the electronic environment. As educational institutions are increasingly held accountable for student learning (Association of American Colleges and Universities [AACU], 2004; National Council for Accreditation of Teacher Education [NCATE], 2003), assessment represents an important way to respond to such accountability.

The COVID-19 euphoria led to some HEIs canceling formal assessments and examination in 2020 (Huber & Helm, 2020). The situation affected transparent, fair, dependable, and evidence-based assessment to academic institutions. There was an unexpected dramatic change of the status quo to a high level of ambiguity. Academic integrity was at stake as lots of assessment criteria were being violated. In the United Kingdom (UK), for example, intervention by academic quality authorities resulted in results downgrading and student lost some university places (Gooblar, 2019). In Week (2021), teachers had to figure out the best way to maneuvre in the transition process and instruction moved to remote learning;

teachers were forced to cope with the untimely and unplanned change. The COVID-19 disruption necessitated the need to have an assessment approach that is part of regular instructional cycle (Harmey & Moss, 2021; Masengu, Ruzive, & Mandongwe, 2022; Week, 2021). Empirical studies done in the UK indicates that teachers had to give formative assessments for student to understand remote learning.

The idea of assessment during the times of disruption constitutes the ability to be creative and consolidate knowledge and skills in different formats (Week, 2021). Practical example to the creativity is the use of hybrid learning mode, which encompasses the preclass, in class, and postclass activities. Students were given the opportunity to replay in-class discussion so that they are in a position to complete an assignment (Harris & Jones, 2021). This level of creativity made assessments quite easy for the lecturer to measure effectiveness of their learning. Other assessment methods incorporated include the use of quizzes, breakout rooms, and the multiple-choice type of examinations completed in Zoom, Google Course Groups, MS Teams groups, Zoom conference calls to mention but a few (Gooblar, 2019). According to Teaching in Times of Disruption, Sheridan Center, Brown University (2020), teaching in times of disruptions require strategy and prioritized asynchronous instruction which allows students not to participate at the same time while concentrating on activities and assignments. The asynchronous learning allows the use of digital learning and design resources such as Google, Panopto, Zoom, and Canvas. Willis (2021) asserts that asynchronous learning focuses on three main components, namely, declutter the curriculum, focus on essential, more depth and breath. This allows students to demonstrate their understanding through diagrams, voice recording, essay media presentation, and question-and-answer sessions.

7.3.3 Innovative formative assessment adopted during the COVID-19 pandemic

Assessment is a very wide topic including every activity that takes place in the learning environment with formative assessment being part of the instructional process (Garrison & Ehringhaus, 2020). Formative assessment provides the information needed to adjust teaching and learning while they are happening. In this sense, formative assessment informs both teachers and students about student understanding at a point when timely adjustments can be made. These adjustments help to ensure students achieve targeted standards-based learning goals within a set time frame (Black 2015).

Several formative assessments have been adopted during the COVID-19 pandemic and most of them will continue to be in use post the pandemic. These included online quizzes, multiple-choice questions (MCQs), gamifying assessments, and activities. Gamification is when game elements are used in nongame contexts that increase participation, excitement, engagement, and competition among students (Lee & Hammer, 2011; Packt, 2019; Smith, 2014). Formative assessments help teachers determine the next step during the learning process since it greatly involves the learners. Clark (2020) affirms that during the pandemic, the adoption of innovative formative assessment tool called Flipgrid increased accessibility and inclusiveness of all learners from different spheres of life. Flipgrid is an online-free-to-use video sharing tool that is classroom friendly allowing students to share their learning (Khan et al., 2021).

Khan et al. (2021) suggest the use of padlets as formative assessment tools during the pandemic. Padlet is a multimedia service that allows for live interaction between student—peers and between students and lecturers. Padlets enabled students to work on tasks, discuss with peers, and write down their findings, then further discuss their findings in live tutorials. Microsoft Teams, Zoom, Google classroom, and WebEx have also been used to facilitate online debates to enhance peer interaction and engagement.

7.3.4 Summative assessment currently adopted and their future use in the education sector

Summative assessments are given periodically to determine at a particular point in time what students know and do not know (Garrison & Ehringhaus, 2020). They are used to evaluate student learning and meeting set outcomes at the end of an instructional unit which is usually a term, semester, or year by comparing it against some standard or benchmark. Gamage et al. (2020) posit that summative assessment usually has a higher weight than other forms of assessment and based on that, students have been seen to be more determined and attentive during summative assessments.

COVID-19 pandemic massively disrupted summative assessments in HEIs that were due to be conducted face to face. Some institutions canceled assessments while others postponed examinations with the hope that the pandemic was short lived (UNESCO, 2020). As the pandemic took longer, Oxford University announced that the "majority of examinations for first-year undergraduates will be canceled, and students will be deemed to have passed except law and medical students" (Oxford

University, 2020). This decision raised questions of allowing progression without certifying those certain skills and knowledge were acquired (UNESCO, 2020). According to Oxford University (2020), the open policy was to make summative assessment less mandatory to ensure students are not disadvantaged by changes in summative assessment induced by COVID-19 pandemic. Virtual assessments were also adopted in medical schools to ensure student progression of learning through scenario-based assessments and simulations. This was criticized of failure to measure the whole set of skills based on Bloom's taxonomy to teaching and assessment (Rutten, Van Joolingen, & Van Der Veen, 2012). Assessing practical knowledge and skills through the observation of student performance on a virtual world is always challenging and complex as both the assessor and student are deemed to be technologically versatile. In practice, "no detriment policies" generally guarantee students a final course grade that is not lower than their average performance before the COVID-19 pandemic outbreak (QAA, 2020, quoted by OECD, 2020).

In an effort to ensure that education is offered to every citizen as a basic right, many institutions have blended traditional and online summative assessments with the hope that as nations continue technologically advancement, online assessments can be done confidently without questions on validity, reliability, and credibility of students' scores. Summative assessment tools generally adopted include controlled examination, open-book examination, essay or report, term paper, critical analysis, portfolio, dissertation, oral presentation, skill performance, and attendance and pop quiz (Orim & Orim, 2020). Student conferences were also adopted in which students present their work-related learning projects virtually using podcast submissions and recorded audios and videos (University of Greenwich, 2020). Some institutions also piloted the use of social media in their summative assessment using Twitter to encourage student active participation during their seminar project presentations.

Studies conducted in various universities that encompass Deakin University, University of Greenwich, Canterbury Christ Church University quoted by Gamage et al. (2020) indicate that COVID-19 pandemic forced institutions to adopt online summative assessments even on practical subjects that required students to exhibit psychomotor skills, conduct laboratory-based tests, or perform social science—based skills. The major summative assessment tools included video-based uploads using Cloud technology, online simulation-based tasks, submitting online portfolio, real-time observed practical/viva via Zoom, or Blackboard Collaborative or take-home exams and open-book examinations that are usually given a 48-h window period to accommodate network or computer challenges and also human challenges such as students with disability and those with limited computer-based skills. Time-constrained examinations were also adopted. The students would download the open-book exams, MCQs, or free-text questions. The students were then expected to answer within the set time usually the normal traditional 3-h time and upload their answers online. Many HEIs, however, do not have online proctoring to facilitate online summative exams invigilation, where they can authenticate the identity of the student and monitor the candidate throughout the exam to ensure that no cheating and breaching of examination regulations.

The authenticity of online examinations lies in ironing out the challenges faced in conducting online examinations. There are high chances of student academic dishonesty, need to measure through direct observation of the student's ability to carry out a practical task, lack of fairness as students are forced to use varying technological equipment such as computer types, Internet bandwidths, which have a bearing on the final score, risk of technical failure as this might be beyond institutional parameters (OECD, 2020). To curb student academic dishonesty, online proctoring has been adopted by many HEIs around the world, although they are concerns of students' privacy as proctoring rely on audio and video recording. To ensure future use of summative assessment, there is need to redesign the summative assessment examinations to suit remote writing and give students flexibility in undertaking the examinations (Garrison & Ehringhaus, 2020; OECD, 2020; United Nations, 2020).

7.3.5 Blended learning and blended assessment during and post the COVID-19 era

The COVID-19 pandemic has created a competitive market in which student acquisition and retention are becoming critical for HEIs. Bashir et al. (2021) assert that many universities adopted new learning and assessment practices to meet the students post-COVID-19 pandemic requirements. Some institutions adopted the blended learning mode that involves some aspects of courses delivered online (Bryan & Volchenkova, 2016; Lalima & LataDangwal, 2017). Other institutions implemented hybrid learning mode which is a combination of online course delivery with face-to-face sessions (Meydanlion & Arikan, 2021).

In O'Byrne and Pytash (2015), hybrid or HyFlex mode or blended learning is defined as a pedagogical approach that includes a combination of face-to-face instruction with computer-mediated instruction. However, it is relevant to note that hybrid learning can be diverse and has an opportunity to provide personalized instruction with some elements of student control over path, pace, time, and place. Looking into the future of learning and assessment researchers such as (Deignan, 2021; Muxtorjonovna, 2020) assert that hybrid learning is futuristic, and it allows students to learn using the hybrid spaces while at the same teacher's tailor make their curriculum and assessment criteria to suit different kinds of environment. Muxtorjonovna (2020) postulates that in hybrid learning and assessment, teachers and student assume an equal responsibility to collaboratively learn in the volatile, uncertain, complex, and ambiguous (VUCA) environment.

Bezuidenhout et al. (2021) and McKenna et al. (2019) agree that the future of successful learning and assessment lies in blended and hybrid mode. Its collaborative nature brings in pluralism which is inclined in the andragogical paradigm. Institutions that do have the capacity and material resources will need to choose among the two approaches to become effective. The next section presents the research methodology.

7.4 Research methodology

This study used Preferred Reporting Items for Systematic Review (PRISMA). It is an international initiative developed by researchers to address the ongoing issue of lack of well-documented and transparent review methods reported in published literature (Todd, 2022). PRISMA differs from the traditional reviews by adopting a replicable scientific process and is meant to lesser chances of errors through an exhaustive search of already published material (Sarkis-Onofre, Catala-Lopez, & Lockwood, 2022; Todd, 2022; Tranfield, Denyer, & Smart, 2003). Liberati, Altman, Tetzlaff, and Gøtzsche (2009) and Wong et al. (2013) concur that PRISMA is another dimension in the creation on knowledge. For Wong et al. (2013), the literature-based methodology constitutes three main parameters, design the literature review, conducting the review and contextual analysis, and writing up discussions. The following key words and phrases were used to identify literature using different search engines: **online assessment, online teaching, and learning, HEI assessments, teaching and learning during pandemic, hybrid learning, HyFlex learning**. Data obtained and collated in the form authors, areas study, findings, and scope.

The literature-based discussion papers covered a period between 2010 and 2022. HEIs' innovative assessment was used to inform the study. A total of 50 research highly indexed articles, publications from HEIs with practical experiences and blogs with proven credentials, were selected from different literature and a sample was drawn based on researchers' convenience and appreciation of the context. A total of 30 literature-based sources were selected after reading the in-depth review of the literature. These papers were used to inform the chapter finding, discussion, and recommendations. The selection of the articles was also based on the year of publication. In this case, literature published from 2012 to 2022 was included in the discussion of findings. Selection of the time frame was based on the convenience of the researchers, relevance, and context of the literature. Most of the research finding is supported by indexed articles; however, purposes of some publications included were to bring robustness in the discussion. The most common theme appearing in the different literature was collated to produce the theme. The findings were discussed and aligned to represent the literature-based finding of the study.

7.5 Discussion of findings

The literature discussion and the collected information from literature are presented in Tables 7.1—7.3. The presented line is in line with the chapter objectives.

7.5.1 Learning and assessment in higher education institutions

Literature on the how learning and assessment was done during and after the COVID-19 pandemic was analyzed and it was found out that pandemic affected the HEIs. Therefore the COVID-19 pandemic came in just to add on to the pandemics that had hit the education sector before. A variety of literature texts that were examined disclosed different opinions regarding the innovative learning and assessment post the COVID-19 pandemic. These opinions are tabled in Table 7.1.

Table 7.1 shows research that investigated assessment in a disruption or pandemic and the opinions of the different scholars were shown. The table also shows the year in which each of the research was performed. Having considered all the research in the table, one concludes that a pandemic or disruption has a huge and negative impact to the education sector. This will then call for a holistic strategy which ensures continuity

Table 7.1 List of scientific papers on learning and assessment in times of disruption used in the literature review (2012−22).

Number	Author and year	Publisher	Title	Opinions on innovative online learning and assessment in times of disruption or pandemic
1	Hoffmann, Hu, de Gelder, Menvielle, Bopp, and Mackenbach (2016)	International Journal for Equity in Health	The impact of increasing income inequalities on educational inequalities in mortality—an analysis of six European countries	Must be transparent, fair, dependable, and evidence-based assessment
2	Harris and Jones (2021)	School Leadership and Management	Leading in disruptive times: a spotlight on assessment	Is usually ambiguous and complex
3	Masengu, Ruzive, and Mandongwe (2022)	DigiTAL2K International Conference on teaching, assessment, and learning	Application of digital technologies in the 21st century. Literature review of experiences, opportunities, and challenges in higher education	Creates an opportunity to embrace technology in a much greater speed
4	Huber and Helm (2020)	Educational Assessment, Evaluation and Accountability	COVID-19 and schooling: evaluation, assessment, and accountability in times of crises—reacting quickly to explore key issues for policy, practice, and research with the school barometer	Is expensive especially for developing and under-developed countries
5	Glied and Lleras-Muney (2008)	Demography	Technological innovation and inequality in health	Is based on technology and nothing else

(*Continued*)

Table 7.1 (Continued)

Number	Author and year	Publisher	Title	Opinions on innovative online learning and assessment in times of disruption or pandemic
6	Harmey and Moss (2021), UNESCO (2020)	Educational Review	Learning disruption or learning loss: using evidence from unplanned closures to inform returning to school after COVID-19	Results in a digital divide among leaners especially in health education groups
7	Gooblar (2019)	Teaching	Helping students revise themselves. The missing course: everything they never taught you about college	The assessment criteria may be violated
8	Week (2021)		Assessing student learning amid disruption	Should be part of regular instructional cycle
9	Harris and Jones (2021)	School Leadership and Management	Leading in disruptive times: a spotlight on assessment	It leads to creativity and consolidation of knowledge and skills in different formats
10	Huber and Helm (2020)	Educational Assessment, Evaluation and Accountability	COVID-19 and schooling: evaluation, assessment, and accountability in times of crises—reacting quickly to explore key issues for policy, practice, and research with the school barometer	Quizzes, breakout rooms, and the multiple-choice type of examinations may be embraced in such times for assessment
11	Willis (2021)	The Centre for Inclusive Education	How can school assessment be fair in a time of COVID-19 disruption?	Assessment may be done through Zoom, Google Course Groups, MS Teams groups, Zoom conference calls

(Continued)

Table 7.1 (Continued)

Number	Author and year	Publisher	Title	Opinions on innovative online learning and assessment in times of disruption or pandemic
12	Harmey and Moss (2021)	Educational Review	Learning disruption or learning loss: using evidence from unplanned closures to inform returning to school after COVID-19	Strategies which may be prioritized include asynchronous mode of instruction
13	Khan, Sivasubramaniam, Anand and Hysaj (2021)	International Journal for Educational Integrity	"e"-thinking teaching and assessment to uphold academic integrity: lessons learned from emergency distance learning	Sickness, Internet access, cost of data may become barriers to online learning and assessment
14	O'Byrne and Pytash (2015)	Journal of Adolescent and Adult Literacy	Hybrid and blended learning: modifying pedagogy across path, pace, time, and place	Hybrid learning is futuristics and it provides students to learn using the hybrid spaces while at the same teacher's tailor make their curriculum and assessment criteria to suit different kinds of environment

in learning and assessment. These results are consistent with the views of Clark (2020), Garrison and Ehringhaus (2020), and Hoffmann et al. (2016), who articulate that pandemics are an obstacle for assessment. They affect planning and scheduling of the assessment instruments, thereby shortchanging the exam boards and the students. Further analysis is presented in Table 7.2 by delving on innovative formative assessment during

Table 7.2 List of scientific papers on innovative formative assessment adopted during the COVID-19 pandemic (2012—22).

Number	Author and year	Publisher	Title	Views on innovative Formative assessment adopted during and post the COVID-19 pandemic
1	Asamoah, Shahrill, and Latif (2022)	Qualitative Report	A review of formative assessment techniques in higher education during COVID-19	There is need to redirect formative assessment to incorporate both informal and formal methods. This can be done through an adopting technologically advanced assessment techniques
2	Wong et al. (2013)	BMC Medicine	RAMESES publication standards: metanarrative reviews	There is need to adopt innovative formative assessment tools to increase accessibility and inclusiveness of all learners from different spheres of life (like developed and developing economies)
3	Iradukunda, and Kumar (2021)	International Journal of Management	The impact of COVID-19 on the education sector in Zambia: a case study on DMI-St	It helps teachers to determine the next step during the learning process since it greatly involves the learners
4	Clark (2020)		How to use Flipgrid in the classroom	Using Flipgrid is excellent as an online-free-to-use video sharing tool that is classroom friendly since it facilitates online knowledge sharing

(*Continued*)

Table 7.2 (Continued)

Number	Author and year	Publisher	Title	Views on innovative Formative assessment adopted during and post the COVID-19 pandemic
5	Khan et al. (2021)	International Journal for Educational Integrity	e'-thinking teaching and assessment to uphold academic integrity: lessons learned from emergency distance learning	Padlets is good during a pandemic since it allows for live interaction between student–peers and between students–lecturers
6	Black (2015)	Principles, Policy & Practice	Formative assessment— an optimistic but incomplete vision. Assessment in education	It informs both teachers and students about student understanding at a point when timely adjustments can be made
7	Luthfiyyah et al. (2021)	EduLite: Journal of English Education, Literature and Culture	Technology-enhanced formative assessment in higher education: a voice from Indonesian English as a Foreign Language (EFL) teachers	It assists students to achieve targeted standards based on learning goals within a set period
8	Alfonsa, Mazario, and Franscisco (2016)	Journal of Technology and Science Education	The use of technology in a model of formative assessment	It provides the information needed to adjust teaching and learning while they are happening

Table 7.3 List of scientific papers on innovative summative assessment adopted during the COVID-19 pandemic (2012−22).

Number	Author and year	Publisher	Title	Perceptions on innovative Summative assessment adopted during and post the COVID-19 pandemic
1	Garrison and Ehringhaus (2020)	Education	Formative and summative assessments in the classroom	There is need to change the focus of summative assessment direction by embracing technology-enhanced assessment in the HEIs.
2	Gamage et al. (2020)	Education Sciences	Online delivery and assessment during COVID-19: safeguarding academic integrity	Online summative assessment is difficult to rely on and hence is not trustworthy. A different person may be writing the exam altogether.
3	Orim and Orim (2020)	10th International Conference on Education and New Learning Technology	Contextual and dispositional factors of information and communication technology utilization among teachers of children with intellectual disability in Nigeria Authors	Online summative assessments can be done singular without questions on validity, reliability, and credibility of students' scores

(Continued)

Table 7.3 (Continued)

Number	Author and year	Publisher	Title	Perceptions on innovative Summative assessment adopted during and post the COVID-19 pandemic
4	Fluck and Hillier (2016)	Brisbane	Innovative assessment with e-Exams. In Australian Council for Computers in Education Conference	Examples of innovative summative assessment may include open-book examination, essay or report, term paper, critical analysis, portfolio, dissertation, oral presentation, skill performance, and attendance, and pop quiz
5	Amin et al. (2021)	Medical Journal Armed Forces India, 77, S466–S474	Case item creation and video case presentation as summative assessment tools for distance learning in the pandemic era	The major summative assessment tools included video-based uploads using Cloud technology; online simulation-based tasks; submitting online portfolio; real-time observed practical/viva via Zoom or Blackboard Collaborate, take-home exams, and open-book exams which are usually given a 48-h window

(Continued)

Table 7.3 (Continued)

Number	Author and year	Publisher	Title	Perceptions on innovative Summative assessment adopted during and post the COVID-19 pandemic
				period to accommodate network, human disability, or computer challenges
6.	Rachmawati, and Hastari (2022)	Education Society	Formative assessment as an innovative strategy to develop English for Special Purposes (ESP) students' writing skills. VELES Voices of English Language	To ensure future use of summative assessment, there is need to redesign the summative assessment examinations to suit remote writing and give students flexibility in undertaking the examinations in cognizance of the various challenges.
7	Borbon and Ricafort (2021)	Sustainable Develop-ment	Summative assessment on student outcomes for tourism program from 2013 to 2017	Another way of dealing with innovative summative assessment challenges may include restructuring of examinations and giving individuals varying papers to avoid sharing of exam-related material during the exam.

the COVID-19 pandemic. As a way of being innovative, educators were found tailor making their assessment to suit the various kinds of environment in which the students were facing. Nevertheless, several challenges were encountered in trying to perform innovative online learning and assessment in times of disruption or pandemic. Some of these challenges include cost of data for those in developing countries, sickness as well as Internet access.

7.6 Innovative formative assessment adopted in higher education institutions during and post the COVID-19 pandemic

A critical analysis was performed on the extent of innovative formative assessment adopted during the COVID-19 pandemic. This was followed by an examination of the possible formative assessment direction which must be taken post the COVID-19. A majority of texts supported the need for HEIs to be innovative in such times as pandemics. Table 7.2 indicates the views posed by a number of scholars regarding innovative assessment in periods of pandemics. Table 7.2 indicates that the innovative formative assessment adopted during the COVID-19 pandemic by several HEIs was very crucial in achieving learning objectives. The table also indicates the examples of innovative formative assessment techniques for formative assessment. It is beyond reasonable doubt that during a pandemic, the only way to have a continuity in HEIs is to implement innovative formative online assessment (Glied & Lleras-Muney, 2008; Harris, & Jones, 2021). This will function as a gateway to engaging students and accomplishing desirable goals. Such a notion is also supported by Khan et al. (2021) as well as Arifuddin et al. (2021) who noted that innovativeness is essential during pandemic. Their argument is critical as it sets a tone and a direction toward stability in higher education as well as increasing participation, excitement, engagement, and competition among students.

7.7 Summative assessment currently adopted and their future use in higher education institutions

A critical review of literature unveiled vast opinions regarding the summative assessment embraced during the COVID-19 pandemic. A handful of these perceptions were collated and displayed in Table 7.3.

Table 7.3 indicates the importance of e-Exams as a significant way to address the serious challenges of handling summative assessments in this globalized world. There is an uncontested agreement on the notion that innovative summative assessment is indispensable with the teaching and learning fraternity, particularly in HEIs. Its importance lies in defining student learning outcomes (Arifuddin et al., 2021; Asamoah, Shahrill, & Latif, 2022; Bardhan, Dey, & Mahonty, 2020; Harmey & Moss, 2021). It was also agreed that the majority of HEIs had challenges in implementing innovative summative assessments during pandemics and disruptions due to the weaknesses which it poses in assessing students' performance. This idea was in the same vein with the perceptions of Gooblar (2019) as well as Willis (2021) who feels there is need to address the challenges which are introduced by the online innovative summative assessment mode. An emphasis was made to redesign the summative assessment to suit remote writing and give students flexibility in undertaking the examinations in cognizance of the various challenges (Borbon & Ricafort, 2021; Rachmawati, & Hastari, 2022). It was also found out that given the wavelength of technological change, embracing technology-enhanced assessment in the HEIs is not an option.

7.7.1 Recommendations

- The COVID pandemic has created a unique opportunity for educational changes that have been proposed before the pandemic but were never fully realized (Zhao & Watterston, 2021). On the post-COVID era, HEIs should implement a curriculum that is developmental, personalized, and evolving.
- The andragogy should be inquiry-based, authentic, and purposeful; and delivery of instruction that capitalizes on the strengths of both synchronous and asynchronous learning. Based on the abovementioned discussions and contributions by major authors on innovative assessment techniques post the COVID-19 pandemic, HEIs should adopt the assessment techniques that best suit their environments as well as situations.
- Basing on a student-centered approach to learning, the future on assessment and evaluation should give students an autonomy to choose between online or physical assessment modes without the institutions regulating on a single mode. Blended or hybrid assessment is highly recommended as the best approach to adopt post-COVID pandemic. This is supported by Deignan (2021) and Muxtorjonovna (2020) who

assert that hybrid learning is futuristic, and it provides students to learn using the hybrid spaces while at the same teacher's tailor make their curriculum and assessment criteria to suit different kinds of environment.

Muxtorjonovna (2020) alludes that with hybrid learning and assessment, teachers and student bear the equal responsibility to collaboratively learn in the VUCA environment. It can also be noted that students in most HEIs are most comfortable with the use of blended learning and blended assessments.

- COVID-19 brought in mixed perceptions toward the authenticity of online assessment and evaluation modes as asserted by Gooblar (2019), Willis (2021) which learners and institutions need to band and adopt to diverse versions of examinations and online proctoring. The pandemic created violation of academic integrity in some institutions (Huber & Helm, 2020) as they implemented online assessments without preparedness, it is recommended that institutions wishing to adopt online-based modes should first draft online educational policies and equip both students and facilitators with relevant expert knowledge to undertake it. Khan et al. (2021) assert that innovativeness is key for the survival of HEIs today and in future, based on that, it leaves the institutions restless to discover more futuristic ways of assessment and evaluation before future disruptions occur, prototypes of different modes of learning and assessment can be tried and tested before their acute need.
- There is need for the HEIs to create collaboration to allow the use of work-based assessment in the form of internships. This will allow the student to have practical experience of the aspect being done using the online platforms.
- Practicum or on campus—based assessment has been introduced into the assessment during the COVID-19 pandemic. The use of practicums will make assessment since practical activities assessed on-campus.
- Industry and HEIs collaboration are becoming more relevant in HEIs assessment. Such interaction will allow experienced specialists to engage universities and offer practical demonstration especially for modules that require practical skills development.

7.8 Conclusion

It can be established that assessment in HEIs in the post-COVID-19 era must change in terms of its strategies. The effect is in modernizing higher education to the digital era. It was also found out that innovative summative assessment has to be applied in such a way as to minimize chances of cheating or other irregularities, as the case may be. Both formative and summative assessment methods that were adopted during the COVID-19 era should be found on their way to the channel of recommended assessment methods post the COVID-19 pandemic. The COVID-19 pandemic also revealed vulnerabilities of both the students. HEIs are expected to adopt technologies that are useful in conducting the different assessments. It can be concluded that this required both entities to have the necessary equipment hence need for funding for the acquisition of the different technologies. The innovative assessments adopted post the pandemic also helped in expanding the definition of the right to education as it addresses the importance of connectivity and access to knowledge and information. HEIs need to be proactive so that they are in a position to respond to environmental changes which are disruptive in nature. The adoption of the best strategy to confront certain situation is the best remedy for competitiveness in modern HEIs.

References

Amin, H. A. A., Khalil, H., Khaled, D., Mahdi, M., Fathelbab, M., & Gaber, D. A. (2021). Case item creation and video case presentation as summative assessment tools for distance learning in the pandemic era. *Medical Journal Armed Forces India*, 77, S466–S474.

Alfonsa, G. L., Mazario, G., & Franscisco. (2016). The use of technology in a model of formative assessment. *Journal of Technology and Science Education*, 6(2), 91–103.

Arifuddin., et al. (2021). Alternative assessments in online learning during COVID 19 pandemic: The strengths and weaknesses. *International Journal of Elementary Education*, 5(2), 240.

Asamoah, D., Shahrill, M., & Latif, S. N. A. (2022). A review of formative assessment techniques in higher education during COVID-19. *Qualitative Report*, 27(2).

Association of American Colleges and Universities. (2004). Our students' best work: A framework for accountability worthy of our mission. *Peer Review*, 7(1), 25–28.

Bardhan, T., Dey, A., & Mahonty, S. (2020). *Online Assessment tools for the teaching and learning: Making ICT more handy*. India: University of Agriculture and Technology.

Bashir, A., Bashir, S., Rana, K., Lambert, P., & Vernallis, A. (2021). Post-COVID-19 adaptations; the shifts towards online learning, hybrid course delivery, and the implications for biosciences courses in the higher education setting. *Frontiers in Education*, 6, 310. Available from https://doi.org/10.3389/FEDUC.2021.711619/BIBTEX.

Bezuidenhout, J., van der Westhuizen, D., & de Beer, K. J. (2021). Andragogy: A theoretical overview on learning theories that impact on benchmarking blended learning at the Central University of Technology, Free State. *Interim: Interdisciplinary Journal*, 3, 1–27.

Black, P. (2015). Formative assessment—An optimistic but incomplete vision. *Assessment in Education: Principles, Policy & Practice*, 22(1), 161–177.

Borbon, M. and Ricafort, N. (2021). Summative Assessment on Student Outcomes for Tourism Program from 2013 to 2017. Available from https://www.researchgate.net/publication/355840581_Summative_Assessment_on_Student_Outcomes_for_Tourism_Program_from_2013_to_2017?enrichId = rgreq-eb63b050e5116e.

Bryan, A., & Volchenkova, K. N. (2016). BLENDED learning: Definition, models, and implications for higher education. *Bulletin of the South Ural State University Series "Education. Education Sciences,", 8*(2), 24–30. Available from https://doi.org/10.14529/ped160.

Clark, H. (2020). *How to use Flipgrid in the classroom.* Available from https://www.hollyclark.org/2020/04/25/infusing-flipgrid-into-your-classroom.

Conrad, D., & Openo, J. (2018). *Assessment strategies for online learning: Engagement and authenticity. AU.* Canada: Press.

Deignan, S. (2021). *Hybrid learning vs blended learning. What is the difference?* – Mentimeter. Available from https://www.mentimeter.com/blog/interactive-classrooms/hybrid-learning-vs-blended-learning-what-is-the-difference.

Fluck, A., & Hillier, M. (2016, September). Innovative assessment with eExams. In: *Australian council for computers in education conference* (Vol. 29). Brisbane.

Gamage, K. A., Silva, E. K. D., & Gunawardhana, N. (2020). Online delivery and assessment during COVID-19: Safeguarding academic integrity. *Education Sciences, 10*(11), 301.

Garrison, C., & Ehringhaus, M. (2020). *Formative and summative assessments in the classroom.* Ohio: Measured Progress.

Glied, S., & Lleras-Muney, A. (2008). Technological innovation and inequality in health. *Demography, 45*(3), 741–761. Available from https://doi.org/10.1353/DEM.0.0017.

Gooblar, D. (2019). *Helping students revise themselves. The missing course: Everything they never taught you about college teaching.* 14–39. Available from https://www.perlego.com.

Harmey, S., & Moss, G. (2021). *Learning disruption or learning loss: Using evidence from unplanned closures to inform returning to school after COVID-19. Educational review.* Routledge. Available from https://doi.org/10.1080/00131911.2021.1966389.

Harris, A., & Jones, M. (2021). *Leading in disruptive times: A spotlight on assessment, . School leadership and management* (Vol. 41, pp. 171–174). Routledge Issue 3. Available from https://doi.org/10.1080/13632434.2021.1887643.

Hoffmann, R., Hu, Y., de Gelder, R., Menvielle, G., Bopp, M., & Mackenbach, J. P. (2016). The impact of increasing income inequalities on educational inequalities in mortality – An analysis of six European countries. *International Journal for Equity in Health, 15*(1). Available from https://doi.org/10.1186/s12939-016-0390-0.

Huber, S. G., & Helm, C. (2020). COVID-19 and schooling: Evaluation, assessment, and accountability in times of crises—Reacting quickly to explore key issues for policy, practice, and research with the school barometer. *Educational Assessment, Evaluation and Accountability, 32*(2), 237–270. Available from https://doi.org/10.1007/s11092-020-09322-y.

Iradukunda, F., & Kumar, A. A. (2021). The impact of COVID-19 on the education sector in Zambia: A case study on DMI-St. Eugene University. *Shanlax International Journal of Management, 9*(2), 9–18.

Khan, R. A., & Masood, J. (2020). *Technology enhanced assessment (TEA) in COVID 19 pandemic.* Available from https://doi.org/10.12669/pjms.341.14354.

Khan, Z. R., Sivasubramaniam, S., Anand, P. & Hysaj, A. (2021). 'e'-thinking teaching and assessment to uphold academic integrity: Lessons learned from emergency distance learning. *International Journal for Educational Integrity, 17.*

Lalima., Dr., & LataDangwal, K. (2017). Blended learning: An innovative approach. *Universal Journal of Educational Research, 5*(1), 129–136. Available from https://doi.org/10.13189/ujer.2017.050116.

Lee, J. J., & Hammer, J. (2011). Gamification in education: What, how, why bother? *Acad Exch Q, 15*(2), 1–5.

Liberati, A., Altman, D., Tetzlaff, J. M., & Gøtzsche, P. C. (2009). The PRISMA statement for reporting systematic reviews and meta-analyses of studies that evaluate healthcare interventions: Explanation and elaboration. *BMJ Journals, 339.*

Luthfiyyah, R., Aisyah, A., & Sulistyo, G. H. (2021). Technology-enhanced formative assessment in higher education: A voice from Indonesian EFL teachers. *EduLite: Journal of English Education, Literature and Culture, 6*(1), 42−54.

Masengu, R., Ruzive, B. & Mandongwe, L. (2022). *Application of digital technologies in the 21st Century. Literature review of experiences, opportunities and challenges in higher education.* Available from https://www.researchgate.net / publication / 357402841 _ Application_of_Digital_technologies _in_the_21_ st_Century_Literature_Review_of_ Experiences_ Opportunities_and_Challenges_in_Higher_Education.

McKenna, K., Gupta, K., Kaiser, L., Lopes, T., & Zarestky, J. (2019). Blended learning: Balancing the best of both worlds for adult learners. *Journal Indexing and Metrics, 31*(4), 139−149. Available from https://doi.org/10.1177/1045159519891997.

Meydanlion, A. & Arikan, F. (2021). Effect of hybrid learning in higher education. *World Academy of Science, Engineering and Technology, International Journal of Social, Behavioral, Educational, Economic, Business and Industrial Engineering, 8*, 1292−1295. Available from https://www.semanticscholar.org /paper /Effect-of-Hybrid-Learning-in-Higher-Education-Meydanl%C4%B1o%C4%9Flu-Ar%C4%B1kan/ cadf0955509611280e28040c4f1854e30b06ca59.

Muxtorjonovna, A. M. (2020). Significance of blended learning in education system. *The American Journal of Social Science and Education Innovations, 02*(08), 507−511. Available from https://doi.org/10.37547/tajssei/Volume02Issue08-82.

National Council for Accreditation of Teacher Education (2003). Professional Standards for the Accreditation of Schools, Colleges and Departments of Education. Retrieved from https://ncate.org.

O'Byrne, W. I., & Pytash, K. E. (2015). Hybrid and blended learning: Modifying pedagogy across path, pace, time, and place. *Journal of Adolescent and Adult Literacy, 59*(2), 137−140. Available from https://doi.org/10.1002/JAAL.463.

OECD (2020). Education at a Glance (2020): OECD Indicators. Paris: OECD Publishing. Available from https://doi.org/10.1787/69096873-en.

Orim, M., & Orim, S. (2020). Contextual and dispositional factors of information and communication technology utilization among teachers of children with intellectual disability in Nigeria. In: *Edulearn 18 proceedings 10th international conference on education and new learning technology.*

Oxford University (2020). Available online: https://www.ox.ac.uk/coronavirus/students?wssl = 1.

Packt (2019). History of gamification in education. Packt https://subscription.packtpub.com/book/web_development/9781782168119/1/ch01lvl1sec09/history-of-gamification-in-education [accessed 1 december 2020].

QAA. (2020). *No Detriment' Policies: An Overview. COVID-19 Supporting Resources.* Gloucester: The Quality Assurance Agency for Higher Education.

Rachmawati, D. L., & Hastari, S. (2022). Formative assessment as an innovative strategies to develop ESP students' writing skills. *VELES Voices of English Language Education Society, 6*(1), 78−90.

Rutten, N., Van Joolingen, W., & Van Der Veen, J. (2012). The learning effects of computer simulations in science education. *Computers and Education, 58/1*, 136−153.

Sarkis-Onoffre, R., Catala-Lopez, F., & Lockwood, C. (2022). How to properly use the PRISMA statement. *Systematic Reviews.* Available from https://doi.org/10.1186/s13643-021-01671-z.

Schleicher, A. (2020). *The impact of COVID 19 on education: Insights from education at a glance.* Available from https://www.oecd.org.

Smith, D. F. (2014). *A brief history of gamification [#infographic]. EdTech focus on higher education.* Available from https://edtechmagazine.com/higher/article/2014/07/brief-history-gamification-infographic.

Snyder, T. (2021). *Educational assessments in the COVID-19 era and beyond.* Available from https://naeducation.org.

The United Nations Educational Scientific and Cultural Organization [UNESCO]. (2022). *Rethinking assessments in the context of COVID-19 — Home.* <https://allchildrenlearning.org/rethinking-assessments-in-the-context-of-COVID-19/>.

Todd, M. (2022). The PRISMA 2020 statement: an updated guideline for reporting systematic reviews. *Research Methods and Reporting.* Available from https://doi.org/10.1136/bmj.n71.

Tranfield, D., Denyer, D., & Smart, P. (2003). Towards a methodology for developing evidence: Informed management knowledge by means of systematic review. *British Journal of Management, 14,* 207—222. Available from https://doi.org/10.1111/1467-8551.00375.

UNESCO. (2020). *Education: From disruption to recovery.* <https://en.unesco.org/COVID19/educationresponse>.

United Nations (2020, August). Policy Brief: Education during COVID-19 and beyond. United Nations. Retrieved from https://www.un.org/development/desa/dspd/wp-content/uploads/sites/22/2020/08/sg_policy_brief_covid-19_and_education_august_2020.pdf.

Walvoord, B. E. (2010). *Assessment clear and simple: A practical guide for institutions, departments, and general education.* San Francisco, CA: Jossey Bass.

Week, T. (2021). Assessing student learning amid disruption. Available from https://www.instructure.com/canvas/resources/all/assessing-student-learning-amid-disruption.

Willis, J. (2021). *How can school assessment be fair in a time of COVID-19 disruption? — The Centre for Inclusive Education.* Available from https://research.qut.edu.au/c4ie/2020/03/27/how-can-school-assessment-be-fair-in-a-time-of-COVID-19-disruption/.

Wong, G., Greenhalgh, T., Westhorp, G., Buckingham, J., & Pawson, R. (2013). RAMESES publication standards: Meta-narrative reviews. *BMC Medicine, 11*(12).

Woolf, S. H., Johnson, R. E., Phillips, R. L., & Philipsen, M. (2007). Giving everyone the health of the educated: An examination of whether social change would save more lives than medical advances. *American Journal of Public Health, 97*(4), 679—683. Available from https://doi.org/10.2105/AJPH.2005.084848.

Zhao, Y., & Watterston, J. (2021). The changes we need: Post COVID-19. *Journal of Educational Change, 22,* 3—12.

CHAPTER 8

Formative assessment in hybrid learning environments

Natalia Auer
Faculty of Education and Society, Malmö University, Malmö, Sweden

8.1 Introduction

One of the impacts of COVID-19 on teaching and learning in higher education has been a change in teaching methods (Auer, 2022; Padilla Rodríguez, Armellini, & Traxler, 2021; Verde & Valero, 2021). Many students and teachers have gained new experiences from learning and teaching with digital technologies. Consequently, expectations and requirements regarding online instruction are changing.

Online formative assessment has not been an exemption to the changes in teaching practice. Since teachers could not prepare ahead of time for these changes, both planned and improvised changes took place, with a large variety of online assessment practices (e.g., Zhang, Yan, & Wang, 2021).

As hybrid learning environments are becoming the new normal— mixed face-to-face (F2F) and online—innovative strategies for online assessment are also needed, as well as a better understanding of how to assess in hybrid learning environments.

Research indicates the value of teacher engagement with online formative assessment during the COVID-19 pandemic (Zou, Kong, & Lee, 2021). Moreover, online formative assessment assisted teachers in monitoring the progress of their students so that they could adapt teaching strategies to students' needs and measure students' understanding of the material (Listyowati, Wiyaka, & Prastikawati, 2021).

However, being positive about formative assessment is not enough to implement effective strategies that will develop learner autonomy (Lee, 2017). The literature also indicates that there is much room for development regarding strategies that takes advantage of the potentials of formative assessment, such as setting learning outcomes and criteria for success,

Digital Teaching, Learning and Assessment
DOI: https://doi.org/10.1016/B978-0-323-95500-3.00013-4

147

promoting learner autonomy, and peer review (Andersson, Boström, & Palm, 2022). Moreover, research on online formative assessment suggests a need to conduct studies that explore how to support teachers' engagement with online formative assessment (Zou et al., 2021). In this context, it is important to have a framework for engaging and supporting teachers in implementing online formative assessment.

8.2 A relevant model for implementing online formative assessment in ways that increase self-regulation by learners

Online formative assessment can facilitate formative and immediate feedback, engagement with critical learning processes, and can promote equitable education (Gikandi, Morrow, & Davis, 2011). These processes are included in Hattie and Timperley's (2007) model, presented in this chapter.

To promote deep learning in online environments, formative feedback should be a dialogic process (Gikandi et al., 2011) and implemented in ways that foster self-regulation among students (Biggs & Tang, 2011). These are also part of the processes referred to by Hattie and Timperley (2007) in their model and can be adapted to online learning environments since the development of self-regulation is relevant in higher education (Gikandi et al., 2011).

The advantages and potentials mentioned previously are closely connected in Hattie and Timperley's model. The teacher designs and shares the learning outcomes[1] with students, students have time to respond, and learning outcomes fit students' needs. Moreover, their model promotes self-regulatory processes.

8.3 The need for a conceptual framework

Embedding formative assessment within online courses, while grounded in theory, needs further research (Gikandi et al., 2011). Hattie and Timperley's (2007) model provides a guide for teachers to provide appropriate formative feedback.

In the online environment, focusing on learning design instead of content is paramount for the learning experience (Conceição & Howles,

---

[1] Hattie and Timperley (2007) utilize "learning goals." The concept of "learning outcomes" emphasizes on the learning process (Biggs & Tang, 2011), therefore the use of the term "learning outcomes" in this chapter.

2019). Even though Hattie and Timperley's (2007) model does not reference online learning, their model can be utilized to online formative assessment. Their conceptual analysis of feedback is particularly useful for those designing and facilitating online courses since their model identifies the circumstances that make feedback effective.

In their systematic qualitative review, Gikandi et al. (2011) recommend a model for the implementation of formative assessment within blended and online environments. In this chapter, I would argue that Hattie and Timperley's (2007) model is appropriate for embedding online formative assessment in hybrid learning environments.

Despite the existence of many studies on online formative assessment in higher education, there is a lack of theoretical frameworks for supporting the design of formative assessment in hybrid learning environments.

This chapter fills that knowledge gap by presenting a framework for implementing online formative assessment in hybrid learning environments. It can be used as a theoretical framework to design online formative assessment that supports self-regulatory processes with technology in hybrid learning environments.

The implementation of online formative assessment based on this framework will be more theoretically robust than online assessments based on the intuition of the course instructor and/or instructional designer. It may also guide conceptual and empirical work among researchers studying online formative assessment in the hybrid learning context.

8.4 Formative assessment and online formative assessment

It is important to clarify the concepts behind the terms used in this chapter, in particular to distinguish between the concepts of assessment and feedback. Assessment relates to "strategies used to evaluate learners' content knowledge, demonstration of a skill or task, development of a product, or experience of a process" (Conceição & Howles, 2019, p. 122). Feedback is "information with which a learner can confirm, add to, overwrite, tune, or restructure information in memory, whether that information is domain knowledge, meta-cognitive knowledge, beliefs about self and tasks, or cognitive tactics and strategies" (Winne & Butler, 1994, p. 5740).

There is a wide variety of formats for assessing students' declarative and functioning knowledge. Declarative knowledge refers "to knowing about things [....]. Functioning knowledge is knowledge based on the academic declarative knowledge base that is put to work" (Biggs & Tang, 2011, p. 92). These tasks include concept maps, gobbets, minute paper, projects, reflective journals, cases, etc. (see Biggs & Tang, 2011 for a full description of formats for assessing declarative and functioning knowledge).

From the several reasons for assessing students, the two most dominant are formative feedback and summative grading. Both have different purposes: the first is ongoing and has the aim of supporting learning; the second measures what students have learned at the end of a course or unit (Biggs & Tang, 2011, p. 195).

Formative assessment is one of the most powerful methods for effective teaching and learning (Biggs & Tang, 2011; Hattie & Timperley, 2007) (for a comprehensive review of formative assessment in the classroom, see McMillan, 2007).

Black and Wiliam (2009, p. 9) define formative assessment as "Practice in a classroom is formative to the extent that evidence about student achievement is elicited, interpreted, and used by teachers, learners, or their peers, to make decisions about the next steps in instruction that are likely to be better, or better founded, than the decisions they would have taken in the absence of the evidence that was elicited."

In this chapter, I use the definition of online formative assessment from Gikandi et al. (2011, p. 2337): "...the application of formative assessment within learning online and blended settings where the teachers and learners are separated by time and/or space and where a substantial proportion of learning/teaching activities are conducted through web-based ICT."

8.5 Using formative assessments online

Formative assessment strategies can be supported by educational technologies. This has several advantages; among others, allowing more than one attempt, providing immediate feedback, guiding reading, and the use of multimedia for assessing functioning knowledge (Biggs & Tang, 2011). Likewise, the dynamic interaction with students in online environments can be enhanced through formative assessment (Oosterhof, Conrad, & Ely, 2008).

In a systematic qualitative review of the research literature on online formative assessment in higher education, Gikandi et al. (2011) identify various benefits of online formative assessment, including improvement of learner engagement with critical learning processes, formative and immediate feedback, and promoting equitable education. Their review provides evidence that online formative assessment has the potential to enhance dialog between the teacher and learner, response time, and clarity in learning outcomes. They recommend that formative assessment needs to be implemented so that it fosters self-regulation by learners. Online formative assessment can promote learners' autonomy, which is one of the characteristics of higher education likely to influence teaching and learning (Jönsson & Eriksson, 2019).

When compared to F2F settings, research indicates that benefits of online formative assessment include immediacy of feedback and flexibility with the submission of assignments (Joyce, 2018). Moreover, online formative assessment differs from F2F settings in that it provides opportunities for interactions with teacher and peers due to the building of collaborative online learning communities, gives time to reflect through asynchronous discussions, and elicits better quality written feedback through the use of computer software (Gikandi et al., 2011).

8.6 Key concepts

There are various terminologies within the field of educational technology which are used synonymously. As a result of the COVID-19 pandemic, many educational institutions adapted their classroom teaching to remote teaching. Although this was far from quality online learning (Hodges, Moore, Lockee, Trust, & Bond, 2020), it gave rise to widely different approaches to the delivery of digital education. With this wide variety of methods to deliver teaching remotely, there was a sudden increase in the number of terms to describe them. In this section, I will clarify the terms online learning, digital learning, blended learning, and hybrid learning.

The term *online* refers to "the connectivity of the learning, teaching and support delivery methods that may be employed by a provider" (The Quality Assurance Agency for Higher Education, 2020, p. 2). The term *digital* relates to "the storage of data but has developed as a term to mean involving or relating to the use of computer technology, exemplified by the use of the terms digital skills or digital literacy" (The Quality Assurance Agency for Higher Education, 2020, p. 3).

Blended learning and hybrid learning are utilized interchangeably when referring to modes of delivery which takes place partly in a digital environment and partly in-person (The Quality Assurance Agency for Higher Education, 2020). The term blended learning is often related to courses with any element of digital learning (e.g., slides, video, searching the web). In fact, today it is difficult not to deliver blended learning, as simply using a PowerPoint presentation is enough to meet the definition. Blended learning also refers to programs that require students to participate onsite for some lessons and engage in digital learning activities for the rest of the course.

In hybrid learning, students can choose whether they attend onsite or remotely. In the United Kingdom, higher education institutions have not used the term "hybrid" as much, but recently it has been utilized to refer to modes of delivery that provide flexibility to students (The Quality Assurance Agency for Higher Education, 2020). In 2005 Beatty (2021) added another dimension to hybrid learning, flexibility, and coined the term "HyFlex." Flexibility refers to students' choice of participation mode per session, topic, or learning activity.

A newer, more complete definition of hybrid learning refers to the blend of "digital and material elements, online and face-to-face spaces, and formal and informal learning and demonstrates how various forms of learning might coexist" (Green, 2022, p. 95). This is the meaning of the term "hybrid" used in this chapter.

8.7 Hattie and Timperley's feedback model

According to Hattie and Timperley (2007), effective formative feedback answers three feedback questions, related to the concepts of Feed Up, Feed Back, and Feed Forward.

Hattie and Timperley's model operates with four levels of feedback related to each feedback question: the level of task performance, the level of process related to how to do a task, the regulatory level, and/or the self or personal level (Hattie & Timperley, 2007).

Feed Up is linked to the learning outcome of the learning process. The feedback is only effective if it is linked to an explicit learning outcome. It is about setting a clear learning outcome: "Your learning outcome is to write one point per section in your description" (it links to learning outcomes in relation to where the student is going).

Feed Back shows where the student is in relation to the intended learning outcomes: "In section 1 you have a point, but afterwards you have the same point in different sections."

Feed Up and Feed Back are prerequisites for Feed Forward to be as specified and efficient as possible. By answering this question, the teacher scaffolds the student learning process toward the learning outcome. The teacher guides the student toward what he or she can do to "close the gap" between the progress that has been made and the learning outcomes, such as by questioning which learning strategies, methods, techniques the student can use. For example: "You have to find the same points and collect them in a section" (it explains the next step, based on Feed Up and Feed Back).

The questions can also be applied to the teacher's own curriculum and thus strengthen the pedagogical reflections on learning outcomes achievement (Hattie & Timperley, 2007).

The focus is on the learning process and on helping the student to develop learning strategies, including summarizing, formulating in their own words, structuring key words by grouping them into categories, awareness of reading purposes, emphasizing important information, etc.

Feedback questions enhance learning when there is a gap. To learn, it is crucial to identify the gap in the student's understanding. If the teacher knows what the student does not understand, they can help to fill this gap. What is powerful with these questions is that they help teachers to identify this gap.

8.7.1 Examples of the three feedback questions

These three forms of feedback do not necessarily have to be implemented linearly. The focus can be put on different levels of feedback, and the three feedback questions can be mixed—it is not a linear process. In practice, the three types of feedback can look like this.

8.7.1.1 At task level

Feed Up: "The learning outcomes for this task were to 1) work with your introduction so that you present the key ideas of the text and 2) minimize the use of the conjunction 'and'."

Feed Back: "You have made a good introduction with the main points of the text; you have removed the conjunction 'and,' but you do not use other conjunctions."

Feed Forward: "Try to use the functions 'search' and 'replace' in word processing software. Search 'and' and replace with 'in addition,' 'besides,' 'furthermore,' etc., then you can vary your language."

8.7.1.2 At process level
This type of feedback focuses on learning processes to understand and design the task. The aim of the feedback at this level is to process information or complete a task. The teacher evaluates and improves students' strategies in solving the task (which strategies should be used, etc.). In hybrid learning environments, one could look at processes using collaborative documents.

Feed Up: "In the task formulation it says that you should summarize what I said and ask some focus points."

Feed Back: "You relate to my feedback. You summarize the main points and set up focus points."

Feed Forward: "Try to summarize what I have said and set up a focus point."

8.7.1.3 At the level of self-regulation
This type of feedback makes the student reflect on their own learning. The student must find out for themselves what the next step may be.

Feed Up: "You should check your concordance errors."

Feed Back: "You have found some mistakes and fixed them."

Feed Forward: "Do you have any idea why this is wrong?"

In the hybrid learning environment, both teachers and students can seek answers to each of the feedback questions.

8.7.1.4 At the personal level
Feedback at the personal level is seldom effective since it is infrequent that praise addresses the three feedback questions (Hattie & Timperley, 2007). Therefore examples at the personal level are not provided.

8.8 Applying Hattie and Timperley's model to hybrid learning environments

When designing formative assessment in online environments, it is crucial to facilitate ongoing and suitable learner autonomy, effective formative feedback, and clarity of learning outcomes (Gikandi et al., 2011). All these characteristics are included in Hattie and Timperley's model (2007). Moreover, effective formative feedback is crucial for successful online formative assessment, particularly regarding immediacy, adequacy, and interactivity (Gikandi et al., 2011).

Hattie and Timperley's (2007) model can be used to enhance dialog between the teacher and learner, facilitate response time, meet individual learning needs, clarify learning outcomes, and provide structure in designing hybrid formative assessment.

8.8.1 Dialog

To promote reflection, formative feedback in online environments should focus on the dialogic process that engages students in reflective thinking (Gikandi et al., 2011). Formative feedback needs to be implemented in ways that foster self-regulation among students (Biggs & Tang, 2011). These are part of the processes referred to by Hattie and Timperley (2007) at the regulatory level.

One of the advantages of hybrid environments is that they offer enhanced interactivity (Gikandi et al., 2011). Although Hattie and Timperley did not include hybrid learning contexts, the model is appropriate for online formative assessment since, in online settings, it is essential that feedback promotes dialog between students and the teacher and among peers (Wolsey, 2008). Their model can improve hybrid learning environments by providing opportunities for interaction.

8.8.2 Time and immediacy of response

As Hattie and Timperley (2007) argue, the model can be used to address the timing of feedback by discriminating between the various feedback levels. For example, at task level, immediate feedback can be beneficial, while at process level delayed feedback is necessary. Hattie and Timperley (2007) explain that complex tasks need more processing to complete the task and delayed feedback is necessary. The asynchronous online environment facilitates this process by providing ample time to respond.

The asynchronous use of online environments is beneficial when questions probe high-level thinking because more time is needed to respond (Biggs & Tang, 2011). More time allows students to answer at their own pace. Educational technology can enhance immediacy and clarity of feedback, but to promote deep learning, it is important to balance immediacy with time to respond (Gikandi et al., 2011). Students need opportunities to review the feedback they receive and reflect before they start a new task. Such opportunities can be suitably enhanced by the three feedback questions.

8.8.3 Learning outcomes

Clarity of intended learning outcomes is a prerequisite for effective online formative assessment (Gikandi et al., 2011). Biggs and Tang (2011) recommend the use of rubrics—an explicit grading scheme—to assess students' performance against learning outcomes. In online learning environments, it is crucial to share rubrics with students and these environments offer opportunities to share and review rubrics (Wolsey, 2008). This process is part of the Feed Up question referred to by Hattie and Timperley (2007).

8.8.4 Individual learning

Identifying learner needs to close the gap is one of the processes in Hattie and Timperley' (2007) model. In online environments, the teacher can better observe students' performance and provide appropriate formative feedback (Gikandi et al., 2011).

Sorensen and Takle (2005) recommend teachers meet the diversity of students by providing support while they engage asynchronously in online environments. It is also crucial that the teacher ask questions in a way that students develop critical inquiry and metacognitive skills (Tallent-Runnels et al., 2006). Hattie and Timperley's (2007) model provides guidelines, so the teacher asks feedback questions that promote critical inquiry and metacognitive awareness.

8.8.5 Design considerations

An effective integration of formative assessment into online environments requires design considerations (Wolsey, 2008). Hattie and Timperley's (2007) model provides a structure for integrating formative assessment in a hybrid learning environment by asking feedback questions that operates at different levels: task, process, self-regulation, and/or self-level.

It is essential that the teacher provides scaffolds to support online learning (Ludwig-Hardman & Dunlap, 2003). Online formative feedback facilitates scaffolded learning. This tailored feedback can engage students in self-regulated learning (Chung, Shel, & Kaiser, 2006). The feedback model provides a guide for facilitating scaffolded learning by setting learning outcomes and offering feedback in relation to identified needs. In addition, their model facilitates assessment strategies so the teacher can provide these scaffolds and students can monitor and self-regulate their learning.

8.9 Conclusion

This chapter showed how hybrid learning environments can support effective feedback, as conceptualized by Hattie and Timperley (2007). Embedding their model in hybrid learning environments can offer an innovative pedagogical strategy to facilitate effective online formative assessment.

Online formative assessment has the potential to enhance dialog between the teacher and learner, and provide response time and clarity in learning outcomes. These advantages are closely connected in Hattie and Timperley's model. The teacher designs and shares the learning outcomes with students, students have time to respond, and learning outcomes fit students' needs. Moreover, their model promotes self-regulatory processes.

Hattie and Timperley's conceptual analysis of feedback is particularly useful for those designing and facilitating hybrid courses since it identifies the circumstances that make feedback effective.

References

Andersson, C., Boström, E., & Palm, T. (2022). Formative assessment in Swedish. *Nordic Studies in Mathematics Education*, *1*, 5–20.

Auer, N. (2022). Emergency teaching in secondary schools in Denmark – 'Some Students Flourish, Some Wither'. In: *INTED2022 proceedings – 16th international technology, education and development conference*. Valencia: IATED. Available from https://doi.org/10.21125/inted.2022.

Beatty, B. (2021). How to use the HyFlex method to teach online and in person at the same. TEACHONLINE.CA. Retrieved from https://teachonline.ca/sites/default/files/webinar-series/slides/hyflex_cn_sep2021.pdf.

Biggs, J., & Tang, C. (2011). *Teaching for quality learning at university*. Maidenhead, UK: Open University Press.

Black, P., & Wiliam, D. (2009). Developing the theory of formative assessment. *Journal of Personnel Evaluation in Education*. *21*, 5–31. Available from https://doi.org/10.1007/s11092-008-9068-5.

Chung, G. K. W. K, Shel, T., & Kaiser, W. J. (2006). An exploratory study of a novel online formative assessment and instructional tool to promote students' circuit problem solving. *Journal of Technology, Learning, and Assessment, 5*(6), 1—27.

Conceição, S., & Howles, L. (2019). *Designing the online learning experience.* Sterling, Virginia, US: Stylus Publishing.

Gikandi, J., Morrow, D., & Davis, N. (2011). Online formative assessment in higher education: A review of the literature. *Computers & Education, 57,* 2333—2351.

Green, J. (2022). Designing hybrid spaces for learning in higher education health contexts. *Postdigital Science and Education, 4*(1), 93—115. Available from https://doi.org/10.1007/s42438-021-00268-y.

Hattie, J., & Timperley, H. (2007). The power of feedback. *Review of educational research, 77*(1), 81—112. Retrieved from http://rer.sagepub.com/content/77/1/81.

Hodges, C., Moore, S., Lockee, B., Trust, T., & Bond, A. (2020). The difference between emergency remote teaching and online learning. *EDUCAUSE Review.* Retrieved from https://er.educause.edu/articles/2020/3/the-difference-between-emergency-remote-teaching-and-online-learning.

Jönsson, U., & Eriksson, A. (2019). Formative assessment in higher education: An example from astronomy. In R. E. Heidi, & L. Andrade (Eds.), *Handbook of formative assessment in the disciplines.* New York, US: Routledge.

Joyce, P. (2018). The effectiveness of online and paper-based formative assessment in the learning of English as a second language. *PASAA, 126—146.*

Lee, I. (2017). *Classroom writing assessment and feedback in L2 school contexts.* Singapore: Springer.

Listyowati, W., Wiyaka., & Prastikawati, E. (2021). English teachers' conceptions of formative assessment. *Journal of Language and Literature, 16*(1), 177—186. Retrieved from http://web.journal.unnes.ac.id/.

Ludwig-Hardman, S., & Dunlap, J. (2003). Learner support services for online students: Scaffolding for success. *International Review of Research in Open and Distance Learning, 4*(1).

McMillan, J. (2007). *Formative classroom assessment: Theory into practice.* Teachers College Press.

Oosterhof, A., Conrad, R., & Ely, D. (2008). *Assessing learners online.* Pearson/Merrill: Prentice Hall.

Padilla Rodríguez, B., Armellini, A., & Traxler, J. (2021). The forgotten ones: How rural teachers in Mexico are facing the COVID-19 pandemic. *Online Learning, 25*(1), 253—268.

Sorensen, E. K., & Takle, E. (2005). Investigating knowledge building dialogues in networked dialogues in networked communities of practice: A collaborative learning endeavor across cultures. *Digital Education Review. 10,* 50—60. Retrieved from http://www.ub.edu/multimedia/iem.

Tallent-Runnels, M. K., Thomas, J. A., Lan, W. Y., Cooper, S., Ahern, T. C., Shaw, S. M., & Liu, X. (2006). Teaching courses online: A review of the research. *Review of Educational Research, 76*(1), 93—135. Available from https://doi.org/10.3102/00346543076001093.

The Quality Assurance Agency for Higher Education. (2020). *Building a taxonomy for digital learning.* Gloucester: The Quality Assurance Agency for Higher Education. Retrieved from https://www.qaa.ac.uk/docs/qaa/guidance/building-a-taxonomy-for-digital-learning.pdf.

Verde, A., & Valero, J. (2021). Teaching and learning modalities in higher education during the pandemic: Responses to coronavirus disease 2019 from Spain. *Frontiers in Psychology, 12,* 1—12. Retrieved from https://www.frontiersin.org/articles/10.3389/fpsyg.2021.648592.

Winne, P., & Butler, D. (1994). Student cognition in learning from teaching. In T. Husén, & T. N. Postlethwaite (Eds.), *International encyclopedia of education* (2nd ed., pp. 5738−5775). Oxford: Pergamon Press.

Wolsey, T. (2008). Efficacy of instructor feedback on written work in an online program. *International Journal on ELearning, 7*(2), 311−329.

Zhang, C., Yan, X., & Wang, J. (2021). EFL teachers' online assessment practices during the COVID-19 pandemic: Changes and mediating factors. *The Asia-Pacific Education Researcher, 30*(6), 499−507. Available from https://doi.org/10.1007/s40299-021-00589-3.

Zou, M., Kong, D., & Lee, I. (2021). Teacher engagement with online formative assessment in EFL. *The Asia-Pacific Education Researcher, 30,* 487−498. Available from https://doi.org/10.1007/s40299-021-00593-7.

CHAPTER 9

Student experience of online exams in professional programs: current issues and future trends

Nga Thanh Nguyen, Colin Clark, Caroline Joyce, Carl Parsons and John Juriansz
Western Sydney University, Sydney, NSW, Australia

9.1 Introduction

The popularity of online learning has surged in recent years. The rapid pivot to the online environment necessitated by COVID-19 has resulted in some universities adopting various forms of online assessment. Online assessment refers to regimes where the design, conduct, communication with staff, and grading, as well as providing feedback on assessment, are performed using various information technology platforms (Alruwais, Wills, & Wald, 2018). Online assessment depends on an Internet connection, which means it can be conducted remotely. While the COVID-19 pandemic continues to necessitate the greater use of online assessment (Jha et al., 2022), it has not prevented many disciplines from continuing assessment practices, such as the use of exams as summative assessments.

Exams have long been common in traditional learning environments to assess student learning. There is still much to be learned and shared as the platforms and technologies supporting online exams continue to evolve rapidly. Unlike other studies, this research examines the impact of two distinct professional disciplines on the practice of online exams and proposes possible avenues and opportunities for sustainable online exam forms. Our purpose in this chapter is not to advocate for exams but to examine innovative approaches that may be applied where such assessments are increasingly unavoidable. This study investigates the value of online exams while exploring current issues and future trends in online examinations as highlighted by the student perspective. It addresses the research question: *What are students' perceptions and experiences of different types of online exams across two professional disciplines?*

Digital Teaching, Learning and Assessment
DOI: https://doi.org/10.1016/B978-0-323-95500-3.00009-2

9.2 Literature review

This section provides a comprehensive review of the relatively sparse online assessment literature on current issues of online exams.

9.2.1 Online exams

A review of recent exam literature reveals many terms used to describe online exams, such as "digital exams" and "computer-based exams." There is inconsistency between contexts. To address this issue, for this book chapter, we use the term "online exams," which refers to exams for which students prepare/bring/use their own devices. Students can choose to sit in their own space at home or on campus. These are considered to be remote exams.

Online exams have proceeded through several generations in terms of sophistication. The first generation is described as traditional paper-and-pencil instruments, conducted at a certain time and in a particular space. Exams, then, were conducted in computer laboratories in electronic format but were simply online forms of paper tests. The next phase is where assessments take the form of interactive e-assessments. Online exams can take many forms, from simple formats submitted via learning management systems with answers on spreadsheets to remote exams with a live invigilator or recorded e-proctored exams (Elsalem, Al-Azzam, Jum'ah, & Obeidat, 2021; Kharbat & Abu Daabes, 2021). Online exams can be taken via different platforms, including online meeting platforms such as Zoom, Teams, or Google Meet. Currently, and especially during the 2020−21 COVID-19 pandemic, the majority of Australian and New Zealand universities have replaced traditional face-to-face invigilated examinations with invigilated online exams (Sankey, 2022), which has enabled university study to continue despite government rules enforcing lockdowns. According to Sankey's (2022) survey data, 51% of universities used online invigilated exams in 2020, while the rest used alternative online assessments. Online exams offer the opportunity to replicate a traditional exam; however, with the rapid transition to online exams, how can we ensure that the student value is maximized while maintaining exam security and respecting student expectations concerning their university experience (Selwyn, O'Neill, Smith, Andrejevic, & Gu, 2021)? There is scant literature discussing differences in online exam formats and their implications for student assessment.

9.2.2 Learners' experiences of online exams

Universities have a responsibility to include student perspectives in the implementation of assessments. From their perspective, there are several advantages to online exams. Remote exams provide students with the opportunity to sit in their own comfortable quiet place and space. According to Butler-Henderson and Crawford (2020), most students are satisfied with online exams and prefer them to paper-based alternatives because they are easy to use, and results are received relatively quickly. Importantly, online exams may provide better access for students with disabilities. Digital-age students prefer computer-based assessments to paper-based assessments as they feel more engaged and find the format more flexible (Butler-Henderson & Crawford, 2020; Selwyn et al., 2021). Students have the benefit of standardized and individualized feedback (Butler-Henderson & Crawford, 2020), which in some cases can be delivered instantly. Some types of assessments such as quizzes can be automatically marked and feedback given to students using feedback studio. The readability of student work would make it easier to mark. Online exams would bring benefits to institutions by reducing assessment costs. Despite this convenience, there appear to be no statistically significant differences between online and traditional exams in terms of student outcomes (Butler-Henderson & Crawford, 2020; Ilgaz & Afacan Adanır, 2020). From the staff perspective, online exams save time and money because they can be delivered and even scored automatically, with results recorded and scored online. This saves marking time and is especially useful for large classes, such as first-year core courses. The collection of data online by electronic tools in a standard format is useful for analysis and comparison between groups of students. There are also logistical advantages in reducing the need to book rooms, print papers, monitor attendance, and store completed scripts.

One consideration in online exams is whether to include an online proctor/invigilator. Academic integrity is a significant problem in online assessment in Australian higher education (Bearman & Luckin, 2020; Bretag et al., 2014). Mitigation strategies in addition to invigilating may include methods such as time stamps on assignment submissions, and biometrics such as facial recognition or keystroke pattern analysis (Sullivan, 2016). The primary justification for the use of online invigilating tools is to reduce cheating by monitoring the use of time (by ensuring that a student starts and finishes at the appointed time), space, by tracking movements by the test taker's eyes, face, or body and resources such as phones or calculators (Lee, 2020). The need for such measures appears to be supported by study findings that noninvigilated students score significantly higher than their invigilated counterparts. Alessio, Malay, Maurer, Bailer, and Rubin (2017) conducted an experiment to compare the results of students in an online test with and without invigilating software, finding that the noninvigilated group scored an average of 17 points higher. This supports survey results that students are more likely to cheat in online than face-to-face classes (Butler-Henderson & Crawford, 2020).

Nonetheless, invigilated online examinations have critics. They create issues concerning ethics and student equity (Allan, 2020). Moreover, it is not clear whether the reduced test scores sometimes observed for invigilated versus noninvigilated exams are due to cheating or to the heightened anxiety that observation by a stranger may cause. Moreover, the difference is not consistent. Ladyshewsky (2015) found no difference between monitored and unmonitored tests, whereas Fawns and Schaepkens (2022) allege that invigilated exams (at least in medicine) engender a sense of "false objectivity that is undermined by the tight script with which examinees must comply in an intensified norm of surveillance" (p. 1). Moreover, the use of surveillance in private spaces using software and human observers in a situation that is legally ambiguous concerning privacy can engender anxiety. It has even been alleged by Barrett (2021) that ethnic minority students and students with disabilities face discriminatory flagging by online invigilators. Barrett (2021) concludes "Remote proctoring software is not pedagogically beneficial, institutionally necessary, or remotely unavoidable, and its use further entrenches inequities in higher education that schools should be devoted to rooting out" (p.1).

9.2.3 Challenges faced and trends in transforming traditional exams

As online education grows in popularity for various reasons, including the move to an online environment due to the COVID-19 pandemic or the flexibility of learning postpandemic, a few common issues have arisen related to online exams (Sankey, 2022). Technical issues around online exams have been caused by different factors such as the Internet, software, and student access to computers (Sankey, 2022). There are also findings that cheating concerns the nature of the exam rather than the format (Bearman & Luckin, 2020). Furthermore, it has been reported that students have posted instructions on how to cheat in online invigilated exams (Selwyn et al., 2021), which tends to reduce confidence in invigilating as a safeguard against malfeasance.

While some researchers (Saha, Pranty, Rana, Islam, & Hossain, 2022; Selwyn et al., 2021) admit there may be a place for invigilated online exams, others support the use of assessment design strategies to minimize opportunities to cheat, especially with high-stakes online exams (Diaz, Linden, & Solyali, 2021). Universities have made great efforts in recent years to adopt and improve online assessments (Sankey, 2021). Reflective strategies and continuous innovation are needed to ensure quality and maintain assessment integrity and fairness in the future. While there is evidence to support the use of invigilated exams to reduce academic dishonesty (Reisenwitz, 2020), there is a lack of research comparing different methods and formats of online exams.

In addition, the reactions of disciplines to external pressures vary within an institution. However, the current literature on assessment during the pandemic does not appear to offer a comprehensive investigation of student experiences of changes across disciplines in higher education. It merely discusses whether short-term responses to the crisis will inform long-term sustainable practices in online exams and assessments. Previous research has not investigated the impact of academic discipline on online invigilated exams to understand the significance of its role in student performance. Current uses of online assessments across disciplines need to be examined to understand their strengths and drawbacks.

9.2.4 Theoretical framework

Vygotsky's (1978) social-cultural perspective suggests that learning and development should be investigated in their social-cultural contexts and with their contextual factors. Constructivism's learning theorists theorize human behavior and experiences as an interaction between the individual and the environment, and others have advanced the perspective that the "fit" between an individual's personality and their environment is especially important for student success and academic decision-making (Pardjono, 2016). By taking a social constructivist perspective, we sought insights into the experience of students in online exams in the context of higher education and this provides not only a lens to analyze students' experiences but also a language to describe the experience.

9.3 Methodology

This study is a report on the implications of the findings of two in-depth case studies with rich data collected over two years of implementing and

piloting three different formats of online exams:
1. Noninvigilated exams via the Blackboard learning management system (noninvigilated exams).
2. Live invigilating by a staff member via the Zoom videoconferencing tool (Zoom-invigilated exams).
3. Artificial intelligence invigilation is supplemented with a live invigilator provided by a commercial invigilating service (live invigilated exams).

As part of a larger study, this research was granted ethics approval from the Human Research Ethics Committee of the study institution in 2020–21 (HREC H13866).

9.3.1 Study setting

The data collected for this project were drawn from the law and medical schools of a federated university of approximately 30 years of age. The law and medical programs have relatively stringent entrance requirements, and potential students are expected to demonstrate a strong academic record for admission. Law is a three-year program consisting of individual subjects with opportunities for placements and internships. Prior to 2020, almost all core subjects used flipped classroom learning approaches with face-to-face invigilated exams and some online assessments using the learning management system. Medicine is a five-year program. In the first two years, students are mainly campus-based, while in the last three years, they are immersed in clinical settings. The program has many high-stakes invigilated exams throughout the five years, and there are some online assessments via the learning management system and workplace-based assessments in the clinical setting. Before the COVID-19 pandemic of 2020–21, these two programs were normally taught and assessed in face-to-face mode, using various blended learning approaches. However, the pandemic necessitated a rapid shift to online program delivery in a relatively short period.

These programs were chosen because both require accreditation by external professional bodies, requiring high entry and qualification standards compared with other university disciplines, and both were normally taught and assessed in face-to-face mode, using blended learning approaches. However, the disciplines and teaching practices of the two schools are rather dissimilar. While both require interpersonal skills and expert judgment, medicine is a life science that requires hands-on practical skills while law is based on written or spoken texts. This creates a basis for comparison of disciplines and the reactions of their students to assessments.

9.3.2 Data collection and analysis

Within the case study approach, in addition to examining curriculum materials, the research team interviewed 29 law and medical students in 11 focus groups conducted via a videoconferencing platform in 2020−2021 (COVID-19 restrictions prevented face-to-face discussions for most of the study duration). The purpose of the interviews was to gain insights from the student perspective into their experience of online exams in the four formats listed previously. The students were interviewed by members of the research team not otherwise involved with their programs concerning topics such as personal coping throughout the pandemic, positive and negative aspects of the change to online learning, and changes to assessment regimes, including examinations.

The semistructured interview protocols were designed by the research team to focus on the topic of interest but allow students to expand on their responses. Each interview/focus group lasted one hour. Zoom automated transcripts were collected after each focus group session, and a team member checked the accuracy of the verbatim transcription by listening to the recording. Participants were deidentified, and only pseudonyms are reported here.

In addition, data were included from student evaluation questionnaires routinely conducted by the schools at the end of each academic year from 2020 to 2022. Student comments on exams were taken from these questionnaires and nonidentifiable data were included in the analysis.

All transcribed student responses were read and discussed by researchers and analyzed using Braun and Clarke's (2006) approach to thematic analysis. The data analysis was inductive and data driven. QSR NVivo 12 qualitative data analysis software was used for coding and organizing into meaningful "nodes," which were then grouped into four categories according to exam format. These codes were further developed through discussion, where they were refined and grouped on multiple occasions until consensus within the research team was reached on the themes that best described students' perceptions of online exams with the research team to create three final themes.

9.4 Results

Overall, common student perceptions of online exams included the convenience of not traveling to campus to sit the exam. Many students acknowledge a different set of skills was required between online exams and written face-to-face exams. Online exams require students to type rather than hand-written their answers. Some students felt disadvantaged by having to type as they found it easier and quicker to handwrite. Flicking between pages of paper exams was deemed far easier than waiting for questions to individually upload in an online exam environment, which made moving between questions much more time-consuming. Other students reported the opposite, preferring to type exams and enjoying the convenience of having access to functions such as spellcheck, delete, and in the case of open-book exams, the facility to copy and paste large chunks of text into their exam responses prepared ahead of the exam.

When students were asked about their experiences of taking exams online, there were shared experiences related to all online exam formats. The student experiences of the invigilated online exams were very different from the experience of all other formats. Undoubtedly, the exam experience of students would benefit from familiarization with the online testing environment through provision of assessment literacy educational modules.

Three themes emerged from the data: (1) the fear of being disadvantaged, (2) online exams: an uncomfortable experience, and (3) the educational value of an online exam.

9.4.1 The fear of being disadvantaged

A common concern for students completing any format of online exam was the "fear" of experiencing technical issues. This fear existed regardless of the online exam format or whether the exam was invigilated or noninvigilated.

> [Y]ou've got all these kinds of fears now, like "what if my computer crashes? What if it freezes?" And then, "what if I uploaded and it doesn't upload on time?" (Telula, law student)

> I faced a lot of issues with my first exam with the invigilator because my answers kept on getting deleted and it kept lagging a lot when I was typing answers and it was taking up a lot of my exam time that was allocated to me... If I need any help, you have to open this chat box and ask and wait for them to reply and stuff and they don't stop the exam time either, so you're using up your exam time to just get help. I think those are the same sort of problems I had. (Indra, medical student)

Students were also concerned about losing their Internet connection during an online exam. As the quote mentioned next demonstrates, failure to submit an exam as a result of losing your Internet connection during an exam would require a student to have to resit the assessment despite having already attempted the exam. Students perceived this as unfair and an unnecessary disadvantage for an issue they had little control over.

> [T]here's always a sort of concern or anxiety about Internet connection during the exam and what to do and everything and the fact that all schools, not just the law school, seem to be adamant that if you didn't submit your thing on time, like let's say you had an Internet connection problem, like in the last five minutes or whatever, then you have no time to whiz down to your brother's granny flat or go to Maccas, or wherever, to get some Wi-Fi, then it seemed unfair to me that you completely fail for something that wasn't your fault. (Christopher, law student)

Students taking online invigilated exams felt disadvantaged by the actions of the online invigilator. Students complained of issues with online invigilators starting the exam session late and once in the exam session experiencing interruptions from their invigilators. For a student to start an online exam, they are required to wait for their online invigilator to open the session. There were multiple instances reported by students of being unable to get into their exams, which added to their stress, as the extract below illustrates. This was not an isolated instance.

> I had a terrible experience, where my invigilator deleted my booked exam session and then could not figure it out, and I nearly missed being able to do the exam. By the time I got in, they'd been mucking me around for an hour and a half, and I was in tears and could not focus on the exam. So I had to put it into special consideration, it was pretty bad actually. (Xena, medical student)

Students reported invigilators interrupting them in the middle of their exams to ensure they were not cheating. Invigilators were reported to interrupt students during the exam by requesting to do checks on the student and their rooms to ensure they were not cheating. The extracts next demonstrate the impact of these interruptions to the quiet exam conditions by online invigilators on student concentration and stress levels. Students feared any movement could be interpreted as cheating. The impact on the student results in them not being able to fully concentrate on completing the exam questions to the best of their abilities.

> ...and halfway through the exam, they kept interrupting me and say, "check something." And I lost my temper. I said, "Hey, I have a few minutes left to finish this. And you have to check something? Where's your due diligence?" (Xavier, medical student)

> I had stomach pain before. I think it was anxiety-related or something and I would catch myself slouching a little bit because it would feel better on my

stomach. And my Invigilator would unmute in the middle of the exam to tell me to sit up straight because my face was in the camera and it was uncomfortable. We also weren't allowed to go to the bathroom for two hours. (Sue, Medical student)

[The invigilating service], my experience in the written exam wasn't ideal just because it kept taking me out of the exam, and then my answer would go. I was just having issues during the exam. (Yasmin, medical student)

Students experienced these interruptions of invigilators making mistakes with their exam allocation times or asking to check students' computer set-up mid-way through exams as creating extra stress. Because they needed either to wait or take time in their exams to deal with the invigilator, students perceived these interruptions as disrupting their test-taking and therefore reducing their marks.

When medical students sat a multiple-choice exam invigilated by academics monitoring student behavior via Zoom, not all students perceived this as an effective way to prevent cheating. Although the invigilator could monitor the student by watching them through the student's computer camera, it was not possible to see what programs the student had open, making it possible for students to use notes or online browsers with answering questions. Students felt disadvantaged by this type of invigilation as they believed it was too easy for other students to cheat and improve their marks.

Online invigilation probably resulted in increased levels of cheating because the tutor can't see what people are doing on their devices (Year 2 survey, medical student)

I believe the invigilation was not adequate in swaying potential cheating, and I am worried this will have an impact on how everyone's marks are scaled. (Year 2 survey, medical student)

9.4.2 Online exams: an uncomfortable experience

Exams, however, they are administered, are commonly considered to be stressful by students. Online exams using online invigilators were reported by students as having extra stressors owing to monitoring by an unknown invigilator who had been given access to their homes and devices. Students reported allowing "strangers" this level of access to their lives made them feel uncomfortable. Students recounted being fearful of any outside noises where they were taking their exams, as these could be interpreted as attempts to cheat.

So while I was doing the exam, the dog just started barking and I was like, "I'm scared. What if they think I'm cheating or something?" I was like, I had to send a text saying "It's not me. It's from the outside." My friends also do exams. So I had a friend who was doing an exam with me and then once he finished he came out and he started screaming. So I'm still doing the exam and he's shouting outside. I don't know, I'm just scared. (Raj, medical student)

To prevent cheating, the online invigilators requested that students rotate their cameras around their rooms to provide them with a 360-degree view to confirm that students did not have other devices or additional notes to help them answer the exam questions. Showing the online invigilators around their rooms made students feel uncomfortable. Some felt this was an invasion of their privacy, whereas others resented having to tidy up their rooms.

[I]t wasn't a particularly pleasant process to go through, because you're showing the invigilator everywhere like in whatever room you're in and you have to clear a table space and I'm a pretty lazy person in that regard. I don't clean my table. (James, medical student)

I felt really uncomfortable that I had to give them like a 360-degree view of my desk and my room. It felt really uncomfortable. (Sue, medical student)

To ensure students were unable to search for the answers online, the online invigilation had access to the device the student was using to take the exam. Students raised concerns about a third party having access to their devices and their personal data, as the exemplar extracts next demonstrate:

It felt quite intrusive knowing that someone random had access to your remote mouse and all the contents of your computer. (Year 1, medical student)

[Online invigilation] seems like an overreach, a massive privacy violation, and a ticking time bomb waiting to burst. The fact that the invigilator has full access over your computer, your data, your open processes, and even your hardware means that any security flaw from their side would result in data breaches and compromised security for all users. (Year 2 medical student)

9.4.3 Students need for authenticity in online exams

For some subjects the move to online exams was viewed by students as beneficial to their learning experience. This included having extra time to complete exams in the online format and more open-book exams.

Having more time to complete online exams was generally viewed as a positive. The extra time allowed varied from 30 to 60 min, and in some cases, students were given more than a day to complete exam questions. In law, students were given 60 min rather than 30 min to complete a multiple-choice paper. Students preferred having more time to complete the online assessments, as the extract next demonstrates students had time to process the information and not rush.

> [I]t gives us more time to read the question, understand it properly and make a good decision. And I mean, due to that lengthy time that we get, I mean, I finished it before one hour, but it boosted my marks really well, besides me being under pressure and doing it [and saying] "I've got 30 minutes left, A,B,C, A,B,C" you know? So I thought that lengthy time was really good. (Ellie, law student)

For law students the benefits of online open-book exams were being able to prepare key content prior to the exam and use this to inform their exam responses. Using the function "control F," made it easier to search through a large volume of notes, helping students locate the relevant information and copy it into their answers in the online exam. The extract next demonstrates the benefits of using prepared electronic documents to complete online exams.

> I did read that same thing in regard to just setting out a skeleton structure of the law, and then apply it. So, that was amazing. That save me a lot of time and stress. So I really like that. And I feel like it's more applicable to real life situations because in real life you don't answer questions on paper with a pen. (Beryl, law student)

> I was able to write out the law, and then in a copy and paste document, copy and paste it in. So it made my exams, much more faster and everything. And I could prepare essays and copy and paste them and stick them in as well. So that was much better, it made me feel like had a lot more time, gave me a lot more confidence in the exam so I didn't need to rush. (Christopher, law student)

Taking open-book online assessments where students were able to use prepared notes was perceived to be a more authentic experience, and realistic of working as a lawyer, as Mara explains in the extract next,

> It is realistic to the real work because we have the access to technology when we are practicing. (Mara, law student)

Completing open-book online assessments over an extended period allowed students to work at their own pace and cover the relevant content to include in the exam, making this a positive learning experience.

> I've kind of thrived more because it's been more towards reading and listening and just internalizing things and then doing your assessment tasks at your own pace, on your own. (Nebo, law student)

Not all law students were positive about the educational merits of online exams. Some law students expressed concerns that the format allowing students to prepare their notes to use in exams was not a reliable measure of competency in that subject. Other students had concerns that being able to use notes in an exam left them feeling like they had not sufficiently learnt the content or allowed them too much time to perfect their answers before submitting their completed exams, making the exams more stressful. With a physical exam, you had to hand the paper in when the time was up, but with online assessments students have more time to complete the exam, allowing students to spend too much time editing and perfecting their answers before submitting.

> I can't help but feel unprepared for next year because with, everything online, the exams were open book, I had all my resources laid out next to me for the open book exams. I did not have to speak in front of a class with people looking at me. So I felt really sheltered and really unprepared. (Lesley, law student)

> [U]nlike physical exams, as I said, where you could just give it away and you don't have to stress about it, just obsessing over going over it — "did I do it right?." That's always been an issue for me because I'm very much a perfectionist and want everything done perfectly. So that was hard. (Christopher, law student)

In medicine, the move to online clinical assessment was considered by many students to be a less stressful experience. When these clinical assessments were face-to-face students were expected to role play taking a patient history or a physical examination with an actor playing a patient with various medical conditions. The student would be given 10 min to demonstrate their clinical skills while a marker would observe the performance and mark the student against the given criteria. The online version had a reduced number of scenarios and rather than demonstrate their skills, students were asked to tell the examiner what they would do in the scenarios. Although many students preferred this type of clinical assessment, reporting it to be less stressful than the face-to-face, many students voiced concerns this was not an ideal way to assess their ability to take histories or examine patients. As the quotes below demonstrate,

> I liked that because I didn't have to do parts of the exam that I find difficult because you weren't face to face, so I couldn't like pretend to listen to the person's chest with a stethoscope or anything. I liked it because it got rid of the hard part that I didn't do, but it's not really good for overall learning. (Zelda, medical student).

> [T]o assess our clinical experience. [A STOVI] was a new exam which was run similar to an OSCE, where we had stations, but it was all video conference and we weren't meant to role play, we were just explain how we would approach

the situation. I didn't enjoy that because I felt like it was a bit vague in terms of what was expected from us. . . .I felt like I could have the knowledge, but I just didn't know how to present it. (Yasmin, medical student)

9.5 Discussion

Most higher education institutions have embraced the concept of online exams and it is unlikely that traditional, paper-based, face-to-face exams will come back into favor. Exam creation, delivery, and marking are generally easier with online examinations, and these result in significant time and financial savings for the institution. Done correctly, online assessments may also be more authentic in the digital age because in the workplace there is ready access to electronic resources. Nevertheless, if this method of assessment is to be accepted by all stakeholders, then the student perspective must be considered.

Students have mixed feelings about online exams: some prefer the online environment while others prefer face-to-face examinations. The convenience of taking the exams at home, the ability to use technology (where permitted), reduced commuting, and flexible timing were all cited as positive aspects. Most negative aspects were reported concerned issues related to technology and invigilation. Some students questioned whether some forms of online assessments validly assessed their knowledge. While law students generally were happy with online assessments, some misgivings were centered around the ability to adequately test their knowledge and skills if all that was required was to copy and paste preprepared material. In medicine, traditional clinical exams involving interactions with patients were acknowledged by educators and students to be difficult, if not impossible, to replicate in an online environment because of limitations in the skills that can be assessed, a finding similar to other studies such as that of Saad et al. (2022).

Invigilation of high-stakes examinations is considered to be a necessary part of these assessments, just as it is for traditional paper-based exams. However, we have shown that in online assessments, some students are not comfortable with the invigilation provisions. There were severe misgivings among some that remote invigilating was an invasion of their privacy. Students were not comfortable showing invigilators their exam spaces, which were often their bedrooms: students come from a variety of different situations, and many do not have the luxury of dedicated study areas.

Privacy and security of their personal computers were also concerns with remote invigilation, where the invigilators were allowed to check their computers for nonpermitted applications. This was despite many reassurances that the invigilator-installed software could not be used for malicious purposes. From an institutional perspective, it is believed that misinformation on the purpose of the checks has spread through social media.

Technology failures were commonly reported and ranged from incompatibility of operating system versions, personal computers that did not meet the required specifications, or poor Internet connections. Such failures often resulted in students missing exam time with no opportunity or provision to make up that time. The only recourse was for students to resit the exam at a later stage causing much disruption and anxiety among students and academics alike. Institutions must respond to this reality by having provisions for students to take examinations in dedicated examination rooms that are fit for online exams and invigilating. This is especially needed to cater to students from disadvantaged backgrounds or circumstances.

Assessments serve several purposes. Formative assessments are designed to provide feedback to students on their learning progress and are considered to be essential in modern teaching practice. Summative assessments provide the institution with information as to whether a student has attained the desired learning outcomes (Lau, 2016). Both forms of assessment shape and drive student learning (Epstein, 2007). To provide an accurate estimate of a student's learning, summative assessments must be valid. That is, the assessment must be appropriate for the content being tested; it must be well constructed and presented to students fairly and equitably (Sullivan, 2011). Fairness and equity are diminished in instances where just prior to being examined, some students must overcome technical barriers, or during the exam when they are interrupted by Internet outages or invigilators. A convenient remedy for these types of issues is to allow students to resit an examination, but this in itself adds to the inequity issue when the resit is conducted during a vacation period or subsequent learning terms.

If institutions are set on continuing with online examinations, then examination platforms must be robust to common Internet problems. Current testing platforms found in learning management systems are not adequate because they rely on continuous and stable Internet connections, as do many of the remote invigilation systems. Institutions must invest in examination platforms that provide a fair testing environment. It may be argued that technology issues are rare, but for the affected students, these disruptions are significant. In the absence of systems that are robust to technical disruptions, test administrators must have contingencies in place to ensure that students are not disadvantaged when tests are disrupted by circumstances beyond their control.

Acknowledging that online assessment and invigilation are here to stay, we urge that the negative impact of these assessments on students is considered, and that effort is put into building systems that ameliorate these concerns.

9.6 Conclusion

This study has sought to investigate student perspectives as to the long-term sustainability and viability of online exams and assessments beyond the utility of their use as short-term responses to the COVID-19 crisis. While online exams continue to be highly valued by both medical and law students for reasons beyond the utility of enabling university study to continue during conditions of lockdown and pandemic, the unyielding challenges associated with academic misfeasance and authenticity of form were cited by students as ongoing concerns. Students appreciated the convenience of online exams but associated online invigilation—especially where externally invigilated—with the attendant invasion of privacy and numerous technical challenges. The lack of contact with classmates and familiar school staff often adds to student stress. It was found that where possible, assessments should be administered in a fashion that avoids or reduces the need for invigilation, applies technologies to reduce academic cheating, and engages students with appropriate summative or formative questioning that reflects authentic assessment of knowledge and skills.

References

Alessio, H. M., Malay, N., Maurer, K., Bailer, A. J., & Rubin, B. (2017). Examining the effect of proctoring on online test scores. *Online Learning, 21*(1), 146–161. Available from https://olj.onlinelearningconsortium.org/index.php/olj/article/view/885.

Allan, S. (2020). Migration and transformation: A sociomaterial analysis of practitioners' experiences with online exams. *Research in Learning Technology, 28*. Available from https://doi.org/10.25304/rlt.v28.2279.

Alruwais, N., Wills, G., & Wald, M. (2018). Advantages and challenges of using assessment. *International Journal of Information and Education Technology, 8*(1), 34–37. Available from https://doi.org/10.18178/ijiet.2018.8.1.1008.

Barrett, L. (2021). Rejecting testing surveillance in higher education. *Social Science Research Network*. Available from https://papers.ssrn.com/sol3/papers.cfm?abstract_id = 3871423.

Bearman, M., & Luckin, R. (2020). *Preparing university assessment for a world with AI: Tasks for human intelligence. Re-imagining university assessment in a digital world* (pp. 49−63). Cham: Springer. Available from https://doi.org/10.1007/978-3-030-41956-1_5.

Braun, V., & Clarke, V. (2006). Using thematic analysis in psychology. *Qualitative Research in Psychology*, *3*(2), 77−101.

Bretag, T., Mahmud, S., Wallace, M., Walker, R., McGowan, U., East, J., ... James, C. (2014). 'Teach us how to do it properly!' An Australian academic integrity student survey. *Studies in Higher Education*, *39*(7), 1150−1169. Available from https://doi.org/10.1080/03075079.2013.777406.

Butler-Henderson., & Crawford. (2020). A systematic review of online examinations: A pedagogical innovation for scalable authentication and integrity. *Computers & Education* (159), 104024. Available from https://doi.org/10.1016/j.compedu.2020.104024.

Diaz, C. M., Linden, K., & Solyali, V. (2021). Novel and innovative approaches to teaching human anatomy classes in an online environment during a pandemic. *Medical Science Educator*, *31*(5), 1703−1713. Available from https://doi.org/10.1007/s40670-021-01363-2.

Elsalem, L., Al-Azzam, N., Jum'ah, A. A., & Obeidat, N. (2021). Remote E-exams during Covid-19 pandemic: A cross-sectional study of students' preferences and academic dishonesty in faculties of medical sciences. *Annals of Medicine and Surgery*, *62*, 326. Available from https://doi.org/10.1016/j.amsu.2021.01.054.

Epstein, R. (2007). Assessment in medical education. *New England Journal of Medicine*, *356*, 387−396. Available from https://doi.org/10.1056/NEJMra054784.

Fawns, T., & Schaepkens, S. (2022). A matter of trust: Online proctored exams and the integration of technologies of assessment in medical education. *Teaching and Learning in Medicine*, *34* (4), 444−453. Available from https://doi.org/10.1080/10401334.2022.2048832.

Ilgaz, H., & Afacan Adanır, G. (2020). Providing online exams for online learners: Does it really matter for them? *Education and Information Technologies*, *25*. Available from https://doi.org/10.1007/s10639-019-10020-6.

Jha, M., Leemans, S. J., Berretta, R., Bilgin, A. A., Jayarathna, L., & Sheard, J. (2022). Online assessment and COVID: Opportunities and challenges. In: *ACE '22: Australasian computing education conference* (pp. 27−35). https://doi.org/10.1145/3511861.3511865

Kharbat, F. F., & Abu Daabes, A. S. (2021). E-proctored exams during the COVID-19 pandemic: A close understanding. *Education and Information Technologies*, *26*(6), 6589−6605. Available from https://doi.org/10.1007/s10639-021-10458-7.

Ladyshewsky, R. K. (2015). Post-graduate student performance in 'supervised in-class' versus 'unsupervised online' multiple choice tests: implications for cheating and test security. *Assessment and Evaluation in Higher Education*, *40*(7), 883−897. Available from https://doi.org/10.1080/02602938.2014.956683.

Lau, A. (2016). 'Formative good, summative bad?' − A review of the dichotomy in assessment literature. *Journal of Further and Higher Education*, *40*(4), 509525. Available from https://doi.org/10.1080/0309877X.2014.984600.

Lee, J. W. (2020). Impact of proctoring environments on student performance: Online vs offline proctored exams. *The Journal of Asian Finance, Economics and Business*, *7*(8), 653−660. Available from https://doi.org/10.13106/jafeb.2020.vol7.no8.653.

Pardjono, P. (2016). Active learning: The Dewey, Piaget, Vygotsky, and constructivist theory perspectives. *Jurnal Ilmu Pendidikan Universitas Negeri Malang*, *9*(3), 105376. Available from https://doi.org/10.17977/jip.v9i3.487.

Reisenwitz, T. H. (2020). Examining the necessity of proctoring online exams. *Journal of Higher Education Theory and Practice*, *20*(1), 118−124. Available from https://doi.org/10.33423/jhetp.v20i1.2782.

Saad, S. L., Richmond, C., Jones, K., Schlipalius, M., Rienits, H., & Malau-Aduli, B. S. (2022). Virtual OSCE delivery and quality assurance during a pandemic: Implications for the Future. *Frontiers in Medicine, 9.* Available from https://doi.org/10.3389/fmed.2022.844884.

Saha, S. M., Pranty, S. A., Rana, M. J., Islam, M. J., & Hossain, M. E. (2022). Teaching during a pandemic: Do university teachers prefer online teaching? *Heliyon, 8*(1), e08663. Available from https://doi.org/10.1016/j.heliyon.2021.e08663.

Sankey, M. (2021). *COVID-19 exam software survey 2020.* An ACODE Whitepaper. Available from https://www.acode.edu.au/pluginfile.php/8244/mod_resource/content/2/eExamsWhitepaper.pdf.

Sankey, M. D. (2022). The state of Australasian online higher education post-pandemic and beyond. *Journal of University Teaching & Learning Practice, 19*(2), 14–26. Available from https://doi.org/10.53761/1.19.2.2.

Selwyn, N., O'Neill, C., Smith, G., Andrejevic, M., & Gu, X. (2021). A necessary evil? The rise of online exam proctoring in Australian universities. *Media International Australia.* 1329878X211005862. https://doi.org/10.1177/1329878X211005862.

Sullivan, D. P. (2016). An integrated approach to preempt cheating on asynchronous, objective, online assessments in graduate business classes. *Online Learning, 20*(3), 195–209. Available from https://doi.org/10.24059/olj.v20i3.650.

Sullivan, G. (2011). A primer on the validity of assessment instruments. *Journal of Graduate Medical Education, 3*(2), 119–120.

Vygotsky, L. S. (1978). Socio-cultural theory. *Mind in Society, 6*(3), 23–43.

CHAPTER 10

E-textbook pedagogy in teacher education beyond the COVID-19 era

Orhe Arek-Bawa and Sarasvathie Reddy
Higher Education Studies, School of Education, University of KwaZulu-Natal, Pinetown, Durban, South Africa

10.1 Background and introduction

Digital transformation became imminent in higher education institutions (HEI) worldwide, including South Africa, following the global lockdown as a result of the COVID-19 pandemic. Many universities that ordinarily implemented face-to-face programs, such as the one where the study was located in South Africa, resorted to remote online pedagogical engagement (Arek-Bawa & Reddy, 2020). In support of the move to online learning, the institution organized workshops for the university community with the aim of facilitating the transition to virtual modes of teaching and learning (Amin, Dhunpath, & Chatradari, 2021; Khoza & Mpungose, 2020; Motala & Menon, 2022). Academics, including those in accounting education in the School of Education (SoE), therefore navigated the learning management system—Moodle asynchronously or synchronously via Zoom, MS teams, and other virtual meeting platforms in their pedagogical endeavors (Khoza & Mpungose, 2020) to deliver the curriculum.

The use of the textbook as the key resource in the accounting curriculum is well established in the literature (Brown & Guilding, 1993; Davidson & Baldwin, 2005; Irsyadillah, Ahmed, & ElKelish, 2021; Mathews, 2001; Ngwenya & Arek-Bawa, 2019; Stevenson, Ferguson, & Power, 2014). In the developing world, the focus hitherto had been on paper-based textbooks due primarily to infrastructure issues (limited access to electricity, Internet, and inadequate technological and digital support systems) (Karuri-Sebina, 2019). To ameliorate those disruptions and infrastructural issues at the start of the full-blown online learning, the university, aided by the Department of Higher Education, supplied the staff and students with data bundles and laptops where needed (Du Preez & Le Grange, 2020). By overcoming the hurdle that

Digital Teaching, Learning and Assessment
DOI: https://doi.org/10.1016/B978-0-323-95500-3.00002-X

constrained e-learning, it is logical that e-textbooks, which have become an integral part of digital learning platforms (D'Ambra, Akter, & Mariani, 2022), replaced paper-based textbooks as the de facto resource in the accounting classroom. While the university provided training support that enabled accounting academics to transmit their curriculum content online, interact with students online, and administer assessments online, there appears to be limited support for using e-textbooks. For the purposes of this chapter, accounting academics refer to those educators who teach the accounting education modules of the Bachelor of Education (B.Ed) program within the SoE.

We contend that e-learning entails much more than using the platform to transmit paper-based content to students. Research has shown that "engagement with e-textbooks and their platforms can improve learning outcomes for students" (D'Ambra et al., 2022, p. 292). Since this is the desired outcome in education, accounting academics should go beyond transmitting content knowledge and assessments from paper-based forms to the online platform. Textbooks, which are also available in the e-format, should be engaged using the features afforded by technology (Nourie, 2021) to enhance learning. After more than two years of virtual education at the research site, the extent to which accounting academics from the SoE engaged in e-textbooks in their pedagogical activities remains unclear.

This chapter sought to provide an understanding of the technological pedagogical practices adopted by accounting academics via e-textbooks by responding to the following question: How do accounting academics integrate e-textbook pedagogy in their online teaching and learning engagement beyond the pandemic era? A case study research design was adopted based on the technological acceptance model (TAM). A qualitative semistructured questionnaire was administered to accounting academics responsible for teaching accounting education modules of the B. Ed program in the SoE. What follows in this chapter is a presentation of the literature that was reviewed, the theoretical framework that underpinned, the study and the research methodology engaged to produce data. Subsequently, an in-depth exposition of the study's findings is presented, followed by the conclusion.

10.2 Literature review

In their simplest form, electronic textbooks, popularly referred to as e-textbooks, are digitized versions of textbooks. Pesek, Zmazek, and Mohorcic (2014) describe different forms of e-textbooks as follows: the digitized textbook, which is basically a digital version of the paper-based textbook (Nourie, 2021; Smith et al., 2013); the rich textbook that includes added features such as video, sound, and assessments; and the interactive textbooks that add more interactive features such as instructive games, analytics, interactive models, and simulators. The interactive features of the e-textbooks make them more attractive to students, and they contain more practice opportunities and activities to engage them in learning (D'Ambra et al., 2022; Nourie, 2021; Pesek et al., 2014; Wiese & Du Plessis, 2014).

Like any other e-book, e-textbooks are read by e-readers or other computers. They usually contain additional features such as interactive links and graphics, supported by standard protocols and a blend of hardware/software (Vorotnykova, 2019; Wiese & Du Plessis, 2014). E-texts are obtainable online and offline and allow users to work with others, jot down notes, or highlight certain sections (Hendrix, Lyons, & Aronoff, 2016; Vorotnykova, 2019). Even though many e-textbooks can be rented and are generally nontransferable (Doering, Pereira, & Kuechler, 2012; Hendrix et al., 2016), lifetime purchases can be made (Elias, Phillips, & Luechtefeld, 2012; Vorotnykova, 2019). Integration with multimedia allows for interaction between academics and students, thereby enhancing communication. E-textbooks accompanied by automated homework grading systems and other resources permit students to perform quizzes and other assessments, communicate with others (academics and peers) as they share notes, and conduct searches for keywords while studying (Doering et al., 2012).

Before online learning became the order of the day, e-textbooks attracted users for various reasons. Primarily, they were considered more convenient, accessible, environmental friendly, and cheaper, with the capacity to search quickly across the text (Baglione & Sullivan, 2016; D'Ambra, Akter, & Mariani, 2022; Doering, Pereira, & Kuechler, 2012; Makwanya & Oni, 2019; Osih & Singh, 2020; Roberts et al., 2021). They are usually more current and may include special features (3D modeling and hyperlinks) and multimedia (Hendrix et al., 2016), which make them more attractive to today's digitized student cohort. E-textbooks can also be customized to suit students' needs and learning styles (Doering et al., 2012; Hendrix et al., 2016). They can be easily integrated with other digital products, enhancing learning opportunities through connections to graphics, animations, explanatory material, supplementary activities, iPod content, animations, and collaborative learning simulations (Doering et al., 2012; Roberts et al., 2021).

Despite the above attractions, technological issues, printing problems, eye strain, distractions (from emails or web surfing), the learning curve on diverse platforms and intermediaries associated with the transition to e-formats hinders the excitement for e-textbooks (Baglione & Sullivan, 2016; Hendrix et al., 2016; Terpend, Gattiker, & Lowe, 2014). Navigating the unique features of e-textbooks can be overwhelming for some students. The paper-based textbook is usually preferred, especially when extensive reading requires more concentration (Elias et al., 2012; Hendrix et al., 2016; Miller, Nutting, & Baker-Eveleth, 2013; Wiese & Du Plessis, 2014). Also, the lack of computer skills, the cost of the device needed to read the content, and limitations arising from digital rights may deter the use of e-textbooks (Doering et al., 2012).

The cost of e-textbooks is a vital issue in transitioning from paper-based textbooks. With the ever-increasing cost of paper-based textbooks (Baglione & Sullivan, 2016; Elias, Phillips, & Luechtefeld, 2012; Makwanya & Oni, 2019; Roberts et al., 2021), some students buy used textbooks, and others rent them from the shop or libraries. Yet some students obtain photocopies illegally, while some borrow from their peers (Hendrix et al., 2016). Even though studies confirm students' preference for paper-based textbooks (Nicholas & Lewis, 2008; Wiese & Du Plessis, 2014), a study conducted by Hendrix et al. (2016) indicated that most students would opt for e-textbooks if it were 25% or more less than the print version. In Baglione and Sullivan's (2016) study, the ideal cost of the e-textbook is about 60% less than that of the paper-based version. For the same cost-related reasons, students from low socioeconomic backgrounds tend to prefer e-textbooks (Miller et al., 2013).

Nonetheless, e-textbooks offer an opportunity for universities to improve the quality of learning (Vorotnykova, 2019). Engaging with e-textbooks and their features can enhance study independence and improve learning outcomes that are pitched at higher order cognitive levels (D'Ambra et al., 2022; Vorotnykova, 2019). Indeed, an initial study by Chaudhri et al. (2013) concluded that students who used an intelligent e-textbook for homework outperformed those who used hard-copy textbooks. Some teachers assert that students' use of interactive e-textbook contributes to the development of technological skills and their ability to think critically (Vorotnykova, 2019). The author further states that high-quality images could be used to ease eye strain, and content that is easy to navigate is likely to reduce the feeling of being overwhelmed. To address the issue of cost, the preferred model is for universities and libraries to secure and negotiate lifetime bulk purchases with publishers at reduced prices (Hendrix et al., 2016; Terpend et al., 2014; Wiese & Du Plessis, 2014; Vorotnykova, 2019). It is our view that this strategy will suit the institution where the study was located, since most students who attend are from poor socioeconomic backgrounds. Thus this chapter contributes to knowledge that will further the adoption of e-textbooks by the university, including its libraries.

A review of related literature suggests that South African students are gradually embracing e-textbooks while acknowledging the paucity of research in the field (Van Schalkwyk & Müller, 2020). In a study conducted at the University of Pretoria, Wiese and Du Plessis (2014) attributed the lag in the use of e-textbook to the perceived ease of working with the familiar paper textbooks and the cost of e-textbooks stating that there is little or no difference between the cost of the electronic and print versions. A more recent study at the University of Fort Hare showed students' preference for e-textbooks rather than paper-based textbooks in their academic work, even though the former is easier for research (Makwanya & Oni, 2019). Another study at the University of Zululand found that postgraduate students use e-textbooks daily but are challenged by limited Internet access and technological skills (Ngema & Masenya, 2020). On the other hand, Van Schalkwyk and Müller (2020) concluded that students' interest in e-textbooks can be enhanced by increased awareness of their environmental benefits and ease of use in addition to their perceived usefulness. The study by Osih and Singh (2020) conducted at a university based in Midrand also showed students' preference for e-textbooks. The studies discussed thus far in the South African context examined students' use and perceptions of e-textbooks. While the outcomes are somewhat mixed, there appears to be a progressive trend toward using e-textbooks in South Africa's HEIs. However, students' approach to their studies is mainly determined by the academics' conduct of their educational activities, which in this case refers to their use of e-textbook (Miller et al., 2013; Roberts et al., 2021; Smith, Brand, & Kinash, 2013; Wiese & du Plessis, 2014) since students will only pay a price for it or try it if academics use it as part of their pedagogical practice (Hendrix et al., 2016).

Smith et al.'s (2013) study on the adoption of e-textbooks in Australia revealed a slow uptake amongst academics primarily due to the lack of awareness of its enhanced benefits over the print version and the perception that it is only a replica of the latter. Kelson's (2016) investigation concluded that the perceived ease of use, perceived usefulness, and cost were predictors in the adoption of e-textbook practices by academics. A recent study (Roberts et al., 2021) conducted in the United States on instructors' engagement with the features of e-textbooks indicated low use levels. A study by Sackstein, Spark, and Masenda (2015) on e-textbooks in a private university in South Africa concluded that lecturers had a negative attitude toward its use due to technical difficulties, lack of skills, and inability to integrate them with teaching, etc. Based on the paucity of research on the use and adoption of e-textbooks by academics (Sackstein et al., 2015), this chapter aimed to ascertain the situation in the SoE by explicitly focusing on how accounting education academics adopted e-textbooks in their pedagogical practice.

10.3 Theoretical framework

The study adopted the TAM developed by Davis (1989) to understand Accounting academics' experiences with adopting e-textbooks in their pedagogical engagement. The original model posits that a user's behavior toward technology is a function of its perceived usefulness, that is, the extent to which the use of the new technology will enhance work and ease of use, that is, how much effort or cognitive work is involved in using the system (Li, 2010; Salovaara & Tamminen, 2009). Features such as hyperlinks, search functions, 3D functionality, or portability may be considered useful, while connectivity problems and lack of familiarity may be deemed burdensome (Terpend et al., 2014). Factors such as availability and adaptability are some attributes that make the e-text comparatively easier, while eye fatigue makes it difficult to read from the screen (D'Ambra et al., 2022; Hendrix et al., 2016; Terpend et al., 2014). Amongst other things, TAM is critiqued for its simplicity, inability to measure the interplay amongst various predictors, and insensitivity to the nature of technology (Salovaara & Tamminen, 2009). Scholars have therefore extended the theory to include other predictors to address the shortcomings. Regarding e-learning, Terpend et al. (2014) extended the model to cover internet self-efficacy, environmental concerns, and cost as likely predictors for adopting e-textbooks.

Internet self-efficacy implies an individual's perceived confidence in Internet use (Terpend et al., 2014). It is believed that digital natives (millennials) with higher Internet self-efficacy will be more open to the use of e-texts (Terpend et al., 2014) than digital migrants. Reducing the environmental impact of paper-based textbooks is considered a motivator for the use of e-textbooks (Gerhart, Peak, & Prybutok, 2017). Lastly, the cost is deemed a key determinant in the adoption of e-textbooks, especially from the student's perspective, due to limited funds (D'Ambra et al., 2022; Terpend et al., 2014). This model was adapted to include habit, substitute, and hedonic motivation (relative pleasure of using e-textbooks compared to print versions) and employed to assess accounting academics' use of e-textbooks which is viewed as a technological innovation in pedagogical practice (D'Ambra et al., 2022; Osih & Singh, 2020; Roberts et al., 2021; Wiese & du Plessis, 2014). Therefore the adapted model used in this research incorporated Internet self-efficacy, perceived usefulness, perceived ease of use, environmental concerns, substitute, habit, facilitating condition, hedonic factors, and cost as likely predictors in the adoption of e-textbooks.

10.4 Research methodology

This research is located within a qualitative, interpretive paradigm using the case study approach. This approach is considered suitable when seeking a detailed understanding of an issue or phenomenon in a real-life situation (Crowe et al., 2011). Case studies help explain or understand "'how,' 'what' or 'why' questions" (Crowe et al., 2011, p. 4), which is what this research is all about. While the case study approach is critiqued for its lack of generalization and or transfer to other contexts due to its specificity, it is found ideal for providing an understanding of a particular phenomenon that may be complex (Bargate, 2012). The case study approach is deemed appropriate for this research as we aimed to understand the e-textbook pedagogical practices of accounting education academics at the SoE.

The case study approach requires that sampling be done according to the uniqueness of the target population to provide an understanding of the phenomenon and not necessarily to obtain a representation (Crowe et al., 2011; Ishak & Abu Bakar, 2014). In line with this approach, all four academics in the accounting education department were purposively sampled for the study, but only three responded. A qualitative semistructured questionnaire was emailed to each academic to explore their views on using e-textbooks in their pedagogy. This was followed by telephonic conversations that probed for further clarifications where necessary. As a subset of the commerce education discipline in the SoE, the accounting education program aims to prepare students to teach the subject in South African secondary schools and other Further Education and Training colleges. It is a 4-year program that provides core and method modules at different levels of study. While the former aims to equip students with the requisite accounting disciplinary knowledge, skills, and values, the latter aims to develop students' pedagogical skills as they apply diverse theories and strategies in disseminating accounting knowledge. The prescribed textbooks used in the core modules therefore cover topics related to the secondary school curriculum and more.

10.5 Data presentation and discussion

The qualitative semistructured questionnaire sought to elicit the participants' views on using textbooks before the pandemic, during the pandemic, and beyond the era of the pandemic. Before the pandemic, the questions aimed to ascertain the resources used in teaching, if the textbook was used, and how it was used. During the pandemic, the questions inquired about academics' use of e-textbooks, how they were used and if the features contained in e-textbooks were useful. It further enquired about the factors that influenced or could influence their use or adoption of e-textbooks and any possible barriers to their use. Beyond the pandemic era, the questions addressed how e-textbooks could be incorporated into the teaching and learning of accounting and how the SoE can facilitate the process. A 5-point Likert scale ranging from strongly disagree to strongly agree was used to elicit the participants' views on the usefulness of the features and factors influencing the adoption of e-textbooks. Apart from the demographic data, others were mainly open-ended questions that allowed academics to express themselves qualitatively.

10.5.1 Before the pandemic

Prior to the transition to online learning, the findings revealed that resources usually used by academics included "chalkboard, laptop, document camera and whiteboard, PowerPoint Presentation slides, Moodle Learning Management Systems, and textbooks." Besides the textbook and the PowerPoint slides, the other resources indicated by the participants were infrastructural and technological hardware and platforms used in facilitating teaching and learning. The textbook and the slides appear to be the participants' principal accounting content knowledge sources. Considering the fact that they sometimes used the "textbook for preparing the PowerPoint presentation," it could be inferred that the textbook was the principal resource in the accounting class, as alluded to previously in the chapter (Brown & Guilding, 1993; Davidson & Baldwin, 2005; Irsyadillah et al., 2021; Stevenson et al., 2014). Similar to the findings of other studies (Abbott & Palatnik, 2018; Davidson & Baldwin, 2005), the participants also found the textbook helpful in their delivery of the accounting curriculum in "planning, sequencing, instruction, assessments and as a reference book with good practical activities." Hence this research confirms the reliance of accounting academics on the use of textbooks in their pedagogical practice.

10.5.2 During the pandemic

The textbooks used in the accounting education core modules are available in print and e-format. The pandemic-induced lockdown, which catalyzed a digital transformation in many traditional universities, simultaneously positioned e-textbooks as integral parts of learning platforms (D'Ambra et al., 2022). However, our findings indicated that during the pandemic, the participants continued to depend on their print textbooks and engaged their use in their online pedagogical practices in the same way they did before the pandemic. Scanned copies of the selected chapters were uploaded on Moodle. Even though the participants navigated teaching and learning via virtual platforms such as Moodle and Zoom, they continued to source their curriculum content from print textbooks. One participant used it in *preparing the lesson by developing PowerPoint presentation* from it, while another stated that *the textbook assisted me in setting the assessments*. The question that then emerges is why would the participants continue with print textbooks while online versions are available? Could it be that they are unaware of the existence of the e-version of the textbook or its functionality or affordance?

The concept of affordance stipulates that technology adoption is a function of the opportunities or benefits the object creates (Smith et al., 2013). From our findings, all the participants agreed that features enabling users to highlight and share content; make and share notes; export text/notes; practice interactive questions or games; use web links to other resources; and access videos and animation are useful in the teaching of accounting education. See Fig. 10.1. Two of them consider the ability to personalize content useful, but one participant was indifferent.

If the participants deemed the features peculiar to e-textbooks useful, why do they persist in using print textbooks in an online teaching environment?

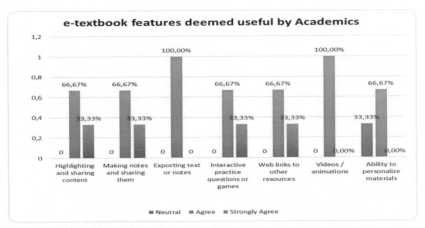

Figure 10.1 E-textbook features.

To answer this question, we explored the possible barriers to adopting e-textbooks. For one participant, *downloading full text* is problematic. The participant may not have used e-textbooks that enabled the sharing/exporting/downloading of the content nor the platforms that make room for text customization (Terpend et al., 2014). Therefore his lack of use of the e-textbook is premised on the nonavailability of the required features, as observed in Roberts et al.'s (2021) study on instructors' use of e-textbook technology in the United States. For this participant, it is possible that the previous e-textbook that he engaged in was the basic version, that is, a replication of the print version in a PDF format that was uploaded on a virtual platform (Nourie, 2021; Smith et al., 2013). Coupled with habitual human nature, this version of the e-textbook provides little impetus for the participant to migrate from the familiar to the unknown (Smith et al., 2013; Van Schalkwyk & Müller, 2020).

Another hindrance to the use of e-textbooks is the *accessibility of E-textbooks due to network connectivity*. Although the institution capacitated the academic community with data bundles that are zero-rated when connected to its learning management systems and website (Du Preez & Le Grange, 2020), power disruptions and connectivity issues are real in the South African context. The implication is that the features and technological content may not be accessible as and when required. This is where the ability to download and own the e-textbook becomes useful, enabling users to work offline. It may be for this reason that one participant argues that an e-textbook *must allow the users to download the full text and not limit me in terms of the number of pages.* However, some publishers in South Africa do not allow downloads for copyright and intellectual property protection reasons. Instead, they include a feature enabling users to work offline to ameliorate connectivity issues. Since some academics are apparently unaware of this feature, publishers need to adopt more aggressive marketing strategies to promote and demonstrate the features of e-textbooks to the academic community.

Other barriers identified by the participants are the *laziness of students* who may insist that *I cannot use them* because *I forgot my laptop at home.* While students may come up with any excuse/reasons to justify their actions, literature (Hendrix et al., 2016; Smith et al., 2013) reveals that academics are at the forefront of technological adoption. When educators model the object's use and affordance, students are more likely to follow (Roberts et al., 2021). *One's preference* and *avoidance of blue screen (vision issues)*, widely documented as drawbacks in e-learning, were also considered barriers to adopting e-textbooks. To this end, there is a need to reduce the discomfort of reading from the screen (Terpend et al., 2014). D'Ambra et al. (2022) suggest that publishers could recommend the optimum screen configuration to enhance learning engagement.

Using the TAM, we further sought to identify the possible factors that may influence the adoption of e-textbooks by accounting academics in the SoE. Fig. 10.2 gives a summary of our findings in this regard.

Going by the extent to which participants agreed or strongly agreed with the specified factors, Internet self-efficacy, habit, and cost are deemed the key drivers in adopting e-textbooks. Others include perceived usefulness, substitute, facilitating conditions, and hedonic aspects. This study thus confirms the work of previous scholars such as Van Schalkwyk and Müller (2020), Gerhart et al. (2017), Kelson (2016), Hendrix et al. (2016), Terpend et al. (2014), and Davis (1989). These authors, together with the participants of this study, agreed that the perceived usefulness of the technology (e-textbook) is a principal motivator for change. Contrary to the findings of Terpend et al. (2014), confidence in using the Internet also stood out as a facilitating factor in this study, enabling the user to overcome the learning curve associated with negotiating the platforms and interfaces of e-textbooks (Hendrix et al., 2016). Nonuse of e-textbook was also adduced to a preference for print, as confirmed by Smith et al. (2013), where academics simply preferred the comfort, feel, and experience of the paper artifact. However, in this case, the participant who strongly disagreed with the features of the e-textbook preferred the

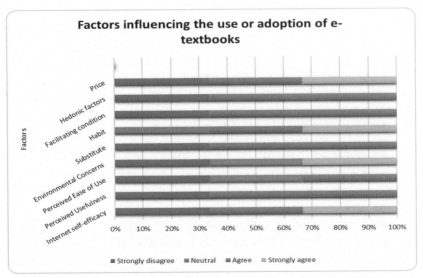

Figure 10.2 Factors influencing the adoption of e-textbooks.

paper-based textbook because of *avoidance of blue screen (vision issues)*. Therefore the producers of this technological resource must be cognizant of the discomfort associated with the effect on users' eyes. In line with the suggestions of other scholars, we advocate a smooth transition from paper-based to e-textbook to ease the discomfort on the eyes possibly "by integrating key features in an intuitive interface" (Terpend et al., 2014, p. 165) or through the use of high-quality images (Vorotnykova, 2019). In addition, hedonic values stood out as one of the predictors of e-textbook adoption in alignment with D'Ambra et al. (2022) findings.

Like Gerhart et al.'s (2017) findings, the participants believed that those in the habit of using a particular textbook format are more likely to continue with it because of prior knowledge and familiarity. On the contrary, the study further indicated that perceived ease of use, which is also a function of the user's familiarity with technology, is not a vital driver of the adoption of e-textbook, just as Gerhart et al. (2017) concluded. Where familiarity is high, users tend to be less concerned with ease of use as a predictor, possibly because using the object comes more naturally. This could be the case in this study as the COVID-19 pandemic catalyzed a digital transformation where academics were compelled to engage digital technologies in their pedagogical activities. Repeated engagement with technology could have enabled a high level of familiarity that minimized ease of use as a construct in adopting e-textbook technology. In other words, while familiarity acted as a motivator in e-textbook adoption through habitual usage, it also served to minimize perceived ease of use as a construct when considering the adoption of the e-textbook. Another consideration in adopting an e-textbook that is impacted by familiarity, as revealed in this study, is *preference*. One participant *preferred print over e-textbook* probably because the academic is more familiar with the former. Familiarity bridges the learning curve (Hendrix et al., 2016) associated with the adoption of a technological innovation considerably. Academics who are unfamiliar with e-textbook technology will spend an extended time learning how to navigate the different platforms, processes, and devices involved in using the electronic resource (Osih, 2020, p. 12). As academics become familiar with e-textbooks through recurrent practice, the likelihood of habitual use and preference for the object increases, hence the need to provide academics with the training, time, and support to facilitate familiarity and the subsequent adoption of e-textbook technology.

The participants further concurred with Gerhart et al. (2017) that the perception of e-textbooks as substitutes for the print version justifies the adoption of the former. Ideally, substitutes contain the same properties and can be used interchangeably to obtain the same result. Yet, viewing an e-textbook as a replica of the print version (PDF format) blurs out the enhanced learning potential derived from the interactive attributes of the e-format (Hendrix et al., 2016; Smith et al., 2013). In that case, for the participant who relied on the textbook (print version) as a critical pedagogical resource and is in the habit of using print textbooks (Wiese & Du Plessis, 2014), there is little incentive to migrate to the e-version (basic PDF format). Thus it would appear that the assumed facilitating factors of habit and substitutes contradict one another and are unlikely to facilitate the adoption of e-textbooks as technology innovation, contrary to the proposition by Gerhart et al. (2017). As such, all the factors enumerated in the adapted TAM model may not hold in adopting e-textbook pedagogy. However, as argued in the preceding paragraph, the key is for academics to become familiar with the (interactive) e-textbooks resource to cultivate the habit of incorporating it in their pedagogical practices.

In line with the findings in other studies (D'Ambra et al., 2022; Hendrix et al., 2016; Kelson, 2016; Wiese & du Plessis, 2014), cost also emerged as a determinant in the adoption of e-textbooks. Besides the fact that students have limited resources, most of the students in the SoE come from poor socioeconomic backgrounds. This crop of students should welcome the cost savings afforded by e-textbook. However, if the students are unaware of the savings affordance of the e-textbooks, they may not be able to tap into them. Hence, the onus is on academics and institutions to promote the use of e-textbooks and their affordance (Wiese & du Plessis, 2014).

10.5.3 Beyond the pandemic

Going forward beyond the pandemic era, the participants expressed an appreciation for the usefulness of the peculiar features of the e-textbook. They are open to adopting e-textbook pedagogy in the teaching of accounting. According to one participant, *E-Textbooks are very helpful because they are user-friendly to both students and the environment; they must be made accessible to all students and lecturers.* Another participant suggested a university-wide approach by stating that the *university must begin to consider approving e-textbooks.* One of them, however, cautioned that it should be *a matter of preference and convenience* so students who *prefer an e-textbook. . .are welcome to use it.* However, academics remain at the center of adopting e-textbook technology because they are responsible for prescribing textbooks for their courses as a collective (department). Therefore one participant asserted that *academics from the School of Education must come together and adopt the use of e-textbooks.* As noted by one participant, *the lecturer must make all the E-books available to students.* They must drive the process of adoption. Nevertheless, they cannot do it without the support of the institution.

The institution is responsible for providing the facilitating conditions for e-textbooks which participants in this study also deemed essential. In addition to the infrastructural hardware, devices, and connectivity that the university already provides, there is a need for training (Nourie, 2021; Roberts et al., 2021; Smith et al., 2013). One participant insisted that *the SoE must provide training to all students and staff on how to use the E-Text book.* Like any other technological adoption, academics need to be educated on how to use the unique features of e-textbooks through professional development workshops, preferably facilitated by publishers' representatives. This will likely enhance the chances of utilizing the technology before adoption. Nonetheless, a flexible approach that will not *compel people to make the switch* is advised because adopting the e-textbook innovation is a process beginning with unawareness until effective use (Roberts et al., 2021).

The library is vital in any university as a repertoire of academic resources. Just as the libraries keep copies of prescribed print textbooks, they could also carry digital versions. As suggested by Wiese and du Plessis (2014), the university, through its libraries, could negotiate better pricing structures and features for e-textbooks with publishers to improve its attractiveness as a viable option to students. Currently, the cost differential between the e-version and print version is about 10% which is not so significant. A study by Hendrix et al. (2016) concluded that 70% of students would opt for e-textbooks if the cost dropped by 25%. The additional discount is more likely attainable through an institutional intervention via the libraries that are established to source books. Since all publishers do not offer the same level of interactivity (Roberts et al., 2021), it is imperative that all e-textbooks acquired allow users to work offline to mitigate connectivity issues while offering some level of learning engagement. Without this feature, adopting the e-textbook as a full online academic resource may not be practicable given the institution's and student body's contextual realities. An entirely online e-textbook administration assumes a consistent supply of electricity and Internet connection which is hardly the case in South Africa since the country is plagued with different stages of load shedding. Outside the university residences, some students struggle to access the Internet from home even though the institution provides data because of the poor network coverage. In addition, a library with an e-textbook collection enhances trialability by students who could do so at zero cost implications (Wiese & du Plessis, 2014). This will further ensure that *every student has equal access to E-Textbook*, as advised by one participant.

Going by the contextual background of the students in the SoE, academics, as the key drivers of technology adoption, must pursue the migration to e-textbook from a cost-effective perspective. Nowadays, many e-textbooks have a special feature that allows for the personalization of content. Using this feature, academics can adapt, amend, or reconfigure content to suit the learning needs of their students. Taking this a step further, academics can adapt, add, remove, or rearrange e-textbooks using the open education resource (OER) model (Roberts et al., 2021; Masuku, Willmers, Trotter, & Cox, 2021; Vorotnykova, 2019) advocated by the United Nations Educational Scientific and Cultural Organization (UNESCO) in 2019 to produce their accounting e-textbooks. OERs are pedagogical materials made available in the public domain at no cost with the permission of the copyright owners to enhance equity and access to quality, affordable education (UNESCO, 2021).

These open resources have two significant advantages that can be adopted by the academic community in the SoE. In the first place, producing their own e-textbooks allows for incorporating indigenous contextual knowledge, thereby aiding the curriculum transformation/decolonization drive (Masuku et al., 2021). In our learner-centered dispensation, this can be done in conjunction with students. For example, students can be asked to develop assessment activities with solutions (part of the pedagogical competencies expected of preservice teachers) for inclusion in the e-textbook. The second advantage is that OER is usually open to everyone at minimal or no cost (Roberts et al., 2021; Masuku et al., 2021). In an institution where most students are from poor socioeconomic backgrounds, the OER route appears to be a more viable option for the students. It, however, comes at a cost to the academics who must make time to produce the e-textbooks. Some institutions that opted for the OER model provided funds for teaching relief while academics compiled their own e-textbooks. This strategy can guide accounting academics as they consider migrating to the e-textbook pedagogy cost-effectively and flexibly.

10.6 Conclusion

As part of a more extensive study examining the digital transformation in the SoE, this chapter sought to understand how accounting academics in the SoE integrate e-textbook pedagogy in their online engagement. Guided by the technology adoption framework, a qualitative approach was used in analyzing the participants' responses to a semistructured questionnaire. The findings revealed that before the pandemic, the participants relied on their print textbooks as the principal resource for teaching. During the pandemic, the findings indicated that they did not utilize e-textbooks in their online pedagogical practices but rather continued to depend on their print textbook due to preference, vision issues, limiting features of e-textbooks, and connectivity issues, among others. While all the participants considered the features of the e-textbook useful in teaching accounting education, Internet self-efficacy, perceived usefulness, facilitating conditions, and cost were some factors that they deemed influential in the migration to e-textbooks.

Of all the factors, the authors consider the savings affordance emanating from the relatively lower cost of the digital version uppermost, considering the contextual background of the students in the SoE. To that extent, this chapter argues for a flexible, cost-effective approach to the migration to e-textbook pedagogy going forward. To facilitate the process, there is a need for the SoE to train academics on e-textbook technology and provide necessary support for academics to familiarize themselves with its affordance and operation. The institution could also capacitate the library to stock e-textbooks and possibly fund academics to produce in-house e-textbooks via OER at zero cost. With the requisite structures and training, accounting academics should become more familiar and comfortable in their e-textbook pedagogy beyond the pandemic era. As they demonstrate the features of the e-textbook in class, students will be more encouraged to use the e-textbooks, thereby actualizing the enhanced learning potential of e-textbook pedagogy in accounting education.

As a case-based study focused on accounting education in the SoE, this chapter may be limited in scope and generalization. Interested scholars with more time and resources can expand the scope to consider other disciplines in commerce education, the entire SoE, the university, or even a cross section of HEIs. This study was based on the views of accounting academics in the SoE. Subsequent research can include the perspectives of the librarians and Information and Communication Services (ICS) officers to provide richer insight. Nonetheless, all academics, especially those engaged in online pedagogy, will find this study helpful. HEIs that aim to enhance students' learning experiences in their digital transformation drive can also benefit from this study. Specifically, insights from this study will be helpful to HEIs that aim to provide quality education in an environment where most of the student body comes from rural or poor socioeconomic backgrounds. Drawing from this study, publishers can tailor the features in their e-textbook portfolio to meet users' needs while improving student engagement and learning. It also makes a valuable contribution to the scholarship of e-textbooks and digital learning, hoping that as the academic community becomes more aware of and engages in this ubiquitous resource, the potential for enhanced learning in a cost-effective manner will materialize.

Acknowledgment

This work is based on the research supported wholly by the National Research Foundation of South Africa (Grant numbers: 138467).

The authors thank the head of the Accounting Education department (Dr. J C Ngwenya) for her critical contribution to refining the research instrument.

References

Abbott, J. I., & Palatnik, B. R. (2018). Students' perceptions of their first accounting class: Implications for instructors. *Accounting Education, 27*(1), 72−93.

Amin, N., Dhunpath, R., & Chatradari, D. (2021). Uncertainties and ambiguities of (Re) learning to teach in the context of crises. In N. Amin, & R. Dhunpath (Eds.), *(Re) Learning to teach in Contexts of Crisis.* In: *Alternation African Scholarship Book Series.* (8, pp. 1−25). CSSALL Publishers.

Arek-Bawa, O., & Reddy, S. (2020). Blending digital and technological skills with traditional commerce education knowledge in preparation for the 4IR classroom: The COVID 19 catalyst. *Alternation African Scholarship Book Series (AASBS), 144.*

Baglione, S. L., & Sullivan, K. (2016). Technology and textbooks: The future. *American Journal of Distance Education, 30*(3), 145−155.

Bargate, K. (2012). Criteria considered by accounting faculty when selecting and prescribing textbooks—A South African study. *International Journal of Humanities and Social Science, 2*(7), 114−122.

Brown, R. B., & Guilding, C. (1993). A survey of teaching methods employed in university business school accounting courses. *Accounting Education, 2*(3), 211−218.

Chaudhri, V. K., Cheng, B. H., Overholtzer, A., Roschelle, J., Spaulding, A., Clark, P., ... Gunning, D. (2013). Inquire biology: A textbook that answers questions. *AI Magazine, 34*(3), 55−72.

Crowe, S., Cresswell, K., Robertson, A., Huby, G., Avery, A., & Sheikh, A. (2011). The case study approach. *BMC Medical Research Methodology 11, 1*(100), 1−12.

D'Ambra, J., Akter, S., & Mariani, M. (2022). Digital transformation of higher education in Australia: Understanding affordance dynamics in e-textbook engagement and use. *Journal of Business Research, 149,* 283−295.

Davidson, R. A., & Baldwin, B. A. (2005). Cognitive skills objectives in intermediate accounting textbooks: Evidence from end-of-chapter material. *Journal of Accounting Education, 23*(2), 79−95.

Davis, F. D. (1989). Perceived usefulness, perceived ease of use, and user acceptance of information technology. *MIS Quarterly,* 319−340.

Doering, T., Pereira, L., & Kuechler, L. (2012). The use of e-textbooks in higher education: A case study. *Berlin (Germany): E-Leader,* 109−123.

Du Preez, P., & Le Grange, L. (2020). *The COVID-19 pandemic, online teaching/learning, the digital divide and epistemological access.* Unpublished paper.

Elias, E. C., Phillips, D. C., & Luechtefeld, M. E. (2012). E-books in the classroom: A survey of students and faculty at a school of pharmacy. *Currents in Pharmacy Teaching and Learning, 4*(4), 262−266.

Gerhart, N., Peak, D., & Prybutok, V. R. (2017). Encouraging e-textbook adoption: Merging two models. *Decision Sciences Journal of Innovative Education, 15*(2), 191−218.

Hendrix, D., Lyons, C., & Aronoff, N. (2016). The library as textbook provider: Administering and assessing a student-based e-textbook pilot. *College & Undergraduate Libraries, 23*(3), 265−294.

Irsyadillah, I., Ahmed, A. H., & ElKelish, W. W. (2021). Do accounting textbooks inculcate global mindsets: An analysis of textbooks adopted in Indonesia. *Journal of Teaching in International Business, 32*(3-4), 262−283.

Ishak, N. M., & Abu Bakar, A. Y. (2014). Developing sampling frame for case study: Challenges and conditions. *World Journal of Education, 4*(3), 29−35.

Karuri-Sebina, G. (September 2019). Sustainable development in Africa through the 4IR. In: *the Proceedings of the 6th annual DHET research colloquium on the fourth Industrial Revolution (4IR): Implications for post-secondary school education and training.* http://www.dhet.gov.za.

Kelson, C. K. H. (2016). A correlation study of the technology acceptance model and higher education faculty e-textbook adoption. Northcentral University.

Khoza, S. B., & Mpungose, C. B. (2020). Digitalised curriculum to the rescue of a higher education institution. *African Identities*, 1–21.

Li, L. (2010). A critical review of technology acceptance literature. *Referred Research Paper*, 4.

Makwanya, C., & Oni, O. (2019). E-books preference compared to print books based on student perceptions: A case of University of Fort Hare students. *International Journal of Information Management*, *13*(12), 236–245.

Masuku, B., Willmers, M., Trotter, H. & Cox, G. (2021). *UCT open textbook journeys.* Cape Town: Digital Open Textbooks for Development and UCT Libraries. Available from https://doi.org/10.15641/07992-2551-8.

Mathews, M. R. (2001). The way forward for accounting education? A comment on Albrecht and Sack 'a perilous future'. *Accounting Education*, *10*(1), 117–122. Available from https://doi.org/10.1080/09639280110050277.

Miller, J. R., Nutting, A. W., & Baker-Eveleth, L. (2013). The determinants of electronic textbook use among college students. *The American Economist*, *58*(1), 41–50.

Motala, S., & Menon, K. (2022). Pedagogical continuities in teaching and learning during COVID-19: Holding up the bridge. *Scholarship of Teaching and Learning in the South*, *6*(1), 7–32.

Ngema, N. S., & Masenya, T. M. (2020). Use of electronic books among postgraduate students in the department of information studies at the University of Zululand. *South Africa. Mousaion*, *38*(2).

Ngwenya, J., & Arek-Bawa, O. (2019). Exploring the quality of Grade 12 accounting education textbooks. *The Journal for Transdisciplinary Research in Southern Africa*, *15*(1), a662. Available from https://doi.org/10.4102/td.v15i1.662.

Nicholas, A., & Lewis, J. (2008). Millennial attitudes toward books and e-books. *Available at SSRN*, 2684872.

Nourie, K. (2021, October). Expansive learning during pandemic teaching: Collaborative digital textbooks in secondary biology courses. In: *European conference on e-learning* (pp. 608-XVII). Academic Conferences International Limited.

Osih, S. C. (2020). E-textbook preferences: A case study of Information Technology students' preferences at a private higher education institution. (Masters dissertation, University of KwaZulu-Natal, Durban).

Osih, S. C., & Singh, U. G. (2020). Students' perception on the adoption of an e-textbook (digital) as an alternative to the printed textbook. *South African Journal of Higher Education*, *34*(6), 201–215.

Pesek, I., Zmazek, B., & Mohorcic, G. (2014). *From e-materials to i-textbooks.* Available from https://www.zrss.si/pdf/slovenian-i-textbooks.pdf. *Ljubljana.*

Roberts, K., Benson, A., & Mills, J. (2021). E-textbook technology: Are instructors using it and what is the impact on student learning?. Journal of Research in Innovative Teaching & Learning, *14*(3), 329–344.

Sackstein, S., Spark, L., & Masenda, T. (2015). E-textbook usage by lecturers: A preliminary study. *Proceedings of the 44 The Annual Southern African Computer Lecturers Association 2015 (Sacla 2015)*, 186.

Salovaara, A., & Tamminen, S. (2009). *Acceptance or appropriation? A design-oriented critique of technology acceptance models. Future interaction design II* (pp. 157–173). London: Springer.

Smith, D., Brand, J.E., & Kinash, S. (2013). Turn on the book: Using affordance theory to understand the adoption of digital textbooks by university lecturers. In *ASCILITE Australian Society for Computers in Learning in Tertiary Education Annual Conference* (pp. 812-820). Australasian Society for Computers in Learning in Tertiary Education.

Stevenson, L., Ferguson, J., & Power, D. (2014). The use of teaching resources in accounting education. In R. M. S. Wilson (Ed.), *The Routledge companion to accounting education*, (pp. 420–446). New York: Routledge.

Terpend, R., Gattiker, T. F., & Lowe, S. E. (2014). Electronic textbooks: Antecedents of students' adoption and learning outcomes. *Decision Sciences Journal of Innovative Education, 12*(2), 149–173.

UNESCO. (2021). *Briefing paper accessible open education resource (OER)*. https://www.unesco.org/en/communication-information/open-solutions/openeducational-resources.

Van Schalkwyk, J. H., & Müller, R. A. (2020). Antecedents of generation Y students' interest and intention to use e-books. *International Journal of Business and Management Studies, 12*(1), 101–115.

Vorotnykova, I. (2019). Organizational, psychological and pedagogical conditions for the use of e-books and e-textbooks at school. *Turkish Online Journal of Distance Education, 20*(3), 89–102.

Wiese, M., & Du Plessis, G. (2014). The battle of the e-textbook: Libraries' role in facilitating student acceptance and use of e-textbooks. *South African Journal of Libraries and Information Science, 80*(2), 17–26.

CHAPTER 11

The death of the massification of education and the birth of personalized learning in higher education

Shamola Pramjeeth[1] and Sarina C. Till[2]
[1]The IIE Varsity College, School of Management, Durban, South Africa
[2]The IIE Varsity College, School of Information Technology, Durban, South Africa

11.1 Introduction

As the Covid-19 pandemic moves to becoming endemic and higher education institutions (HEIs) begin to revert to teaching and learning pre-Covid days, one must ask:

Can teaching and learning revert to the "old ways" and discard the lessons learnt during the pandemic, the changed learner, and technology's important role in education?

Have students (secondary school and tertiary students) evolved in their learning styles, and are they ready to revert to the old face-to-face classes? Or do HEIs need to evolve and redesign their teaching and learning strategies to suit the post-Covid students? Students (both secondary school and tertiary) have become accustomed to their lessons being split between in-person contact, both online and in-person and purely online.

Covid-19 forced HEIs into online learning in the form of unplanned emergency remote teaching and learning (ERTL) to ensure the safety of their staff and students and the completion of the curriculum (Hodges, Moore, Lockee, Trust, & Bond, 2020). It is important to note that ERTL cannot be compared to online learning or distance, or e-learning, argue Groarke et al. (2020). ERTL is a sudden unplanned temporary shift in face-to-face or blended teaching modes of delivery to an alternate, fully remote mode due to crisis circumstances with the intent to return to the previous mode of learning once the crisis is over (Bond, Bedenlier, & Marín, 2021). Such a sudden change in pedagogy does not allow for the creative and

Digital Teaching, Learning and Assessment
DOI: https://doi.org/10.1016/B978-0-323-95500-3.00012-2

focused design of curriculum and teaching and learning strategies to suit the mode of delivery. Stakeholders were unified in agreement that there was no clear vision of effective teaching and learning during the pandemic (OECD, 2020) or the appropriate pedagogies to be used.

Hodges et al. (2020) advise that courses delivered online in reaction to a catastrophe or crisis are significantly different from well-planned online learning experiences; however, they provide an impetus for HEIs to understand the differences and emergence of new learnings when analyzing ERTL that occurred during the Covid-19 pandemic. Maseleno et al. (2018) note that with the implementation of technology and connected learning pedagogies, the manner in which students learn has changed, resulting in less reliance and the active participation of the educator in the process. The pandemic has accelerated this change dramatically. Lee (2021) highlights that Covid-19 has been a catalyst to student-centric learning allowing for the creativity and collaboration parts of their minds to be activated.

As academics at a private HEI (PHEI), we were always interested in how students learn using technology. This became even more of a question when learning moved unexpectedly to purely online during the Covid-19 pandemic. The researchers' exploration into students' online learning behavior began when the first hard lockdown was announced in April 2020, and they were asked to pivot from face-to-face classrooms to an online space. To ensure standardized delivery across the PHEI, the institutional learning management system (LMS) was used as the delivery medium for online lectures. A structured lesson plan was created that included video content, additional resources, and short quizzes to allow the students to work through the prescribed course material. To save space on the LMS, all video content was hosted on YouTube as unlisted playlists, which would not allow students or others to find the content through an Internet search. Unfortunately, one playlist was accidentally marked as public. Students discovered this very quickly and opted to abandon the structured lesson plan created on the LMS for the YouTube channel. Instead of locking down the playlist, the researchers followed their students' online behavior to understand their behavior better.

Thus, this chapter reflects on the students' online behavior and their teaching and learning preferences during ERTL resulting in the birth of the next-generation teaching and learning approach that integrates active learning, authentic learning constructivism, personalized learning, and problem-based learning, hence creating an enhanced relevant student learning experience that equips them with the required skills to prepare them for a technology-driven working and learning world.

11.2 Literature review

The literature review briefly explores online learning and unpacks the personalized learning pedagogy that guided this study.

11.2.1 Online learning

Learning has traditionally been classroom-based, and as technology, advanced HEIs began introducing it into their teaching and learning strategy. This inclusion has created a technology-enhanced teaching approach (Peng, Ma, & Spector, 2019) with online learning, further changing the approach to teaching and learning (Maseleno et al., 2018).

Due to technology, learning has evolved from e-learning, the use of the Internet to deliver educational resources and teaching, to mobile learning (m-learning), accessing learning resources through personal mobile devices, to ubiquitous learning (u-learning), a hybrid of e-learning, and mobile learning that allow learners to learn at any time and in any location (Suartama, Setyosari, Sulthoni, & Ulfa, 2020) and finally to smart learning (s-learning) (Adu & Poo, 2014).

Peng et al. (2019, p. 1) define s-learning as an amalgam of "smart devices technologies (such as the Internet of Things, wearable devices) and intelligent technologies (such as learning analysis, cloud computing." With s-learning, Peng et al. (2019) note that technology enables tracking of the learning process, early recognition of learning patterns, the ability to connect different groups of learners and allows for easy interaction among learners and facilitators. S-learning accommodates various types of students based on their needs and varying learning styles, times, and preferred places of learning. This results in greater flexibility, adaptability, engagement, motivation, and effectiveness of learning for the learner.

Branch and Dousay (2015, cited in Darkwa & Antwi, 2021) write that effective online education is achieved through carefully planned instructional design. Hodges et al. (2020, citing Means, Bakia & Murphy, 2014) identify nine key dimensions for an effective online education design, modality, pacing, student—instructor ratio, pedagogy, instructor role online, student role online, online communication synchrony, the role of online assessments, and source of feedback. Within each of these dimensions, various options exist; however, the effectiveness of the options changes based on the growing class sizes, which will inevitably affect the quality of feedback. Further, the student's traits, learning preferences, skills and what best addresses their learning needs play a crucial role. Students differ in their personalities, interests, and learning styles and with time, this changes as well, writes Peng et al. (2019). The instructor's traits, skills, level of comfortability and confidence in engaging in online delivery also need to be factored in as they will impact the student's learning experience. Interaction between students, students, and instructors, as well as students and the content, plays a key role. Determining the correct content to cover in online learning is not the only the key component to consider. One needs to consider how the instructor will support various interactions, manage large class sizes, ensure quality feedback and engagement, and different student personalities, learning styles and means of communication are critical to the learning process.

Learning is recognized as a social and cognitive activity, not just a matter of information transmission; in this approach, it necessitates an investment in a learner support environment and platforms relevant to the learner, which takes time to discover and construct (Hodges et al., 2020). Kim and Bonk (2006) assert that for students to influence their learning, the constructivist approach must be applied to the online course design to ensure it allows for applicability, synergism, and practicality. A finding from a pedagogical practice survey found that 40% of educators felt online teaching must include data analysis, data simulation and activities that are interactive (Mpungose, 2020).

With ERTL, these considered and carefully designed processes and activities are often omitted due to the emergency of the situation. At the PHEI understudy, content and resources used in face-to-face contact sessions were used online, on a medium that both students and instructors were unfamiliar with, with no changes to teaching strategies taking place.

As technology adoption increases and becomes an even more integral part of a student's life, it is vital to ensure that HEI's teaching and learning strategy aligns more with the s-learning approach, with resources explicitly curated for online and for the transformed technologically enabled learner. Thus online education implemented during the ERTL is a short-term solution to the pandemic and calls for a review of the learning experiences, content, and lessons learnt to design an education and learning experience that addresses the new needs of learners and communities.

11.2.2 Personalized learning

The concept of personalized learning, where learning is student-centered, can be traced back to Confucius's "teaching students according to their aptitude" and Socrates's elicitation teaching theory, cites Peng et al. (2019, p. 1). Personalized learning is an educational strategy that aims to tailor learning to the strengths, needs, skills, and interests of each student (Chatti, Jarke, & Specht, 2010, p. 79). It is a shift from teacher-centered education to a learner-centered pedagogy to attain the "full awareness of the learner" (Kaminskiene & DeUrraza, 2020, p. 3). According to UNESCO (2017), education must connect with the learner on a personal level for it to be impactful. Thus, for learning to be effective, it should be about the learner's holistic development.

In the personalized learning approach, each student receives a tailored learning plan based on their requirements, acquired knowledge and learnings, and preferred learning style that is cocreated with the teacher. Greater flexibility is employed in the teaching and learning strategies and curriculum design, with the pacing of learning using personalized, differentiated assessment practices (Kaminskiene & DeUrraza, 2020).

A wide range of educational programs, learning experiences, instructional methodologies, and academic-support strategies are created jointly with individual students to cater for their unique learning needs, learning styles, interests, goals, and preferences. This approach assists learners in better understanding themselves, their competencies, and what is expected of them, thus, becoming key agents of their learning journey (Li & Wong, 2020). Lee (2021) writes that "education tailored to students' individual levels will help them accumulate knowledge and improve their ability to use it."

To ensure effective learning, quality feedback to the learner is required. Lim et al. (2021) established that feedback based on learning analytics and personalized learning was well received and actioned by students. However, Tsai, Perrotta, and Gašević (2020) argue that student empowerment should not be considered to have occurred due to the implementation of learning analytics only. The intertwined power relations within a dynamic, complex education system and that between humans and machines must be considered "when presenting learning analytics as an equitable process to enhance student agency and educational equity" (Tsai et al., 2020, p. 554). Learning analytics is dependent on a personalized approach for both educators and students.

Peng et al. (2019) advise that the s-learning environment enabled by advancements in technology and smart devices encourages personalized and adaptive learning development and integration. The role of technology in this learning sphere is used as a tool to aid and reinforce learning, and the role of the teacher changes to one of a facilitator (Forbus, 2018). Students can now blend technology easily to socialize and learn in their own ways and time; however, HEI teaching and learning still need to evolve to factor in this new type of learner; hence further research is necessary.

11.3 Research methodology

This work builds and expands on a previous conference proceeding by Till and Adam (2021) which explored how students interacted with online content during the Covid-19 pandemic in 2020. From this study, an initial and incomplete personalized learning framework was developed. This research included the data from the initial and subsequent surveys to delve deeper and formalize the initial personalized learning framework.

This study was exploratory in nature and employed a mixed methods methodology as the researchers wished to have an in-depth understanding of the student's online behavior and the motivations for their behavior. This approach allowed the researchers to delve deeper into the observed online trends, such as time of study and durations spent on online videos, by cross-referencing and contextualizing the observed online behavior with the responses provided in the surveys and interviews. Data were thus collected through probing online surveys and interviews targeting computer science undergraduate students (for two modules that were first and third year), YouTube channel analytics, and informal WhatsApp chat data. Researchers first used an initial probing survey issued in April 2020 to gather information regarding the student experience of the online material and video content. A follow-up survey was administered in April 2021, exploring the student experience of the same content and platforms in a hybrid environment. The YouTube analytics were consulted, which in combination with the student responses from the second survey, prompted the informal WhatsApp chats as well as the final survey.

11.3.1 YouTube analytics

A YouTube channel containing prerecorded videos covering course material and recorded online lectures created in March 2020 is still in use today. The analytics data for two years (2020–21) was collected and analyzed to better understand student behaviors during the full lockdown and when lectures resumed on campus. Both the default and advanced YouTube analytics of the YouTube channel were consulted. Data such as the time slots of student activity, number of views per video, click-through rates, duration of watch time per video, video sharing behaviors, and device types used to view content were gathered using the above-mentioned tools.

11.3.2 Online surveys

Using purposive sampling (Campbell et al., 2020), three probing Microsoft Forms online surveys were issued between April 2020 and November 2021. These surveys were exploratory and were not piloted. The first survey was administered in April 2020 to explore how students were initially experiencing the online content during the full lockdown. Three simple questions regarding the online resources and lectures provided were asked: (1) which resources worked for you and why?, (2) which resources did not work for you and why?, and finally, (3) what would you like us to know about the online resources? This survey was issued to all the first- and third-year computer science students (500 students) as it focused on two modules offered in these years of study as a reference point. The survey received 217 responses. A second survey was issued in April 2021, asking students to rate their experience with the online video content, in particular, also asking what worked for students and what did not work for students, and if they had additional information, they wished to share, this survey received 198 responses. The final survey was issued in November of 2021 based on the YouTube channel's data and the previous survey's responses. This survey enquired about the devices students used to study in conjunction with online resources, the platforms they preferred to use, the times of the day they studied and, most importantly, detailed their ideal learning experience along with the devices they would use in this learning. The final survey received 135 responses.

11.3.3 Informal WhatsApp chats

The institution in question has offered student support through the use of class WhatsApp groups and WhatsApp groups dedicated to student support through peer tutors (tutors were a year further in their studies than the students they were tutoring) since 2013. WhatsApp communications are well adopted and ingrained in the running of qualifications.

Students opt-in to use the WhatsApp groups and are free to leave these groups at any time. The researchers initiated group discussions on the use of video content, learning times, the use of online platforms, and student online behaviors on these WhatsApp groups. The researchers would pose a question such as "Why do you make use of YouTube playlists instead of the lesson plan on [The institutional LMS]." Any student who wished to participate in the discussion could then join it and give their input. A total of four WhatsApp group chats representing around 487 students were analyzed.

11.3.4 Focus groups

Two online focus groups were conducted to understand better the observed student behavior and the responses to the survey questions. The first focus group took place in February 2021 and included 10 students. This focus group probed areas such as the preferences for different online platforms, the study times observed on the YouTube analytics, video watch time durations, and the students' study and learning methods in 2020. The second group took place in November 2021 and included seven students.

11.3.5 Qualitative data analysis

The researchers met online and created a code book to code the qualitative data gathered from the focus groups and informal WhatsApp chats. During the coding phase, the researchers remained in communication to discuss and agree on new codes assigned as the data analysis took place. Using the finalized code book, the researchers used thematic analysis to generate themes. The researchers met online once more to discuss the generated themes to cross-check and validate the themes to ensure the necessary scientific rigor was present in the qualitative data analysis (Castleberry & Nolen, 2018).

11.3.6 Quantitative data analysis

The survey data were cleaned by removing incomplete and duplicate records. Descriptive statistical analyses were performed on the data.

11.3.7 Ethical considerations

Ethical clearance for this study was obtained in July 2020 and reaffirmed in November 2021 by the researcher's institution. The study abided by the ethical guidelines of research and the institution by ensuring informed consent was obtained for both the survey and focus group participants. The surveys were anonymous, and students could opt out at any point in the survey. The focus group data were anonymized before transcribing the data. All the data pertaining to this study are stored on a secure data cloud only accessible to the research team through a username and password.

11.4 Results and discussion

11.4.1 Student learning: when?, what time?, using what device?

From the analysis of the YouTube data, it is evident that students across all years of study were most active online and working through learning content after 12 p.m. or midday (see Fig. 11.1). This is an interesting finding because the institution schedules all its first- and third-year lectures from 08:30 a.m. to 12:30 p.m. Only second-year students attend classes between 12:30 p.m. and 15:30 p.m.

This finding was further validated when the researchers analyzed the survey data (survey 3), with 31% of the surveyed students indicating that they preferred to study in the mornings, followed by 38% preferring the afternoons, as per Fig. 11.2. In fact, 62% of the students indicated

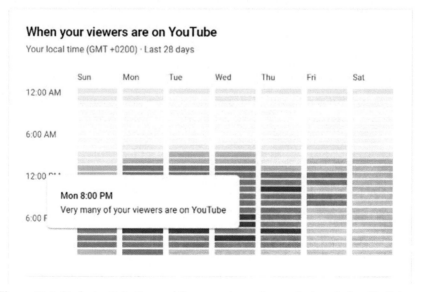

Figure 11.1 Student activity times while consuming online content posted on YouTube.

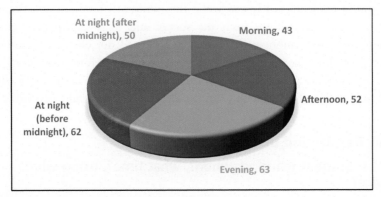

Figure 11.2 Student study time preferences.

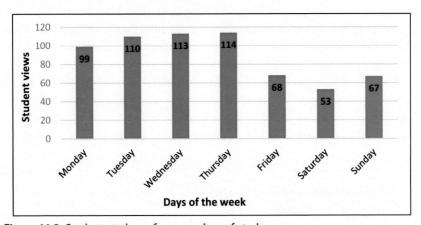

Figure 11.3 Student study preferences: days of study.

that their ideal study and learning time is in the evening before midnight. In comparison, 50% were found to study after midnight (see Fig. 11.2).

Regarding the days of the week, students preferred most to study and learn, per Fig. 11.3, on a Thursday, followed by Wednesday. A moderate number of students indicated they study on Saturdays and Sundays. This directly correlates with the data gathered from the YouTube channel analytics (see Figs. 11.1 and 11.3).

Reflecting on the qualitative data, it further validated these findings with students providing responses such as:

I study really well at night... I work at my best during the evening—
Participant 13

Studying at night also is advantageous because of the peacefulness and the ability to work uninterrupted.—Participant 11

Students further indicated that they use more than one device when they study and have strong personal preferences regarding the usage of these devices. The predominant device is a laptop (122 respondents); however, these devices are paired with a smartphone, smart television or gaming console, or even wearable devices depending on the student's preference or availability. This finding was prevalent in both the survey and YouTube data, as per Figs. 11.4 and 11.5.

From the above, it can be noted that students blend resources and choose devices and time slots to match their personal study times. It is further evident that the current educational models do not match the optimal times of study, use of devices, or days of study of their students.

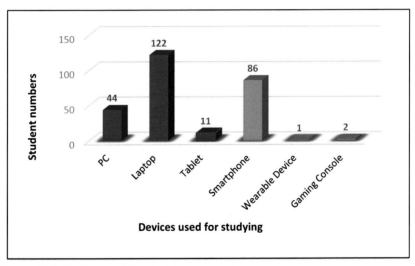

Figure 11.4 Devices used for studying: survey data.

☐ **Total**	**27,357**	**1,732.9**	**3:48**
☐ Computer	18,427 67.4%	1,246.8 72.0%	4:03
☐ Mobile phone	8,092 29.6%	378.9 21.9%	2:48
☐ Tablet	588 2.2%	42.2 2.4%	4:18
☐ Game console	164 0.6%	53.7 3.1%	19:37
☐ TV	84 0.3%	11.2 0.7%	7:59

Figure 11.5 Devices used for studying: YouTube data.

11.4.2 Student learning: which resources?

Learning resources and platforms are no exceptions to the rule; even here, students presented strong preferences regarding what they use when they are learning (see Fig. 11.6 and Table 11.1). The highest scoring platforms for "This is my go-to space" are not resources curated and provided by the PHEI but rather resources such as online tutorial websites (24%) such as Geeks4Geeks, C# Corner, W3School, and Stack Overflow (22%. Stack Overflow is a popular discussion board for software developers and students where the Stack Overflow community answers questions regarding software errors) and YouTube videos (19%). Only 3% of the students elected the institutional LMS as their go-to space for learning resources. When students were asked what resources they frequently used, 36% indicated the institutional LMS, and 58% stated the institutional content-sharing platform. It should be noted that the content-sharing platform was also used to stream and record online lectures.

In comparison, personally sought out resources such as online tutorials (45%), YouTube videos (46%) and technical documentation (41%) received a comparative rating. Based on the findings, it can be seen that students find and curate their own resources to facilitate their learning in a way that

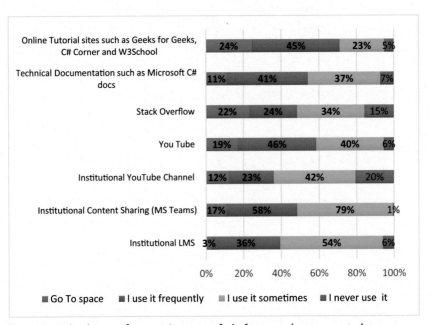

Figure 11.6 Student preferences in terms of platforms and resources to learn.

Table 11.1 Students' preferred learning resources and platforms.

Resource type	Platform	Go-to space (%)	I use it frequently (%)	I use it sometimes (%)	I never use it (%)
Institutional content	Institutional LMS	3	36	54	6
	Institutional content-sharing (MS Teams)	17	58	79	1
	Institutional YouTube Channel	12	23	42	20
Personal content	YouTube	19	46	40	6
	Stack Overflow	22	24	34	15
	Technical documentation such as Microsoft C# docs	11	41	37	7
	Online tutorial sites such as Geeks for Geeks, C# Corner, and W3School	24	45	23	5

makes sense to them and fits into their learning preferences and contexts. Conversely, this could indicate that the resources provided by the institute were not deemed helpful, appropriate, or interesting by the students.

11.4.3 Student learning: support-seeking behavior

The researchers wanted to ascertain what students considered the ideal support mechanism in terms of content, platforms, and lecturer and tutor involvement. Only 11% of the students elected face-to-face interventions such as workshops and sessions with lecturers. However, 55% of the students selected a blend of video content, tutor-led WhatsApp groups and other online resources. The students provided comments such as:

> I like having videos to watch at any time with[sic] WhatsApp support to assist as I require. Very effective. It gives people like myself who work as well, time to do our daily jobs and come back and study with full guidance and assistance.—Participant 15

A specific focus on access to resources in their own time and space is evident and aligns with the findings detailed in Section 11.4.1.

which describes the times, days, and platforms students prefer for learning and studying.

> Something like WhatsApp where all the information will be stored in one place, and we can all just refer back to it in our own time, workshops (especially online) never really have as much participation as I've seen on those groups.— Participant 20

Students further blend video resources and access to support tutors in an online space, not necessarily during traditional working hours, but still, require some face-to-face support from lecturers. Students commented as follows:

> I appreciated the WhatsApp workshops held by the tutors. Those helped us very much as tutors helped with any queries also. Video content has also been a strong support mechanism for me as I could go back to videos to revise and recall.—Participant 6

> Workshops are helpful. Especially ones that are relating to the PoE/task/assignments.—Participant 18

Finally, there is a need for a shared online space where students can meet to leverage video content, share online resources, and leverage peer learning. One student commented:

> I find discord a very nice platform to use, I use it every day to communicate with friends, and it is extremely easy to jump into a voice chat with them and share your screen; the text chat channels can also be used effectively while in voice chat and screen sharing.—Participant 7

11.4.4 Student learning: how they blend technology, resources, platforms, and content to create their personal braid

When asked what students believed the perfect learning experience was, 46% of the students indicated that they preferred a blend of either online or face-to-face lecturer engagement, online video content that they can access in their own space and time and additional resources such as Stack Overflow posts and online tutorial sites. One student stated the following alluding to the blending of resources, thus allowing for reinforcement of learning:

> A concept taught, a tutorial available that can be rewatched, an activity on the same, a real-life scenario of where it can be used.—Participant 6

Other students noted the use of different resources for specific learning needs and content:

It depends on what I'm doing. StackOverflow for code usually. YouTube for concepts. The institution LMS-related resources for lecturer-specific content.—*Participant 16*

Hard to say as I use all resources differently for different things, e.g., For practical work, I use the internet, websites, youtube etc. while for theory, I use institution LMS and teams.—Participant 10

Even within this blend, students showed further personalization preferences, such as preferring tutorial websites to video content. Students provided comments such as:

W3Schools, GeeksForGeeks, C# Corner, etc., I prefer reading the documentation instead of watching a video on the subject.—Participant 4

However, some students preferred only video content:

YouTube is my preferred method of learning. YouTube videos give specific solutions to specific problems.—Participant 7

YouTube videos because I can pause and repeat and refer back to a certain section if needed.—Participant 5

In contrast to the blended approach, 13% preferred only face-to-face contact in a traditional classroom setting, and 16% preferred to work through content on their own time, in their own space, with the option of reaching out to a lecturer or tutor when they require additional support.

Well, I would like to work in a [sic] quiet place with my own personal space and working on problems but also require help if I get stuck somewhere; I like to break down tasks and do them one by one rather than having everything due or done quick. I would also like a review lesson before any of our assignments are due, which helps or boost my confidence.—Participant 4

The researchers finally asked the students which online platforms and tools they preferred to use the least and to motivate their answers. The students indicated that they do not use the curated resources placed on the (Institutional LMS) because they do not learn as much from the content curated by the lecturer as they do from content they source for themselves. Students provided comments such as:

[Institutional LMS] I don't learn much from there as I do from external resources.—Participant 9

I don't use [Institutional LMS] that much as, I don't learn much from there as I do from external resources a video rather than reading as this is a practical course after all. I have nothing against [Institutional LMS]. Some students prefer it; personally, I don't.—Participant 1

Textbooks and [Institutional LMS]. Lecturers mostly upload reading material on Institutional LMS, which I barely ever look at.—Participant 4

From the findings, it is evident that students' preferred learning times, days, and use of learning devices do not match what is provided by traditional lecturing timetables and classrooms offered by the PHEI understudy. Students want the option to study any time from 6 a.m. to 2 a.m. on any day of the week. There is also a wide range of preferences for learning, either in the morning or in the evening. Chatti et al. (2010, cited in Zerbini, & Merrow, 2017) explain that mismatching students' time-of-day preferences can have detrimental effects on student learning and assessment, with the participants in his study scoring lower in tests and assessments scheduled outside of their preferences. The same can be said for students' ability to study effectively outside of their time-of-day preferences. Realistically, it is impossible to offer traditional lectures at a suitable time that is optimal for all learners. It is, however, possible to make resources in the form of video content such as recorded lectures, concepts, and other YouTube videos, as well as online tutorials, documentation, and additional learning resources available online. The study findings further indicated that students prefer to curate their own resources that match their study preferences and needs. According to Densmore, Bellows, Chuang, and Brewer (2013), this is accomplished by building a more appropriate, braided channel of communication through repetitiveness or complementing opportunities. This finding ties in well with a constructivist learning and teaching approach, which states that learning occurs when students leverage their own internal frameworks and prior knowledge to construct knowledge in their own minds (Vygotsky, 1978).

In addition, it was established that students use a wide range of devices to digest learning content and often use more than one or a nontraditional device such as a gaming console or a wearable device to access and digest their learning content. Based on the YouTube analytics of the channel since its inception in 2020, the channel had 79,115 views as of July 21, 2022, with students' maximum viewing time for a video being 3 min and 25 s before they lose interest and end the video. The average video watching time is significant for lecturers when they are creating content to ensure the video does not exceed 3 min in duration. Information should be presented in short burst of information blurbs that attracts and retains the student's attention while providing the pertinent information in a snapshot.

11.5 Student-centric framework for personalized learning

Building on the research findings presented by Till & Adam (2021) on hybrid learning and braided technologies for teaching programs in a post-Covid-19 world that explored student online learning behavior during the Covid-19 pandemic and this study's findings, the following student-centric framework for personalized learning designed by the researchers is put forth. The proposed framework builds on the conceptual framework postulated by Till & Adam (2021) that proposed the key resources student need access to for effective learning to take place and the guiding teaching and learning pedagogies that need to be in place, which serves as the first and second levels—the foundation and the pillars, in this study's proposed framework, as per Fig. 11.7. It is important to note that paper presented by Till and Adam (2021) analyzed the student behavior during the pandemic (2020) at the PHEI understudy here, while this study looks at the same student behavior over 2020−2021.

The proposed framework has four levels:

The first level is "The Foundation"—it refers to the institution ensuring their teaching and learning align with the pedagogies of

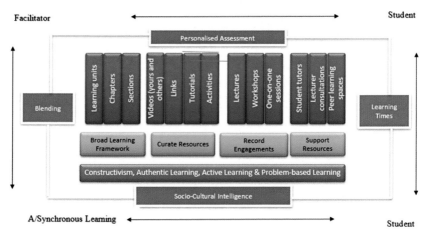

Figure 11.7 Personalized learning framework for higher education. *Framework modified and adapted from Till, S., & Adam, E. (2021). Hybrid learning and braided technologies for teaching programming in a post-COVID19 world. In:* Digital2k—Conference on teaching, assessment and learning in the digital age.

constructivism, authentic learning, active learning, and problem-based learning, helping to build the attributes of inquiry, critical and solution-based thinking. Students take personal ownership of their learning and are real-world problem-solvers.

The second level is "The Pillars"—the institution needs to provide key resources for students to access. These resources are a broad-based learning framework; curated resources, recorded engagements; and support resources.

The third level is "The Walls"—the institution needs to ensure that the resources put in place allow for learning to occur at any time and place. The institution's culture and environment should embrace and integrate sociocultural intelligence principles into its teaching and learning strategy. A review of its assessment methodology to factor in personalized assessments that cater to the different student competencies and weaknesses should be done by moving away from a one-size-fits-all approach. Finally, the institution needs to ensure that it has the infrastructure and systems in place that will enable students to blend resources and technology easily.

The fourth level is "The Players"—the final level is the people. The lecturer now plays the role of the facilitator, and there is a two-way relationship between the student and the facilitator and student and student. They work in unison to craft and reinforce the students learning. The other key aspect is creating an environment that encourages peer-to-peer learning and support. Further, learning should be synchronous or asynchronous, depending on the student's requirements. Flexibility is critical to the success of this learning; thus it is essential to remove barriers that prevent optimal learning from occurring that promote personal and academic development and growth.

11.6 Implications and the way forward

Based on the study findings, it is essential to factor in the universal design for learning (UDL) teaching approach, active learning, and authentic learning enabled by s-learning as HEIs begin to rethink their teaching and learning strategies. UDL is a teaching method developed by Universal Design for Learning (n.d.), which "is a framework to improve and optimise teaching and learning for all people based on scientific insights into how humans learn" (Universal Design for Learning, n.d.). UDL strives to meet the "needs and abilities of all learners" while removing needless barriers to learning. This entails creating a "flexible learning environment in which information is presented in multiple ways" (Burgstahler & Cory, 2008; Universal Design for Learning, n.d.). Students participate in learning in various ways, with a range of alternatives to prove learning has taken place, thus making it inclusive and transformative.

Incorporated into this approach should be the authentic learning pedagogy (ALP). ALP affords students the opportunity to engage with and address current real-life activities, situations, and problems using practical everyday resources and tools (Herrington, Parker, & Boase-Jelinek, 2014, p.23), enhancing their critical thinking and problem-solving skills, and better preparing them for the dynamic working environment. In his study, Lee (2021) found that students were dissatisfied with having lab classes via the Zoom platform due to the indirect and passive learning experiences. Lee (2021) postulates that with the use of "virtual reality, augmented reality, image recognition and eye-tracking technologies" to address the challenges associated with "scientific experiments, engineering prototyping and other hands-on activities."

The above have high cost and cultural implications for institutions that follow a traditional teaching approach. This learning approach calls for institutions to reinvent their teaching and learning strategies; amend policies and regulations; acquire, implement, and embrace new technology infrastructure and systems; and create a culture that embraces personalized learning, flexibility, and adaptability among all stakeholders.

11.7 Conclusions

Online learning, which has evolved to s-learning, allows for flexibility in teaching and learning, which can occur anywhere, anytime and across multiple devices and platforms. To enrich online learning, communication and content are often braided to students using various communication channels, allowing for reinforcement of the channel and content, as evident in this study. Students easily blend technology, resources, platforms, and content to create their personal braid to suit their learning needs, styles, and times. However, online learning has a reputation for being of lesser quality than face-to-face learning, which could be due to the lack of knowledge on the effectiveness and benefits of online learning and how to effectively braid communications and content. Thus, based on the study's findings and the ability of students to create their own personal braid to suit their needs as they learn at different times and days, it is imperative for HEIs to begin relooking at their teaching and learning strategy by factoring personalized learning as HEIs begin to cater for the new normal with a technology savvy learner. With HEIs adopting personalized learning pedagogy and having a better understanding of how to braid communications effectively, it will assist students' online and offline learning experiences resulting in greater student engagement and understanding of the content being studied, improving relations with the facilitator

11.8 Limitations

This study was based on a single PHEI in South Africa; thus, to ensure greater generalization of findings to public institutions and other private institutions, it is advised that this study is replicated. As this study was based on the computer science discipline, it is further recommended that the study be replicated using other disciplines. The surveys used in this study were probing in nature and thus not piloted. WhatsApp groups are ingrained in the running of the qualification used in this study, but some students might not have felt comfortable replying on this platform.

References

Adu, EL, & Poo, DCC (2014). Smart learning: A new paradigm of learning in the smart age. In *Paper presented at TLHE 204: International conference on teaching and learning in higher education*, National University of Singapore.

Bond, M., Bedenlier, S., & Marín, V. I. (2021). Emergency remote teaching in higher education: Mapping the first global online semester. *International Journal of Educational Technology in Higher Education, 18*, 50. Available from https://doi.org/10.1186/s41239-021-00282-x.

Branch, R. M., & Dousay, T. A. (2015). *Survey of Instructional Design Models* (5th Edition). Bloomington: Association for Educational Communications and Technology.

Burgstahler, S., & Cory, R. (2008). *Universal design in higher education: From principles to practice*. Cambridge, MA: Harvard Education Press.

Campbell, S., Greenwood, M., Prior, S., Shearer, T., Walkem, K., Young, S., ... Walker, K. (2020). Purposive sampling: Complex or simple? Research case examples. *Journal of Research in Nursing*. Available from https://doi.org/10.1177/1744987120927206.

Castleberry, A., & Nolen, A. (2018). Thematic analysis of qualitative research data: Is it as easy as it sounds? *Currents in Pharmacy Teaching and Learning, 10*(6), 807−815.

Chatti, M. A., Jarke, M., & Specht, M. (2010). The 3P learning model. *Educational Technology & Society, 13*(4), 74−85.

Darkwa, B. F., & Antwi, S. (2021). From classroom to online: Comparing the effectiveness and student academic performance of classroom learning and online learning. *Open Access Library Journal, 8*, e7597. Available from https://doi.org/10.4236/oalib.1107597.

Densmore, M., Bellows, B., Chuang, J. & Brewer, E. (2013). The evolving braid: How an organisation in Uganda achieved reliable communications. In: *Proceedings of the sixth international conference on information and communication technologies and development* (pp. 257–266): Full Papers – volume 1 (ICTD' 13). New York, USA: Association for Computing Machinery.

Forbus, A. (2018). *What's the role of the teacher in a personalised learning classroom?* Thomas B. Fordham Institute. Available from https://fordhaminstitute.org/national/commentary/whats-role-teacher-personalized-learning-classroom.

Groarke, J. M., Berry, M., Graham-Wisener, L., McKenna-Plumley, P. E., McGlinchey, E., & Armour, C. (2020). Loneliness in the UK during the COVID-19 pandemic: Cross-sectional results from the COVID-19 psychological wellbeing study. *PLoS One*, *15*(9), e0239698.

Herrington, J., Parker, J., & Boase-Jelinek, D. (2014). Connected authentic learning: Reflection and intentional learning. *Australian Journal of Education*, *58*(1), 23–35. Available from https://doi.org/10.1177/0004944113517830.

Hodges, C., Moore, S., Lockee, B., Trust, T., & Bond, A. (2020). *The difference between emergency remote teaching and online learning.* EDUCAUSE Review. Available from https://er.educause.edu/articles/2020/3/the-difference-between-emergency-remote-teaching-and-online-learning.

Kaminskiene, L., & DeUrraza, M. J. (2020). The flexibility of curriculum for personalised learning. *Society. Integration. Education. Proceedings of the International Scientific Conference*, *3*(0), 266–273. Available from https://doi.org/10.17770/sie2020vol3.5009.

Kim, K. J., & Bonk, C. J. (2006). The future of online teaching and learning in higher education: The survey says. *Educause Quarterly*, 22–30.

Lee, K.H. (2021, October 29). *The educational 'metaverse' is coming.* THE Campus Learn, Share, Connect. Available from https://www.timeshighereducation.com/campus/educational-metaverse-coming.

Li, K. C., & Wong, B. T. M. (2020). Features and trends of personalised learning: A review of journal publications from 2001 to 2018. *Interactive Learning Environments*. Available from https://www.tandfonline.com/doi/abs/10.1080/10494820.2020. 1811735.

Lim, L. A., Dawson, S., Gašević, D., Joksimović, S., Pardo, A., Fudge, A., & Gentili, S. (2021). Students' perceptions of, and emotional responses to, personalised learning analytics-based feedback: An exploratory study of four courses. *Assessment & Evaluation in Higher Education*, *46*(3), 339–359. Available from https://doi.org/10.1080/02602938.2020.1782831.

Maseleno, A., Sabani, N., Huda, M., Ahmad, R., Jasmi, K. A., & Basiron, B. (2018). Demystifying learning analytics in personalised learning. *International Journal of Engineering and Technology*, *7*(3), 1124–1129. Available from https://doi.org/10.14419/ijet.v7i3.9789.

Mpungose, C. (2020). Emergent transition from face-to-face to online learning in a South African University in the context of the Coronavirus pandemic. *Humanities and Social Sciences Communications*, 7. Available from https://doi.org/10.1057/s41599-020-00603-x.

OECD. (2020). *The impact of COVID-19 on student equity and inclusion: Supporting vulnerable students during school closures and school re-openings.* OECD policy responses to coronavirus (COVID-19). Available from https://www.oecd.org/coronavirus/policy-responses/the-impact-of-covid-19-on-student-equity-and-inclusion-supporting-vulnerable-students-during-school-closures-and-school-re-openings-d593b5c8/.

Peng, H., Ma, S., & Spector, J. M. (2019). Personalised adaptive learning: An emerging pedagogical approach enabled by a smart learning environment. *Smart Learning Environments*, *6*(1), 1–14. Available from https://doi.org/10.1186/s40561-019-0089-y.

Suartama, I. K., Setyosari, P., Sulthoni, S., & Ulfa, S. (2020). Development of ubiquitous learning environment based on moodle learning management system. *International Journal of Interactive Mobile Technologies (iJIM)*, *14*, 182–204. Available from https://doi.org/10.3991/ijim.v14i14.11775.

Till, S., & Adam, E. (2021). Hybrid learning and braided technologies for teaching programming in a post-COVID19 world. In: *Digital2k—Conference on teaching, assessment and learning in the digital age.*

Tsai, Y. S., Perrotta, C., & Gašević, D. (2020). Empowering learners with personalised learning approaches? Agency, equity and transparency in the context of learning analytics. *Assessment & Evaluation in Higher Education, 45*(4), 554—567. Available from https://doi.org/10.1080/02602938.2019.1676396.

UNESCO. (2017). *Training tools for curriculum development: Personalised learning.* UNESCO International Bureau of Education. Available from https://unesdoc.unesco.org/ark:/48223/pf0000250057.

Universal Design for Learning. (n.d.). *Center for teaching innovation.* <https://teaching.cornell.edu/teaching-resources/designing-your-course/universal-design-learning> Accessed 22.07.22.

Vygotsky, L. S. (1978). *Mind in society: The development of higher psychological processes.* Cambridge, MA: Harvard University Press.

Zerbini, G., & Merrow, M. (2017). Time to learn: How chronotype impacts education. *Psych Journal, 6*(2). Available from https://doi.org/10.1002/pchj.178.

CHAPTER 12

New online delivery methods beyond the era of the pandemic: varied blended models to meet the COVID-19 challenges

Shravasti Chakravarty

General Management, Xavier School of Management (XLRI), Delhi-NCR, India

The importance of technology in education has a new-found meaning with the advent of the pandemic. Many institutions and organizations have moved away from traditional classroom teaching practices toward a more holistic format by incorporating technological advancements to varying degrees. The most prolific outcome of this change has been in the modality of information transfer since the classroom teacher is no longer limited to the confines of the traditional place of study. They can now reach the students in the comfort of their homes or workplaces, as required. This proves the inroads that blended learning and flipped classroom scenarios have made. In this chapter, I have attempted to capture how the new modality affects the mathematical abilities, information and communication training (ICT) skills, and understanding and using English as a foreign language among "International Foundation Programme" students in Uzbekistan. The chapter starts with a note on the context in which the data has been collected. Next, what is meant by blending is highlighted, followed by an explanation of the half-and-half model of information transfer. Three case studies detailing the blended learning format are presented. The findings of the study are discussed in terms of the advantages of using blended learning, challenges, and possible solutions to using the new system of delivery. Some challenges that need to be explored further are highlighted. The chapter ends with a note on the policy-level changes taking place to propel Uzbekistan further into the domain of digital literacy and beyond.

Digital Teaching, Learning and Assessment
DOI: https://doi.org/10.1016/B978-0-323-95500-3.00014-6

12.1 Background to the study

The year 2019 was a red-letter day for the education system in Uzbekistan: UNICEF stepped in with technical assistance to enable the country to propel itself toward a more holistic approach of education that catered to students irrespective of their learning differences. However, very soon, the pandemic brought a massive disruption in the process as more than 6.2 million learners in the country were affected by it. The biggest challenge faced was the inconsistency in access to effective education, especially in the distance learning mode. As a result of UNICEF's intervention, when schools reopened in December 2020, it was accompanied by reforms in the education system in the means of evaluation and in proper training for teachers to cater to students with different intelligence types. This heralded the onset of various blended learning programs that incorporated sessions in remedial learning. The "International Foundation Programme," run in various universities, has its roots in this step taken by the government with support from UNICEF. These programs aim to identify the areas of academic weakness and provide scaffolding for them. Learners are, therefore, reoriented for long-term educational benefits. In sync with the guidelines laid down by UNICEF, program guidelines were redesigned to include audiovisual materials for distribution at two levels: to the administration and the teachers to make them aware of the required changes and by the teachers themselves in the modality of information transfer carried out within the classroom. This policy had a beneficial effect across the country; 9825 schools (98 percent of schools in the country), expecting to benefit 4,437,262 students across the school years, were influenced by the decision. UNICEF developed and distributed more than 30,000 informational, educational, and communication materials related to remedial education. A total of 10,000 copies of the guidelines to support blended learning were also shared nationwide among teachers and parents. A total of 500 teachers were trained to implement blended learning techniques effectively.

The school education system in Uzbekistan that benefitted from the UNICEF policy continues till grade 11 after which students get into Lyceums. These are special schools in which learners study for a year before proceeding toward universities for their undergraduate studies. English exists as a foreign language in the country and students have access to it only within the confines of the classroom. They are exposed to it as a medium of instruction for the first time only after entering the university, thereby giving it the position of a foreign language. Furthermore, only students who are enrolled in international universities get this exposure. Consequently, most such international universities require students to undergo a year-long bridge course to reduce the gap. In the foreign universities that have established branches in the country, this is known as the International Foundation Studies/Programme. These universities have been started under the direction of the Ministry for Development of Information Technologies and Communications of the Republic of Uzbekistan.

As stated earlier, the International Foundation Studies/Programme prepares students for an undergraduate degree at university. Thus the curriculum is specifically designed for students to attain the correct level of qualifications and skills to propel them forward. A foundation year gives students the academic and English skills, both in terms of content as well as language, to progress toward an undergraduate degree. While there are many permutations and combinations of subjects that students can opt for, the three compulsory subjects include English, mathematics, and ICT.

12.2 Blending the classroom: established norms

The history of blending the classroom can be traced back to the early 1800s when Sir Isaac Pitman used it to propagate the use of the shorthand technique. The meaning of blended then was limited to the notion of taking the teaching−learning process outside the confines of the classroom. However, with the changing trends in modern technology, the term "blending" now refers to a host of ideas ranging from face-to-face (F2F), flipped workshops, webinars, and hybrid learning apps to name a few. The Online Learning Consortium (erstwhile Sloan Consortium) defines it as one that "integrates online with traditional face-to-face class activities in a planned, pedagogically valuable manner" (2014). Therefore merely making the physical class communicative is not enough. It is imperative to ensure the flow of communication even in the blended learning mode. To attain this goal, innovation took place both in the methodology of teaching adopted and in the technology that is used. One such outcome is the learning management system (LMS) that has become a repository for the A to Z of the teaching−learning process in the postpandemic era (Nguyen, 2021). Blended learning techniques, today, therefore, corroborate the principles of effective classroom management as well as communicative teaching−learning. The advantages of blending the classroom include increased teacher−learner interaction, interlearner interaction, improved amount of learner autonomy through self-regulation, and ability to access their higher order thinking skills (HOTS). While the different formats of blending have numerous components, some common characteristics found across the blended format are as follows:

- All the teaching-learning materials are always at the disposal of the learners both in print as well as electronic formats.
- The teacher is no longer the 'sage on the stage,' instead, they essay the role of the 'guide on the side' (King, 1993): they are available to propel students in the right direction. Knowledge is co-created by the teacher and learners in sync.
- The channels of communication between the teacher and learner extend beyond the duration of the session and the locale of the classroom. It takes place both in a synchronous and asynchronous manner according to the convenience of both stakeholders.

(adapted from Bonk & Graham, 2006; Watson, 2008)

As discussed earlier, even before the onset of the pandemic, different kinds of blending have been followed the world over for making classrooms learner-centric: flipping is one of them. This flipped classroom ranges from the standard flipped model where the teacher assigns homework to the faux-flip model in which videos are shown in class while the teacher goes around attending to individual student's needs thereby, saving time. Thus blending the sessions enables learners to plan and organize their learning more effectively by increasing the flexibility of the knowledge dissemination process. Consequently, learners now access materials at their own pace, thereby, increasing their level of independence and motivation. This leads to higher learner autonomy which in turn increases creativity among learners by making them adept at using HOTS. It encourages them to develop metacognitive awareness. The efficiency of the education system also increases since learners can better identify their learning needs. The onus of knowledge dissemination is no longer the sole responsibility of the teacher but the prerogative of the learners themselves. The teacher, therefore, becomes an assistant to the learner during the process of knowledge transaction (Zhelnova, 2006).

So far, we have looked at the concept of blending and flipping the classroom. In the next section, the half-and-half model of blending and flipping the classroom that was adopted by an international university will be explained. Then, the different kinds of blending that were adopted by specific subject teachers will be highlighted.

12.3 The half-and-half model

In keeping with the directives of the government, the international private university that I was teaching at also adopted the blended learning format to ensure that the education process continued uninterruptedly. The total strength of students was 160 for the academic year 2020−21. Each class comprised 40 students in accordance with the directives of the Ministry of Education, Uzbekistan. Therefore the first step was to divide the students into four sections. During the nonpandemic years, all students of a particular section attended the physical classes together. However, in keeping with the Ministry of Health directives for COVID safe protocols, each section was subdivided into two groups: A and B. Each week, student−teacher in-class interaction was carried out between Monday and Thursday. On Days 1 and 3, group A students attended the class in person and group B students joined in using Microsoft Teams (MS Teams). On Days 2 and 4, students from group B attended the F2F class, and group A students attended it online. This schedule was maintained across the semester. Every two weeks the students were made to change their groups to facilitate the experience of interacting with the maximum number of students. The groups remained constant across the three subjects that the students were studying as part of their curriculum. This format of systematically grouping the students was identified to maintain parity as the half-and-half model.

As discussed earlier (Section 12.1), the academic level of the students was at par with the internationally recognized plus two levels: both in terms of age (in most cases) and years of formal academic exposure. Therefore the sessions were planned to last 55 min. This was longer than the average 45 min duration that lessons in school last and slightly shorter than the hour-long sessions that a typical undergraduate class runs for. A total of 5 min were officially set aside for marking attendance and the actual classes lasted 50 min. An unwritten rule was to ensure a 50−50 student−teacher talking time. However, this rule could not be implemented when following the half-and-half model of classroom instruction since it was sometimes difficult to get the students who were attending the sessions online to speak up. Consequently, the majority of the students' talking time was utilized by those attending the sessions in the F2F mode. While this standard format was adopted by the university at the policy level, individual teachers had the autonomy to design their classes and implement the components of blending and flipping classrooms based on their individual preferences, teaching styles, and the subject in which instruction was being provided.

In this research, I have used the case study methodology for data presentation since the information was collected from a small group of participants from one private university in Uzbekistan. This qualitative descriptive research involves data collection through participant and direct observations, interviews, protocols, tests, examinations of records, and collections of writing samples. The narrative accounts of the participants themselves also form a part of the data. Such research is grounded within a specific context and the focus of this methodology is on exploring and describing the phenomenon being researched. It is the preferred method when there is little control over the events which are based on real-time scenarios. Similar to the suggestions made by Berkenkotter, Huckin, and Ackerman (1988) (Becker et al., 1994−2022), this study exemplifies a critical instance case study since the data were collected from hybrid classrooms to explore the research problem in greater detail. Adhering to the norms of the methodology data was collected across an academic year from teachers teaching across the curriculum, and the learners by using classroom observation, questionnaires, and semistructured interviews.

In the next segment, a detailed description of the course content across the three subjects (mathematics, ICT skills, and English) is elucidated. This is followed by a description of the classroom processes. Each case study ends with a sample task used during the blended learning session.

12.4 Case 1: the English class

12.4.1 Components of the syllabus

To restate, English is present in the Uzbek context as a foreign language (Introduction). Kapustin (2007) states that especially in the context of foreign language learning, blended learning instruction needs to be both instrumental and meaningful specifically in engineering universities such as the present site for data collection. Blended learning needs to be focused, and the teacher should be at the helm of things. However, it should vie toward making the learners independent in terms of the use of the target language. Therefore, in keeping with the suggestions made by Bondarev and Bakulev (2012), this course focuses on all four English communication skills—reading, writing, listening, and speaking leading to the undergraduate degree. The syllabus followed here is in keeping with the requirements of the IELTS exam; it is the symbolic rite of academic passage among aspirants of study abroad programs. A high IELTS score is essential for securing better jobs both nationally and in international organizations. Some of the components of the English syllabus include grammatical aspects like idioms and phrases, foreign words loaned from other languages, homophones and homographs, onomatopoeic words, and functions like using maps and giving directions, understanding paralinguistic features, introducing oneself, using small talk, using paralinguistic features to one's advantage, reading on different areas, understanding, and deciphering academic reading pertaining to different subjects, writing different types of letters and essays.

12.4.2 Classroom processes

The typical English class could be clearly demarcated into the presentation, practice, and production model of information transfer. It started with a recapitulation of the previous lesson. The teacher used review questions and pop quiz techniques based on the lesson already completed. Toward the beginning of the academic semester, the questions would incorporate only the information disseminated in the previous class. However, with the progression of the session, the first segment turned into a revision of the syllabus covered until that point. The half-and-half model proved handy during this stage of the lesson plan. Quizzes were set on MS Teams. These were accessible for online and F2F groups synchronously. Using technology helped to save valuable time that would otherwise be spent in sharing the handout and evaluating the responses. It freed time to discuss the results and explain the mistakes made. This phase lasted around 7 min of class time. The next step comprised introducing the topic for the day. Depending on the lesson, pretask Socratic questions were used extensively to create interest among learners. This developed their higher order and out-of-the-box thinking skills. Once the session moved toward the topic, the teacher started her instruction and explanation of it. The presentation of information usually lasted 20 min. The next 15 min comprised an activity to make the students practice the task and clarify their doubts. The usual format for this was individual work leading to pair work and group work, eventually culminating into a whole class activity. Like the classroom groups, MS Teams breakout rooms were created that enabled the students to work in smaller units on the given task. Then the teacher led the students to the production stage of the session. Here students worked individually using the concepts introduced in the session. This lasted 7 min. The last 5 min were for recapitulating the lesson, clarifying further doubts, and assigning work for the subsequent session.

12.4.3 Sample task from the English class

Following is an example of a task that was taken up in the blended English class. Fig. 12.1 is a snapshot of the extension of the blended lesson. After the initial instructions on asking questions for interviewing people in the online class, students were given hands-on practice the following day in the classroom. The lesson was then taken forward to the production stage when they interviewed foreigners in the places of tourist interest in Tashkent. The production stage was video recorded and uploaded on the LMS for future reference (A video sample can be accessed on the following link: https://www.facebook.com/shravasti/videos/1463015487432363). Using Facebook to showcase the work was inspired by the findings of Özmen & Atıcı (2014,a,b). The teacher also provided feedback and assessed the learners on their performance during the hands-on activity. Thus the tenets to improving the delivery system of knowledge in the postpandemic era that UNICEF is vying for in Uzbekistan were also adhered to by the teacher of this course.

12.5 Case 2: the information and communication training class

12.5.1 Components of the syllabus

The educational environment that makes use of electronic resources and other technical means to augment the teaching—learning process is known

Figure 12.1 Excursion based on the lesson "Developing interview skills."

as the ICT class. Once a novelty associated with informatizing environments, it is now synonymous with modern pedagogical techniques. It is instrumental in making the notions of blended learning and flipped classrooms a reality especially, as a fallout of the COVID-19 pandemic (Magdaminkhodjaevna, Payzieva, Shaumarova, & Nagmatova, 2020). The syllabus for the course comprises making the students acquainted with the theoretical knowledge of the basics of computer hardware and software; office automation, including editing and word processing; creating excel sheets and tables; and making PowerPoint presentations. Learners are introduced to various social media platforms, management tools, measurement and reporting techniques, and concepts of online advertising. A segment of the syllabus also deals with the concept of the World Wide Web, basic tags, HTML elements, and web designing tools such as Dreamweaver, Fireworks, Firefox Developer, and Photoshop. The last section of the syllabus introduces artificial intelligence, data analysis, blockchain, virtual reality, augmented reality, machine learning, the Internet of things, robotic process automation, and business intelligence. The practical component of the subject requires learners to apply all the aforementioned concepts and create word documents, excel sheets, presentations, creating Facebook and Twitter channels, creating basic HTML pages that are linked and populated with text and images.

12.5.2 Classroom processes

The ICT sessions focus on providing learners with hands-on experience in using technology. This is important since, in alignment with the developmental policy of the country at the ministry level, Uzbekistan is turning into the next IT hub of central. Forbes magazine reports

> Their government has spent a small fortune training IT workers, too, in hopes it can now pitch itself to Silicon Valley as an outsource partner. The tech talent is there. A lot of it is Russian anyway. And the English language skills are there.
>
> (Rapoza, 2022)

In the site for data collection, the ICT classes were conducted in computer laboratories. All labs are fitted with a whiteboard on one face of the wall which is visible across the room. The teacher's desk is equipped with a master computer that is connected to all the other machines over an intranet monitoring system. Fig. 12.2 is a screenshot of a video lesson that is uploaded on the LMS for the learners to access at their convenience. Learners go through the lesson before the session. In class, the teacher

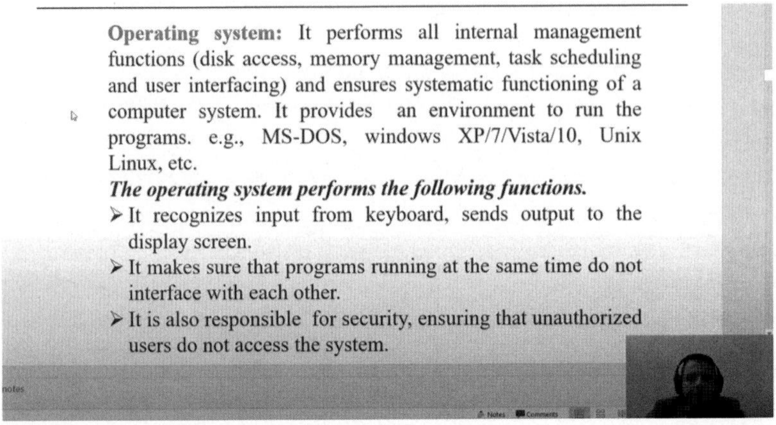

Figure 12.2 ICT video lesson based on "Different operating systems." *ICT,* Information and communication training.

provides practical experience in the computer laboratory. Any other difficulties faced in understanding the lesson are clarified by the teacher during the session.

12.5.3 Sample task from the information and communication training class

The teacher used a twofold process to monitor learner progress: students were expected to respond to theoretical questions, and as the practical component, they performed simple computer operations such as creating files and folders, storing data on excel sheets, and making videos using the software preloaded in the systems. Fig. 12.3 is a sample of the assignment leading to formative assessment.

12.6 Case 3: the mathematics class

12.6.1 Components of the syllabus

The mathematics syllabus was predominantly a revision of the components that learners were exposed to in the lyceums. This was necessitated by the loss of academic rigor because of the onset of COVID-19. Furthermore, most students learnt the concepts in their first language: Russian or Uzbek. However, now they needed to familiarize themselves with the English equivalents of the keywords to become on par with other undergraduate university students at the international university.

Student's Name: _____   Enrolment No.: _____

Assignment Title/Description:

> - Compare primary memory to secondary memory. Why do we need RAM and other secondary storage devices?
> - What is software? What are the different types of software? Discuss high-level and low-level programming languages. Why do we need them? Provide examples.
> - What are the common characteristics of an IP Address?
> - Describe URL address and Email address?

Assignment Objective:

> Students should be able to understand and analyze the information from module 1. Basic understanding of computer systems and its components is expected to be achieved.

Module and Topic(s) Covered:

> **Module I: Hardware and Software Concepts**
> History of Computers, Processing Devices, Memory Devices, Input and Output Devices, Storage Devices (Primary & Secondary). Software – Types of software. Introduction of Internet, IP address, URLs & Email address, Internet Applications (Email, Video Conferencing, Instant Messaging)

Figure 12.3 Assignment based on Module 1 of the ICT syllabus. *ICT*, Information and communication training.

The syllabus thus comprised set theory, functions: Cartesian product of sets, relations, pictorial diagrams, domains, real-valued functions, different types of functions, trigonometric functions, subtraction and transformation formulae, matrices, determinants, and system of linear equations (Cramer's rule) trigonometry, functions, derivatives of a function, derivatives of trigonometric functions, indefinite integral, and theorem of calculus.

12.6.2 Classroom processes

For implementing the half-and-half model of blended learning, the mathematics teacher encountered numerous issues such as (1) difficulty in explaining the subject without F2F interaction; (2) tracking students' homework and assignments in real time; and (3) evaluating their knowledge across the semester. In the semistructured interview that was conducted, he said:

Monitoring students' thinking is the main barrier to online math education. One day I allowed all the students to unmute during the discussion and question time. It was a catastrophe. Toddlers sobbing, family members conversing, and even a little boy telling all about his new dress-up outfit could all be heard. I had to reconsider how I delivered the information and how I wanted the students to respond. Without interaction, I can't imagine taking math class effectively. (T3)

To overcome these challenges, he used the flipped classroom method wherein he prerecorded the lesson and uploaded it onto the LMS. A sample problem accompanied the theoretical explanation. Learners went through the problem and solved the practice questions. Next, during the class, students were required to send back their solved responses on the "Telegram" mobile app since that required less Internet bandwidth. The teacher would invite some students to turn on their cameras and explain the solution to the rest of the class. He stepped in to scaffold the lesson only when required. To ensure optimum classroom interaction and put into practice the tenets of formative assessment practices as earmarked by UNICEF and Ministry of Education policy (2021), marks were allotted for classroom participation.

12.6.3 Sample task from the mathematics class

Fig. 12.4 is a sample of the text shared by the teacher before class. This was accompanied by an audio explanation of the solution.

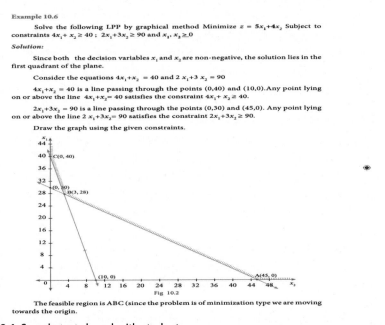

Figure 12.4 Sample text shared with students.

12.7 Results and discussion

The incorporation of blended learning techniques using the half-and-half model posited numerous benefits for the teaching—learning process at the data collection site. However, there were certain challenges that the instructors faced when using the blended learning modality for classroom interaction. In this section, I will highlight these varied experiences along with the solutions that were arrived at by the teachers teaching the course.

12.7.1 Using different digital tools simultaneously

The most consistent experience that the different instructors on the courses shared was their experience of using a multitude of digital technology to ensure a seamless blended learning experience for the learners. For catering to the needs of the online students, all the teachers went live on MS Teams during every session. The laptop was placed facing the teacher on the teacher's desk, sometimes elevated to adjust to the level of the smart board. This ensured that both groups were able to view the lesson. Using the digital platform allowed the lesson to be recorded, thereby enabling students to access the explanation asynchronously. This was especially useful for clarifying doubts during the end-semester exams: over and above the inputs from the teacher, they had ready access to the explanations provided. This resulted in making everyone tech-savvy which in turn is a direct contribution to nation-building practice (UNICEF, 2021).

12.7.2 Interaction with other learners

Another interesting outcome of blending the lessons in the half-and-half format was the familiarity that developed among learners of a specific group. The smaller yet consistent groups enabled many introverted learners to open up sooner and express themselves during the sessions. Also, interacting from behind the screen initially acted as a buffer, a safe haven of sorts. Eventually, it became easier for such learners to speak freely when they met in class. Since the groups remained constant across the three subjects throughout the semester, learners became aware of the learning styles of their group members and could work in unison on the assignments and group projects that formed a part of the formative assessment systems. Case study 1 is an example of this positive effect of blending the classroom.

12.7.3 Access to the resources

The next advantage of blending the classrooms by flipping them was the ease of availability of the resources. Most teachers uploaded prerecorded explanations of difficult concepts on the LMS: students had unlimited access to those, thereby creating multiple rounds of explanation. After that as well, they could get their doubts clarified in class. The availability of knowledge in this manner eased the learning process. In this way the learning gap that often exists among students was reduced considerably, in turn making optimal utilization of the limited session time. Case studies 2 and 3 are examples of these benefits of using the half-and-half blended learning model.

Every coin has two sides. Similarly, blended learning has its challenges too. Some of those encountered at the data collection site are presented below along with the measures taken by the teachers to overcome them.

12.7.4 Movement of the teacher in the classroom

Many teachers are in the habit of walking around the classroom while teaching. This is a good practice for classroom management and has the added benefit of making leaners feel more included even though they may be seated toward the back of the class. However, during the blended learning sessions, to be visible to the online students, this movement was restricted. This sometimes resulted in lesser involvement of the at-risk students sitting in the class.

The problem created on account of technology was also countered by using another digital platform: every time the teacher performed an action, especially when teaching nonverbal communication, she asked one of the students to record the segment and send the video to the "Telegram" group of the section. This ensures that the students had synchronous access to the demonstration even when the teacher moved away from the direct view of the camera.

12.7.5 Greater involvement of online learners

Another problem that was encountered by the teacher was the ability to monitor the given task—especially for the online group.

The solution to this problem was also arrived at by making use of the "Telegram" group: just as the teacher shared her video, the students were asked to share their written responses on the group which was then publicly accessed in the classroom by the teacher. The teacher accessed the "Telegram" desktop app and opened the responses sent by the students. The laptop was always connected to the smart board and screen-sharing options were activated therefore ensuring that both the F2F and online groups were able to view the content simultaneously. The responses were then discussed as a whole class activity with consent from the student. This garnered an atmosphere of being in a mutually inclusive shared safe space for all.

12.7.6 Limited exposure to learners

Using the half-and-half blended format led to students interacting with fewer learners. In some cases, this was beneficial; however, it impacted their social and professional skills when interacting with different students. This problem was seldom encountered in the traditional classroom since teachers had the liberty to create different groups in every session. This posed a problem for students in the digital age, especially on account of the pandemic since interactions and attendance to the offline classes were strictly monitored on account of governmental strictures.

The solution to this problem that many teachers arrived at was to merge students from groups A and B in a manner that during any given session half, the group attended the online session and the other half was in class. In this way, during group work, teachers were able to ensure continuity of interaction among both sets of learners. This also made the online students feel included during the in-class activity.

12.7.7 Motivating students

Across the three compulsory subjects, teachers identified the issue of procrastination among learners specifically when they attended the online session. Numerous reasons were responsible for this which included but were not limited to technological challenges that Akçayır, and Akçayır. (2018) highlight in their study. These include students residing in remote areas, frequent power disruptions, and low bandwidth that the country has: especially in the outskirts of Tashkent city.

As discussed earlier, to motivate them, teachers often took to sharing the material beforehand to ensure asynchronous learning. Reminders for classes were uploaded to the LMS every day in sync with the suggestion made in the study conducted by Davis and Abbitt (2013).

12.7.8 Aversion to new technology

Another related difficulty encountered by the teaching fraternity was students' lack of technological literacy and poor time management skills. Studies (Chen, Yang, & Hsiao, 2016) show that often students are immune to accepting new ways of learning since they are intimidated by technology. Coupled with this is the wide array of online LMS options that confuse the already baffled students even more (Prasad, Maag, Redestowitz, & Hoe, 2018). Therefore blending the classroom posed challenges for the teachers.

The compulsory ICT course was the solution to this problem wherein students got a first-hand experience of using technology to aid in the process of their academic endeavors; the ICT teacher provided support at the absolute basic level.

So far, we have looked at the positives of using the blended learning format, followed by identifying certain challenges to which solutions were found by the teachers themselves. However, some problematic scenarios emerged when blending the lessons to which solutions are elusive. Some such instances are discussed next.

12.7.9 Mode of instruction

While most of the problems encountered could be solved by the ingenuity of the teachers during the blended learning sessions, the mathematics teacher posed a unique problem. He believed that instruction in the subject required direct F2F live interaction and dialog between teacher and students. This echoed the concerns raised by other practitioners and was not always possible in the online blended format (Rasheed et al., 2020). Further, his teaching style necessitated a physical blackboard to explain the steps and formulae in real time. He referred that students watch him carefully while listening to the running commentary to understand the hidden concepts. Often, on account of technological challenges problems were encountered in this stage of the lesson. This further hampered the teacher's ability to read the students' facial expressions and clear doubts instantly.

12.7.10 In-class practices

Similar to the findings of a study conducted earlier (Ocak, 2011) teachers also stated that a single F2F in-classroom lesson took almost twice the time to prepare than the online class. There was bare minimum interaction from the learners. Therefore, sometimes, it appeared that online classes were easier than offline classes for teachers. They believed that the syllabus can be completed within a short period in an online class. They surmised that students need writing practice (paper and pen) to understand mathematics effectively but there is no role for paper and pen during an online class. This carries into the offline session wherein students often attend the sessions without "something to write on and something to write with." Consequently, such learners struggle while appearing for the mathematics examination.

To counter these two issues raised by the practitioners themselves, research needs to be conducted. This can focus on the methodology of teaching, teacher autonomy, and using appropriate technology to overcome challenges.

12.8 Conclusion

The different formats of blending the sessions that teachers adapted to suit their teaching needs are evident from an analysis of the method of delivery of lessons. The half-and-half model of blended learning that is followed in the private university that forms the site for data collection of the present study is unique in terms of the method of delivery of content. Teachers have the autonomy to carry out their sessions based on the requirements of the subject they teach. However, to minimize the learning gaps among students, a higher component of formative assessment will be more effective than the summative assessment measures that are more convenient and useful in the traditional classroom. The quality and quantity of feedback provided to the learners should be enhanced to enable learners to better identify their learning goals. Emphasis should also be laid on remedial lessons especially those that are made available in the blended format. To make the process easier, UNICEF (2021) is now engaged in developing guides to help teachers transition into a more inclusive, blended learning curriculum across the education system of Uzbekistan. These are being adapted by most international universities in the country.

The chapter highlighted the education system found in Uzbekistan. This was followed by an overview of the different kinds of blended learning that have been identified over time. The half-and-half model of blended learning that is followed at a private international university in Uzbekistan has been described. Detailed information about the variety of blending found across the core subjects taught at the university has been presented in-depth. Some of the difficulties identified in the blended learning contexts and their possible solutions have been highlighted in the discussion section. The chapter ends with an overview of the steps being taken at the policy level to engineer changes in the modality of online education delivery methods in the aftermath of the pandemic.

Conflict of interest

I have no conflicts of interest to disclose.

Acknowledgment

I take this opportunity to thank my former colleagues Dr. Supriya Banerjee, Mr. Azimjon Rasulovich, Dr. Pranav Shrivastav, and Dr. S. Priyan. This chapter would not have seen the light of day without their valuable contributions. Correspondence concerning this chapter should be addressed to Shravasti Chakravarty, General Management, XLRI Delhi-NCR, Jhajjar, Haryana, India.

References

Akçayır, G., & Akçayır, M. (2018). The flipped classroom: A review of its advantages and challenges. *Computers & Education, 126,* 334−345.

Berkenkotter, C., Huckin, T. N., & Ackerman, J. (1988). Conventions, conversations, and the writer: Case study of a student in a rhetoric Ph.D. Program. *Research in the Teaching of English, 22,* 9−44.

Bondarev, M. G. & Bakulev, A. V. (2012). Fundamental principles of andragogy as the basic principles of the modern concept of language training in an engineering university. In: *Collection of articles on the materials of the II international scientific and practical conference.* TTI, SFU, pp. 67−72.

Bonk C. J. & Graham C. R. (2006). *Handbook of blended learning: Global perspectives, local designs.* San Francisco, CA: Pfeiffer Publishing.

Becker, Bronwyn, Dawson, Patrick, Devine, Karen, Hannum, Carla, Hill, Steve, Leydens, Jon, ... Palmquist, Mike (1994−2022). *Case studies. The WAC clearinghouse.* Colorado State University Available at. Available from https://wac.colostate.edu/resources/writing/guides/.

Chen, S. C., Yang, S. J., & Hsiao, C. C. (2016). Exploring student perceptions, learning outcome and gender differences in a flipped mathematics course. *British Journal of Educational Technology, 47*(6), 1096−1112.

Davis, D. R., & Abbitt, J. T. (2013). An investigation of the impact of an intervention to reduce academic procrastination using short message service (SMS) technology. *The Journal of Interactive Online Learning, 12*(3).

Kapustin, Yu. I. (2007). *Pedagogical and organizational conditions for the effective combination of full-time education and the use of distance education technologies* (PhD dissertation). Russia: Moscow State University.

King, A. (1993). From sage on the stage to guide on the side. *College Teaching, 41*(1), 30—35.

Magdaminkhodjaevna, N. M., Payzieva, R. A., Shaumarova, N. S., & Nagmatova, M. N. (2020). Effective combination of different teaching methods, teaching models and technologies in blended learning. *Psychology and Education, 57*(8), 589—595.

Nguyen, N. (2021). A study on satisfaction of users towards learning management system at International University — Vietnam National University HCMC. *Asia Pacific Management Review, 26*(4), 186—196.

Ocak, M. A. (2011). Why are faculty members not teaching blended courses? Insights from faculty members. *Computers and Education, 56*(3), 689—699. Available from https://doi.org/10.1016/j.compedu.2010.10.011.

Online Learning Consortium. (2014). <https://onlinelearningconsortium.org/news_item/the-sloan-consortium-changes-name-to-online-learning-consortium/> Accessed 12.10.22.

Özmen, B., & Atıcı, B. (2014a). The effects of social networking sites in distance learning on learners' academic achievements. *European Journal of Open, Distance and E-Learning, 17*(2), 61—75.

Özmen, B., & Atıcı, B. (2014b). Learners' views regarding the use of social networking sites in distance learning. *The International Review of Research in Open and Distributed Learning, 15*(4).

Prasad, P. W. C., Maag, A., Redestowitz, M., & Hoe, L. S. (2018). Unfamiliar technology: Reaction of international students to blended learning. *Computers and Education, 122*, 92—103.

Rapoza, K. (2022). *Techies from Russia, Belarus, Find Solace in Uzbekistan. Can they attract western outsourcers?* Forbes. <https://www.forbes.com/sites/kenrapoza/2022/07/03/techies-from-russia-belarus-find-solace-in-uzbekistan-can-they-attract-western-outsourcers/?sh = 1f0f71357bb2> Accessed 29.07.22.

Rasheed, R. A., Kamsin, A., & Abdullah, N. A. (2020). Challenges in the online component of blended learning: A systematic review. *Computers and Education, 144*(103701).

UNICEF Education Case Study: Uzbekistan. (2021). <https://www.unicef.org/media/107911/file/Curriculum%20reform%20to%20meet%20the%20individual%20needs%20of%20students%20(Uzbekistan).pdf> Accessed 09.10.22.

Watson, J. (2008). Blended learning: The convergence of online and face-to-face education. *North American Council for Online Learning*, 16.

Zhelnova, E. (2006). *"The 8 stages of blended learning: A review of the article "Missed Steps" by Darlene Painter, Training & Development magazine, July 2006"* [Electronic resource]. Available from http://www.obs.ru/interest/publ/?thread = 57.

CHAPTER 13

Digital teaching and learning: the future of ophthalmology education

Tony Succar[1,2], Virginia A. Lee[3], Hilary Beaver[3] and Andrew G. Lee[3,4,5,6,7]

[1]Massachusetts Eye and Ear, Harvard Medical School, Boston, MA, United States
[2]Department of Ophthalmology, Faculty of Medicine and Health, The University of Sydney, Sydney, Australia
[3]Department of Ophthalmology, Blanton Eye Institute, Methodist Hospital, Houston, TX, United States
[4]Departments of Ophthalmology, Neurology, and Neurosurgery, Weill Cornell Medicine, New York, NY, United States
[5]Department of Ophthalmology, University of Texas Medical Branch, Galveston, TX, United States
[6]Department of Ophthalmology, University of Texas MD Anderson Cancer Center, Houston, TX, United States
[7]Department of Ophthalmology, University of Iowa Hospitals and Clinics, Iowa City, IA, United States

13.1 Introduction

The rapid and exciting advances in digital technology have advanced the delivery of medical education in ophthalmology. The benefits of e-learning are well documented in the literature in terms of increased accessibility to education, efficacy of delivery, cost-effectiveness, learner flexibility, and interactivity (Sinclair, Kable, & Levett-Jones, 2015). Additional benefits include decreased travel time for both educators and learners, subsequent elimination of travel expenses, and enhanced outreach opportunities unrestrained by cost or geographic distance (Al-Khaled et al., 2022; Lim & Lee, 2020).

In light of the COVID-19 pandemic, medical education experienced abrupt disruptions as medical students were temporarily removed from patient contact and social distancing measures were put in place among students and staff. Teaching took place remotely as components of the medical curriculum were migrated online, and students completed virtual clerkships, and assessments and took part in novel online electives. Thus while the pandemic and its variants negatively impacted the delivery of ophthalmology graduate medical education with strict restrictions placed on face-to-face interactions and onsite education, it also provided a force to drive digital transformation for teaching ophthalmology. In response to the pandemic, several educational strategies were implemented with modified curricula in ophthalmology as outlined in a recent review (Succar, Beaver, & Lee, 2021). The pandemic demonstrated multiple benefits of online learning, as well as its necessity in an interconnected global learning environment (Al-Khaled et al., 2022). Many of the tools that educators relied heavily on during the pandemic for continued learning, for example, videoconferencing and sharing of imaging via web-based platforms, were already present before the global lockdown but were utilized more frequently and with a larger scope during the pandemic (Al-Khaled et al., 2022). This larger community utilizing online education technology allowed for increased access to resources and lectures, adding to the expertise and discussion. It will be beneficial to continue those aspects of online learning that have demonstrated added value to in-person education (Al-Khaled et al., 2022).

One worldwide cross-sectional survey-based study evaluated the implementation of tele-education (e-learning) in ophthalmology during the COVID-19 pandemic and compared training systems in several institutions before the pandemic. This study demonstrated that there was a statistically significant increase in the use of virtual training in ophthalmology during the COVID-19 pandemic era (Chatziralli, Ventura, & Touhami, 2020). Specifically, before the pandemic, approximately 48% of participants did not use e-learning modalities, while about 60% reported that their institutions did not provide facilities nor appropriate software for e-learning. During the pandemic, there was a switch to distance learning, with Zoom being the most preferred platform for synchronous tele-education, supporting a large number of participants and giving the ability to share content. Availability of e-learning facilities and the academic character of institutions were found to be associated with the use tele-education (Chatziralli et al., 2020). However, it should be noted that although most institutions managed to maintain the teaching hours for theoretical training at a satisfactory level, the surgical training was dramatically decreased during the pandemic due to the suspension of elective surgeries in most of countries. The lack of practical training was probably the driving force behind the more negative perspectives on the quality of training during the pandemic (Chatziralli et al., 2020). Increased experiences with tele-education had positive impacts on survey respondents for their future role in ophthalmology curricula. Approximately 83% of participants believed that the experience gained during the pandemic regarding tele-education will be used for future training in ophthalmology, with about 30% perceiving no barriers in adopting e-learning (Chatziralli et al., 2020).

A recent review of the current modalities for digital learning in ophthalmology was conducted and included the following key findings (Al-Khaled et al., 2022):

1. Web-based programs were shown to be effective for acquiring knowledge in ophthalmology (Al-Khaled et al., 2022).

2. Virtual ophthalmic training curricula, web-based society meetings, and online examinations served a role as additions to in-person activities and may replace certain activities in the future (Al-Khaled et al., 2022).

3. Telesurgery and surgical simulators, including artificial intelligence (AI)-based systems, have been developed for ophthalmologists and trainees (Al-Khaled et al., 2022).

4. There is a need for trainee education in the operation of teleophthalmology programs (Al-Khaled et al., 2022).

Based on these findings, the following recommendations were made (Al-Khaled et al., 2022):

1. Problem-based learning via online platforms was shown to statistically improve diagnostic competency of users. Remote learning via commercially available telecommunication technology, without the incorporation of a flipped classroom approach, provides passive learning at most. Interactive programs, whether virtually or in-person, should be the mainstay of education during training (Al-Khaled et al., 2022).

2. Surgical, as well as clinical simulators allow for a hands-on experience to repeatedly practice diagnostic and interventional techniques. Automated feedback allows users to immediately identify and reform their performance. This may reduce the cost to the system, as well as complications in patient care, in the long term (Al-Khaled et al., 2022).

In addition, there has been a recent shift toward the use of online resources to obtain clinical and surgical knowledge. This technology provides opportunities to improve the quality and accessibility of educational materials across international boundaries and to those in rural environments. As virtual methods continue to have a more prominent presence in medical training, curricula must be established for virtual medical school clerkships, simulated surgical training, teleophthalmology, and AI programs. These methods have the potential to reach ophthalmology trainees around the world to supplement their training experiences and strengthen their skillsets (Al-Khaled et al., 2022). Web-based curricula for ophthalmology clerkships in medical school have been developed and commonly involve using Zoom (Zoom Video Communications, Inc., San Jose, CA) to virtually meet with mentors to discuss the material and reference YouTube videos to provide step-by-step instruction on the use of examination instruments such as the direct ophthalmoscope (Al-Khaled et al., 2022).

In response to the challenges faced by the pandemic, this chapter describes two revolutionary digital teaching platforms which we developed and successfully implemented to help mitigate the difficulties encountered in educating medical, undergraduate, and pregraduate students (Succar, Lee, Karmonik, & Lee, 2022; Wendt, Abdullah, & Barrett, 2021).

The first digital teaching program which we developed was for pregraduate and undergraduate students to enhance interest and to increase academic exposure to basic clinical, research, and educational domains in ophthalmology (Succar et al., 2022). The second program which we developed was a virtual ophthalmology rotation (VOR) to allow medical students to continue their ophthalmic education remotely in both completely virtual and hybrid learning environments; to conduct and present research projects from home; and to network with faculty and prepare for residency applications via Internet platforms (Wendt et al., 2021). Each of these programs will now be discussed in greater detail.

13.1.1 Digital teaching program one: an academic ophthalmology curriculum for preprofessional students

An academic curriculum model for pregraduate and undergraduate students was developed by our group to enhance interest and to increase academic exposure to basic clinical, research, and educational domains in ophthalmology (Succar et al., 2022). The Houston Methodist Hospital (HMH) Academic Institute offers a 10-week summer student research program that matches HMH faculty members with students from multiple levels (e.g., high school, college undergraduates, and medical school). Students undergo prerequisite virtual training; attend weekly didactic lectures given by mentors, invited speakers, and other local leaders; shadow health-care providers in active clinical settings as observers; participate in active research projects; present at local conferences; and are encouraged to eventually publish their work. In the realm of graduate medical education, students leveraged a preexisting online digital platform (neuro-ophthalmology with Dr. Andrew G. Lee) on YouTube and created a novel and unique Web series (EyeWonder) aimed at a peer (high school and college level) target audience. These short videos provide learners with easy-to-follow, short, videos on selected and requested topics in a YouTube format (Succar et al., 2022). The HMH internship consists of three programs: the Summer Undergraduate Research Internship (for undergraduate students interested in translational research), the Rosenberg Summer Surgical Fellowship (for undergraduate students interested in surgical shadowing), and the Summer Internship Program for high schoolers (for high school students over the age of 16 interested in translational research). We describe the structured curriculum from our first Summer Internship Program for high schoolers in ophthalmology (Succar et al., 2022).

The participants learn about the doctor—patient relationship, medical professionalism, systems-based practice, communication and interpersonal skills, and practice-based learning. They participated in daily "peer-to-peer" and "peer-to-near-peer" teaching and learning activities. Examples of "peer-to-peer" teaching and learning include fellows answering questions during the Socratic method learning sessions and thus indirectly teaching other fellows and residents about correct or incorrect answers in real time (Succar et al., 2022). Other examples include resident presentations at ophthalmology grand rounds (peer-to-peer) under the supervision of the faculty member who acts as moderator for the session but did not necessarily create the content for the case presentation or discussion slides. In contrast, "peer-to-near-peer" includes residents and medical students teaching our HMH high school interns about topics that these "peers" and "near-peers" actually have more experience and expertise (e.g., how to dress professionally in the clinic, how to introduce yourself to patients as a nonphysician). Peer-to-near-peer teaching and learning also frees the faculty member from lower level educational tasks (Succar et al., 2022).

The learners contextualized specific clinical cases and learned valuable presentation communication skills by presenting at the Departmental Weekly Ophthalmology Grand Rounds Conference. In the domain of clinical research, the learners completed institutional review board (IRB) applications for two research projects and completed 4—5 h of learning modules on research ethics (e.g., Helsinki) and research protections for human subjects (Succar et al., 2022). The learners participated in virtual and real meetings about active research projects in neuro-ophthalmology, including "Artificial Intelligence to Detect Optic Disc Abnormalities by Hand-held Fundus Photography"; "Trends in anti-VEGF use in ophthalmology during the COVID-19 pandemic"; and "Negative Pressure Goggles to Assess Spontaneous Venous Pulsations." Learners participated in medical research projects and contributed alongside medical students to coauthor several

EyeWiki articles [American Academy of Ophthalmology (AAO)]. The learners authored EyeWiki on the following topics: polyarteritis nodosa, painful tic convulsif, and bilingual aphasia (Succar et al., 2022).

Academic medicine relies heavily upon the "apprenticeship model" for clinical training. High school students interested in medicine as a career have few opportunities for real-world exposure to the medical field. An introduction to all three legs of the tripartite mission of an academic medical center, medical education, clinical and biomedical research, and patient care, is critical to understanding the nature and workings of medicine (Succar et al., 2022). Over the course of the HMH Summer Research Internship, we constructed and implemented a program that incorporated direct clinical experience, the basics of clinical research, and novel platforms for virtual peer-to-peer medical education. The structured curriculum included hands-on experience with the IRB application process for research, creating EyeWiki articles and developing a YouTube educational platform (Succar et al., 2022). This structured, academic curriculum is specifically aimed at pregraduate and undergraduate students interested in potential careers in ophthalmology to create and sustain a pipeline of potential candidates starting at an earlier point in training. Our program benefits from direct participation and financial support from a major academic medical center (HMH) in a large urban environment (Texas Medical Center, Houston, TX) (Succar et al., 2022).

This program benefits from an existing robust infrastructure within a designated HMH Summer Research Internship program that is specifically designed for preprofessional students at multiple levels (high school, undergraduate, and graduate) (Succar et al., 2022). The stated goal of the program is to create a sustainable pipeline of academically minded students to continue with multiyear summer participation at higher levels of training to recruit high-quality applicants to ophthalmology as a career downstream. We hope that our model might be helpful to other like-minded and interested ophthalmology programs and eventually generalizable to other programs in our local medical center and also across the country (Succar et al., 2022).

13.1.2 Digital teaching program two: a virtual COVID-19 ophthalmology rotation

A VOR was developed by our group to allow medical students to continue their ophthalmic education remotely in both completely virtual and hybrid learning environments; to conduct and present research projects from home; and to network with faculty and prepare for residency applications via Internet platforms (Wendt et al., 2021). This novel virtual elective designed for medical students provided high-quality exposure to ophthalmology despite the challenges posed by the pandemic. The elective includes a virtual curriculum that teaches the core anatomy, diseases, and concepts of neuro-ophthalmology; opportunities to study unique cases through morning reports, research opportunities, and grand rounds presentations; clinical experience via patient encounters; and assessments in the form of oral and written examinations (Wendt et al., 2021). Each of these domains will now be discussed.

13.2 Clinical knowledge

The virtual curriculum is the foundation of our neuro-ophthalmology elective, developed to cover most of the level-1 topics established by the North American Neuro-ophthalmology Society (NANOS) Curriculum on the Neuro-Ophthalmology Virtual Education Library (NOVEL) (Wendt et al., 2021). These level-1 topics are recommended by NANOS for medical students and cover a variety of foundational topics in neuro-ophthalmology. The core components of the virtual elective include morning report, grand rounds, research experience, patient encounters, and oral examination (Wendt et al., 2021).

The level-1 topics are divided across the twenty days of the elective in a progressive manner, so that concepts build upon each other. Students will learn relevant physiology and anatomy in week 1, followed by clinical signs and symptoms in week 2. In week 3 and 4, students learn a variety of diseases relevant to neuro-ophthalmology (Wendt et al., 2021). In addition to the core components of the elective, students are provided links to EyeWiki articles and YouTube didactic videos by an expert source corresponding to each topic. Finally, a brief multiple-choice exam will be administered at the end of each week to assess students' mastery of the coursework and to provide feedback for course improvements (Wendt et al., 2021).

13.3 Morning report

Students are expected to attend and participate in a virtual neuro-ophthalmology morning report daily during the elective. Morning reports, like grand rounds, are relatively well suited to a virtual format and can be transitioned to a videoconference platform (Wendt et al., 2021). Through involvement in a virtual morning report, students receive similar value as attending in-person rounds, such as improving their clinical and basic science knowledge, developing clinical decision-making, and learning how to present cases. We have implemented a number of strategies to facilitate student participation in virtual morning reports (Wendt et al., 2021). Students are expected to respond to questions throughout the report from the attending physician. If there are many medical students in the elective, a select number may be assigned each day as "active" participants who are designated to answer the morning's questions. Alternatively, students may alternate in a queue to answer questions. To further aid student engagement, at each morning report, one student is expected to send via email the night before and then provide a very brief presentation on a relevant topic (Wendt et al., 2021). This "med-student minute" is an effective way to reinforce material from the virtual curriculum while adding clinical context. Additionally, a weekly student-run morning report session is facilitated by a medical student, providing an opportunity to lead and present a case to an audience. Students can evaluate the effectiveness of each of these methods via a postelective survey. We anticipate that video-based morning reports and conferences could be used in the future. The virtual nature of these conferences allows for increased medical student attendance due to decreased travel constraints and the ability for students at a different institution to attend (Wendt et al., 2021).

13.4 Grand rounds

An enrolled student is required to present at least one case during the elective at the institution's neuro-ophthalmology grand rounds via videoconference. The student should confer with fellows and/or the attending physician to find an appropriate case to present, cumulating in a formal slide deck presentation (Wendt et al., 2021). The presentation should include an introduction slide with a "focused stem" summary, relevant past medical and ocular history, physical examination including images where possible, representative imaging studies and pathology (if relevant), diagnostic procedures, and a "take-home message" summary slide (Wendt et al., 2021).

13.5 Research experience

The elective also facilitates student exploration of neuro-ophthalmology research. Students are expected to compose an article to be published on the AAO EyeWiki website, write a case report based on a unique patient encounter during the elective, and/or contribute to a neuro-ophthalmology book chapter (Wendt et al., 2021). The research component of the elective is well suited to a virtual format (Wendt et al., 2021).

13.6 Patient encounters

Patient encounters are a challenging component of a course to conduct virtually, and where possible, in-person encounters are preferred. In this elective, some students may still participate in in-person patient encounters, in which they accompany and assist an attending physician during a history and physical examination (Wendt et al., 2021). The patient examination room is situated in a manner that follows social distancing guidelines by using floor "X" stickers to mark appropriate safe distances from others. When these accommodations are not possible, such as for students enrolling in the elective as an away rotation, virtual encounters will be provided via video chat on tablets mounted on rolling stands. Through this methodology, students will observe the entirety of the patient encounter and may be taught and questioned by the attending in a similar manner to in-person students (Wendt et al., 2021). Though virtual students cannot carry out any of the physical examination, they may be asked to observe and evaluate signs which the attending physician elicits. Virtual students may also interact with the patient by asking follow-up questions after the history. Both virtual and in-person students may be asked to construct a differential diagnosis, describe a management plan, or write notes following these patient encounters (Wendt et al., 2021).

13.7 Oral examination

An oral examination was administered virtually during the last week of the elective by the course director. The purpose of the oral examination is to assess the student's ability to communicate their acquired knowledge in neuro-ophthalmology in a well-organized, succinct manner. The oral examination will serve as an opportunity for the student to demonstrate their ability to develop a differential diagnosis and make clinical decisions about diagnostic testing and treatments for common neuro-ophthalmic conditions (Wendt et al., 2021). A typical oral examination will involve a case selected by the course director. The case will be presented to the student by the course director, followed by prompted questions by the course director to facilitate discussion. The student will be expected to answer questions relating to patient history, examination findings, differential diagnosis, and treatments. The student will be graded based on their ability to demonstrate proper clinical approach and reasoning, rather than their memorization skills. Our oral examination format is modeled after the American Board of Ophthalmology's oral examination for graduating ophthalmology residents seeking board certification (Wendt et al., 2021).

Virtual teaching conferences, didactics, and clinical experiences are innovative tools that are transforming medical education and will likely play a larger role in the future as educational technologies continue to develop (Wendt et al., 2021). The virtual nature of these experiences is useful to foster community between students and faculty at different academic institutions. This elective format is easily adaptable to other ophthalmology subspecialties and provides utility to other institutions navigating this new virtual environment (Wendt et al., 2021).

13.8 Conclusions

The COVID-19 pandemic resulted in active curricular innovation and transformation, with the advancement of ophthalmology medical education. Implementation of these novel digital teaching programs developed by our group have provided students with high-quality exposure to ophthalmology education, clinical care, and research despite the challenges posed by COVID-19. Digital teaching and learning will represent a significant portion of ophthalmology education in the future. While the COVID-19 pandemic presented an unprecedented challenge for education, positive outcomes of the pandemic included wider access to online educational platforms globally. In ophthalmology, lectures were rapidly converted from "face-to-face" to online video conferences, using several platforms, such as Zoom, Skype for business, and Cisco Webex, which ensured the safety of students and the efficiency of the educational activities (Chatziralli et al., 2020). Ophthalmology webinars have also been described effective teaching tools in enhancing knowledge acquisition and active participation (Mayorga, Bekerman, & Palis, 2014). To ensure enhanced learning experiences, it is critical that any new innovations should be competency-based, which has been shown to be more effective than content-based curricula (Succar, McCluskey, & Grigg, 2017). Future research should focus on evaluating the impact of this curricular transformation to virtual learning environments on student performances, as well as implementing longitudinal assessment strategies for clinical competence in workplace-based practice. Embracing these changes will enable training programs to rise to the challenges of COVID-19 and ensure the provision of high-standard education for the future (Chatziralli et al., 2020). These educational innovations will persist even after the end of the pandemic because they have proven that face-to-face learning is not required for all aspects of the ophthalmology curricula (Succar et al., 2021). Optimizing teaching available through evidence-based digital education will lead to graduates who are highly trained in eye examination skills, resulting in improved patient eye care through timely diagnosis, referrals, and treatment.

References

Al-Khaled, T., Acaba-Berrocal, L., Cole, E., Ting, D. S. W., Chiang, M. F., & Chan, R. V. P. (2022). Digital education in ophthalmology. *Asia-Pacific Journal of Ophthalmology*, *11*(3), 267−272.

Chatziralli, I., Ventura, C. V., Touhami, S., et al. (2020). Transforming ophthalmic education into virtual learning during COVID-19 pandemic: A global perspective. *Eye (London)*, *35*, 1459−1466.

Lim, A. S., & Lee, S. W. H. (2020). Is technology enhanced learning cost-effective to improve skills?: The Monash objective structured clinical examination virtual experience. *Simulation in Healthcare*. Available from https://doi.org/10.1097/sih.0000000000000526.

Mayorga, E. P., Bekerman, J. G., & Palis, A. G. (2014). Webinar software: A tool for developing more effective lectures (online or in-person). *Middle East African Journal of Ophthalmology*, *21*, 123−127.

Sinclair, P., Kable, A., & Levett-Jones, T. (2015). *JBI Database of Systematic Reviews and Implementation Reports*, *13*(1), 52−64, Jan.

Succar, T., Beaver, H. A., & Lee, A. G. (2021). Impact of COVID-19 pandemic on ophthalmology medical student teaching: Educational innovations, challenges, and future directions. *Survey of Ophthalmology*, *S0039-6257*(21), 00098−00099.

Succar, T., McCluskey, P., & Grigg, J. (2017). Enhancing medical student education by implementing a competency-based ophthalmology curriculum. *Asia-Pacific Journal of Ophthalmology*, *6*(01), 59−63.

Succar, T., Lee, V., Karmonik, C., & Lee, A. (2022). An academic ophthalmology curriculum as a model for introducing preprofessional students to careers in ophthalmology. *Journal of Academic Ophthalmology*, *14*, e 45−e51. Available from https://doi.org/10.1055/s-0042-1743413.

Wendt, S., Abdullah, Z., Barrett, S., et al. (2021). A virtual COVID-19 ophthalmology rotation. *Survey of Ophthalmology*, *66*(02), 354−361.

Further reading

Kaup, S., Jain, R., Shivalli, S., et al. (2020). Sustaining academics during COVID-19 pandemic: The role of online teaching-learning. *Indian Journal of Ophthalmology*, *68*, 1220−1221. Available from https://doi.org/10.4103/ijo.IJO_1241_20.

CHAPTER 14

"Online education which connects" adopting technology to support feminist pedagogy—a reflective case study

Upasana Gitanjali Singh
University of KwaZulu-Natal, Durban, South Africa

14.1 Introduction

The COVID-19 pandemic has resulted in a major involuntary shift to online teaching, learning, and assessment. This pandemic has propelled the adoption of technology in the classroom. As a digital practitioner prior to COVID-19, I have been passionate about introducing technology for assessment purposes in the courses I taught. Thus, when the forced move to the online space was introduced by the pandemic, I began to search for more meaningful ways of student interaction in the digital world. As Maboloch (2020, p.3) outlines "online learning is not just about the use of technology … the set of values people have will influence online learning." The knowledge creation process expected of a student is more essential in the digital space. Often, the adoption of technology in education simply means "dumping" content onto a digital platform. However, once the material is made available to the students, there needs to be methods adopted by the educator to ensure that the student and the educator can engage in an environment that fosters critical thinking. One such method includes testing both the analytical and critical skills of students. This research will add to the body of literature on how technology can be implemented to facilitate the adoption of feminist pedagogy and foster engagement, collaboration and a sense of responsibility among students.

14.2 Background

14.2.1 The South African context

Access to South African higher education was deemed as a privilege during the apartheid era. Postapartheid, Higher Education Institutions (HEIs) opened their doors to all race groups in South Africa. Funding opportunities for the low-income groups were made more freely available and in recent years higher education, in particular, at public institutions, has become far more accessible. Despite its accessibility, higher education at South African public institutions is often plagued with violent student disruptions which, over the past 5 years, have become almost a biannual event. So much so that we, as lecturers, factor in extra time for disrupted lectures and assessments, when planning for the semester. This has been one of the leading reasons for a drive to adopt blended learning approaches, in particular at the traditionally face-to-face public HEIs in South Africa. Then came COVID-19 which literally pushed us all to fully online, rather than the blended approach. So, while "saving the academic year" was the buzzword in the early stages of the pandemic, each HEI, with varying resources, infrastructure, and planning, embarked on their own journey to complete the academic year online. This brought about many challenges from both the academic and student perspectives—lack of knowledge, access issues, lack of technology, social isolation, lack of support, and lack of study space (Singh, Proches, Blewett, & Leask, 2020). The pandemic highlighted and exacerbated the digital divide in higher education, as I experienced myself with my students. The development of the digiFEM framework (Molele, 2020) is my proposed model to reduce the gender digital divide in the South African context, based on my interaction with female academics and businesswomen during this pandemic.

14.3 My positionality

Rosso (2021, p.424) posits that the compassionate teaching strategies used to help students learn amid the pandemic inherently undercut academic standards and that these teaching strategies were not previously needed, during the so-called "normal time" that preceded the pandemic. However, my belief is that prior to and post the pandemic, students benefit the most from "learner-centered" teaching strategies that encompass collaboration, engagement, and reflection, which I attempt to include in my classroom irrespective of the mode of delivery. Being a female, from a nonwhite race, in a male-dominated discipline, created in me a passion to empower females and encourage them to adopt STEM (science, technology, engineering, and mathematics) careers. Thus during my interaction with students in their early years of entry to higher education, I spent time sharing my journey and encouraging them by enlightening them on the possible career paths within the technical fields.

14.4 Literature

Cooper (2015, p.48) believes, "traditional teaching in higher education is largely didactic," which resulted in a significant number of the youth being forced to live "wasted lives." Giroux (2020) outlines that while pedagogy, in general, offers educators a set of theoretical tools that aid in promoting "both reason and freedom" in the learning process, critical pedagogy is not simply applying a generic "set of strategies and skills" to aid teaching, but rather it is dependent on the "context, students, communities, and available resources." Young (2020) adds that the goal of critical pedagogy "is to encourage students to think about the way they are being taught and how they, as students, fit into a broader social and cultural context." Thus if applied correctly, critical pedagogy should enable students to not only find a job, but also develop in them the ability to form their own "beliefs, practices, and social relations"(Giroux, 2020). Stommel (2019) as cited in Young (2020) highlights that we need to think about who our students are, think about the sort of communities that they live in, think about them as more than just bodies in a classroom, but think about how they actually engage with their world. And it is really focused on not only having them learn knowledge in a classroom, but also learn how to read their world and be participants in the communities that they live in. Shrewsbury (1993) expands this definition, stating that "feminist pedagogy is engaged teaching and learning. . . engaging with materials, engaging with each other and continually reflecting." Chick and Hassel (2009) ask some pertinent questions of feminist pedagogy in the online classroom—"Do students communicate with each other regularly? Do they collaborate? Do they learn from each other? How does the instructor relate to students? Do students have a voice? Do students take a leadership role in the classroom?" Stommel (2019) further introduces the concept of critical digital pedagogy, asking educators to reflect on what their classroom looks like when engaging students online. Thus educators could question how the digital interface changes the way that students relate to the educator, as well as to one another; if the digital space limits our ability to find agency; and whether the digital environment enhances student engagement? Jeyaraj (2020) found that students were in agreement that successful critical pedagogy includes "participatory forms of learning such as the co-construction of knowledge" especially where educators are not the sole expert of the "authorized knowledge." The COVID-19 pandemic has posed a challenge to educators, policy makers, and institutions worldwide and forced them to rethink how human beings interact with each other, and more generally, "how human beings are affected by, a much wider set of biological and technical conditions" (Maboloch, 2020). In particular, Maboloch (2020) suggested that educators have had to address "the underlying vulnerabilities and evaluate the virus as a threat to academic experiences and access to a fair education," and in some ways reevaluate the role of pedagogy in the teaching process. With the sudden shift to online learning during the COVID-19 pandemic, Maboloch (2020) suggests that technology can facilitate the personal interactions and engagement between educators and students while still providing meaningful experiences. To facilitate more engaging and innovative adoption of technology to facilitate greater interaction and collaboration for students, the ASSET Framework highlights the importance of digital pedagogy as an essential skill which academics need to develop/embrace in the shift to the digital space (Singh, 2020b). One of the key skills highlighted in this framework is that of digital pedagogy, which in simple terms refers to knowing which technology tool is best suited to the content being taught and/or assessed.

In the South African context, most research on critical pedagogy seems to be focused on school education. As Cooper (2016) outlines that the implementation of critical pedagogy should encourage students to reflect on their "sociopolitical contexts, catalyzing transformative actions and, in turn, changing oppressive structural conditions." This is the need of the hour in South Africa, "a country that has suffered from widespread human rights violations and is currently one of the most unequal societies worldwide" (Cooper, 2016). However, he adds that the "South African educational research remains fixated on explanations for South African students' poor performance in, for example, literacy and numeracy tests ... rather than aiming to develop young people who possess the skills necessary to participate in a modern knowledge economy and, simultaneously, produce self-reflexive citizens committed to attaining social justice." Perumal (2014) highlights, "the material tensions of enacting critical pedagogy in disadvantaged South African educational contexts are rendered all the more poignant when teachers themselves emanate from and function within contexts that are debilitating." This was precisely the situation highlighted during the sudden transition to the online space during the COVID-19 pandemic. Singh & Nair (2020) highlighted the plight of academics in higher education in Africa who clearly outlined the lack of access to connectivity, devices, and conducive environments to support their teaching online, with the added stress of the nonideal forced work-from-home situation. The academics also expressed their students' lack of access to connectivity, devices, conducive environments, and knowledge of online learning environments/platforms as another concern.

I am of the strong belief that every student in the classroom needs to be an active participant. The days of the lecturer being the "sage on the stage" are over, where students are no longer simply passive consumers of knowledge. I believe that the classroom should foster mutual respect, consider social justice and equity, develop a shared responsibility for learning, and promote empathy for each other.

14.5 My journey—an exploration of my teaching through the lens of critical feminist pedagogy

As a senior lecturer in the discipline of Information Systems and Technology (IST) at a public HEI in Durban, South Africa, who has attempted to introduce technology into her classroom over the past 5 years, I believe that one of the positive effects of the pandemic we face is the propelling of the move to digital teaching, assessment, and learning. I was forced to rethink and redesign a third-year module from a fully face-to-face mode of delivery to a fully online mode of delivery, in IST which focuses on Information Technology (IT) Consulting and IT Strategy for our group of final-year B. Com IT students, who are specializing in IT. Since this was the first offering in a fully online mode, I felt it necessary to critically reflect on my experiences with this shift.

14.6 Methodology

As a digital practitioner, particularly in online assessment, prior to COVID-19, I was keen to introduce innovative and engaging methods of adopting technology into her traditionally face-to-face classroom to engage with students in the medium which resonates with the techno-savvy student generation. While it was understandably difficult to embrace this change fully for technology-related modules, particularly those which required practical lab sessions, I chose to experiment with adopting feminist pedagogy principles in a soft-skill IT module with topics on IT Strategy and IT Consulting. Thus the class that formed the basis for this reflective case study is a small final-year IT module, at a South African public university, with 34 students registered.

As is typical of any South African HE classroom, the student diversity was prominent with respect to race, social, economic, and digital capital. The majority of the students were male, which clearly highlights the gender digital divide present in STEM subjects in South Africa (Singh, 2020a).

Based on my own personal beliefs, as described in the section earlier, the delivery of the content for this module was developed using a variety of methods to promote engagement, collaboration, and communication, in this "new norm" of online learning. My online classroom was developed to facilitate engaged teaching, encourage engaged learning, promote continued reflection, recognize that students are no longer simply passive consumers of knowledge, foster mutual respect, develop a shared responsibility for learning, and promote empathy for each other.

Through informal feedback from students, the researcher aimed to understand the extent to which some of the questions posed by Chick and Hassel (2009) were addressed in her attempt to "connect" students in the online environment, through the implementation of technology to support feminist pedagogical principles.

The first engagement that I had with the students was aimed at understanding who the students in the classroom were, especially since this was the first time I was interacting with this group of students in 2020. While some aspects of the diversity can be ascertained from the registration list, it is essential for that online connection, to have a "face to a name." Through an online discussion forum created on the prescribed learning management system (LMS), Moodle, students were invited to introduce themselves and post a picture of themselves. Students responded well to this activity, with some students using their wit, humor, and creativity in introducing themselves.

This activity was created prior to the commencement of the module in an attempt to understand the diversity present in the class prior to the first "live" online lecture session.

The challenge faced with this activity was that due to the extension of registration for 2 weeks into the semester, there were many students who registered late and did not participate in this discussion activity.

So additional methods were adopted to understand who the students were in the classroom. At the beginning of the first online session, I requested students to introduce themselves briefly and switch their videos on if they were comfortable doing so. To make the students more comfortable, I ensured that my video was always on, so that students could connect visually to her. It must be noted that while some students participated in live introductions, many others were "silent."

I needed to find a method that students would be comfortable with in making visual contact with them, so that I could "see" them as I would typically in a face-to-face session. In the first two sessions of the semester, I spent time letting the students get to know me, interacting with each other, and giving them the space to freely discuss, engage, and socialize during the online sessions. Further, while the sessions were recorded, for students who may have been unable to attend, prior to uploading these recordings, I ensured that the social talk and nonacademic discussions were trimmed. Thus over the period of 2 weeks, I was able to get students to engage and build trust in the community which was set up. The final activity proposed for recognizing the diversity in the classroom worked like a charm. Youngsters today are typically fixated with selfies and photographs, so, in week 3 of the semester, I invited students to a "Class of 2020" group photo. At this session, we had full attendance, and students were in their highest spirits.

The above activities made me realize that while technology is an enabler in the online classroom, there is no "one-size-fits-all" approach. Multiple activities have to be experimented with to engage students fully. An early reflection indicated that the adoption of online discussion forums for nonacademic, social interaction helped to reduce the social isolation that students were facing, which was exacerbated by the pandemic. As Aderibigbe, Dias, and Abraham (2021) suggest that students commit to and engage in online discussions better when there is an effort by faculty to support and provide guidance of the learning platform, as well as provide exciting topics. I held weekly discussions with students on various nonacademic contents, ranging from soccer results to their comfort and challenges with the online move, to create a socially comfortable atmosphere across our computer screens. I also provided guidance during the early stages of the modules for students on an individual basis, especially for those who faced challenges with understanding the Zoom and Moodle environments (as these were prescribed by our institution). Baber (2021) highlights, "social interaction has a positive significant impact on the effectiveness of online learning."

14.7 Analysis and discussion

Informal feedback gathered from students at the end of the topic indicated, as depicted in Fig. 14.1, that the biggest factor that affected their learning was the "economic" diversity. Gender and race diversity seemed to have a minimal effect on their learning. Likewise, the race, gender, and economic status of the lecturer had no effect on their learning. However, an interesting comment made by one student highlighted the reality of the gender digital divide. "I enjoyed having a female lecturer after many other modules had male lecturers."

I acknowledge that based on student feedback, in the next iteration of the module, ways of promoting students' power and authority in the online classroom would need to be explored. Judy and Eleanor (2020) suggest that taking cognizance of the student voice in the classroom speaks with the notion that "non-participation in regular life ... contributes to young people feeling isolated or marginalised." On the contrary, they add that "being consulted and listened to implies acceptance and membership of a community or society which promotes 'the feeling of an increased sense of belonging' and generates 'a greater positivity about learning'." It was encouraging to note, being the first attempt at a fully online delivery, under unprecedented circumstances, 50% of the students felt challenged to explore something new.

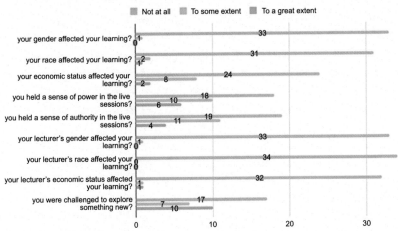

To what extent did you feel that...

Figure 14.1 Students' feedback on the role of diversity and authority.

To promote engaged learning, I invited special local and international experts and practitioners to deliver guest lectures to provide an opportunity for students to engage in meaningful discussions regarding their careers. While this was common practice with me, especially in exit-level modules, during face-to-face classes where local experts often participated, the move to the online space allowed the inclusion of international experts with little effort. Thus not only were students exposed to developments with respect to the module content from a global perspective, but they also had to learn to adapt to different cultures, accents, and consider time zones to accommodate these international guests. Observation of the interactions during these sessions highlighted that students were comfortable asking questions and engaging with industry experts in the online environment, compared to the previous face-to-face sessions. Discussions were centered around not only the content they delivered, but more vibrant conversations about the reality of the work world, career prospects, and future studies advice. One student commented that the component of the module most enjoyable was "the guest speakers and their live video presentations...sharing their experiences and knowledge of the aspects we learn(ed) in the module." It was clear that these guest sessions helped to relate the theory to the practical application in the "real world."

To support engaged teaching, and recognizing that students are no longer simply passive consumers of knowledge, I adopted online breakaway sessions during some of the classes. This further allowed students to take responsibility for their learning, and then reconnect with the group to share their insights on case studies and readings. It was noted that students felt more comfortable to discuss with peers during these smaller group sessions than they were to express their opinions in the larger class group. In the initial few online sessions, I would have to resort to cold calling to get students to engage. As students moved into using breakaway rooms and discussing with their peers in these small groups, they became more confident to speak in the larger group. It was evident that the breakaway sessions helped them reinforce that their thinking was acceptable to the class, and the lecturer.

Fig. 14.2 presents that students were encouraged to take both an active and shared role in the learning process. Majority of the students indicated that in this module, they saw the lecturer's role, as that of a facilitator; the student's role, as one of an active learner; and their classmates' roles, as collaborative learners.

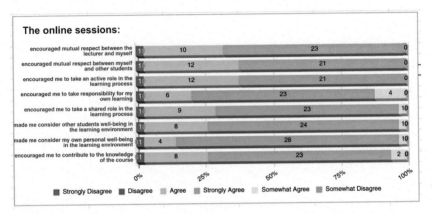

Figure 14.2 Highlights of the online sessions.

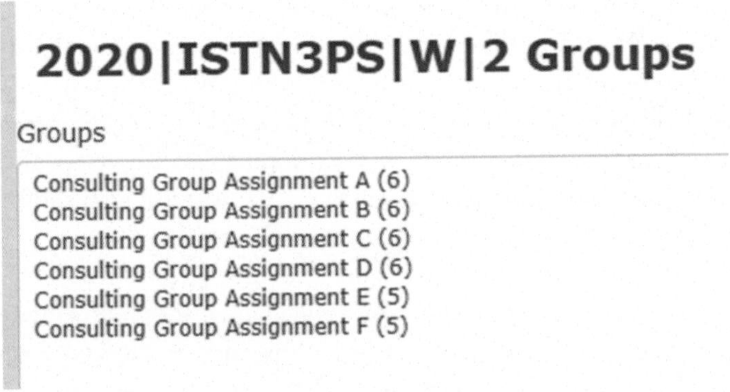

2020|ISTN3PS|W|2 Groups

Groups

Consulting Group Assignment A (6)
Consulting Group Assignment B (6)
Consulting Group Assignment C (6)
Consulting Group Assignment D (6)
Consulting Group Assignment E (5)
Consulting Group Assignment F (5)

Figure 14.3 Automatic student grouping by the LMS. *LMS,* Learning management system.

The implementation of a group assignment with the submission of a written group document, as well as an online presentation component, forced students to engage with, and understand, their fellow students (some of whom they had never met personally). Further, through this assignment, they developed empathy for their fellow classmates with respect to access, technology, and infrastructure limitations. Despite the above challenges, they had to still ensure that the task assigned was completed. The assignment was detailed on the LMS and students were randomly allocated to groups by the LMS (see Fig. 14.3). I chose to use the random allocation method so that students become comfortable with working with team members that are not necessarily known to them previously, as is often the case in the "real world."

The details of the assignment were outlined to students with clear instructions on the LMS (see Fig. 14.4).

Instructions of where to upload the document and how to save the file, together with submission deadlines, were clearly explained. For the presentation component of the assignment, understanding that some students may face technical issues with connection, data access, and electricity interruptions, an allowance was made for some group members to submit prerecorded presentations that other members of the group could play during the presentation. In addition to posting the assignment on the LMS, I directed students to view the details of this assignment through an announcement on the LMS noticeboard (see Fig. 14.5), as well as provided an opportunity for discussion during the live online session.

While I expected there would be difficulties in students locating and communicating with other group members in an online environment,

Assume that you are a group of IT consultants (Groupings created on Moodle, please locate your team members and identify your own group leader).

You are required to identify any SA entity which was affected by the COVID-19 pandemic.

Prepare a 2 page report outlining the following:

1. Briefly describe the following based on the entity's existence prior to the COVID-19 pandemic
   o Business Strategy
   o Organisational Strategy
   o IT Strategy
2. Explain how their IT Strategy changed during the COVID-19 pandemic to support their business and organisational functions, thus ensuring that they survive this pandemic.
3. Outline the recommendations that your consulting practice has to enable them to take advantage of emerging technologies to support their sustainability and profits post the COVID-19 pandemic.

The report should be submitted via the Moodle site as Group Name.pdf (Group A.pdf) by Friday 23rd October 2020 @ 20:00. Groups not adhering to the above instructions will obtain a ZERO for the document submission portion of this assignment.

This assignment contributes 10% towards your Final Module Mark.

A group presentation of this project is to be delivered on Monday 26th October during our live online sessions.

1. Each member of the group is expected to deliver some content for a max of 2mins, with audio and video on (If a member of the group is concerned about network connection, then that contribution may be recorded prior to the session, but it is the responsibility of the group leader that there is a seamless transition between the live and recorded content of the presentation). Note that the entire presentation CANNOT be recorded.

2. The total presentation time allocated is 12 mins, with 3 mins for QnA, per group.

Figure 14.4 Extracts of assignment details.

Assignment details
by Upasana Gitanjali Singh - Thursday, 8 October 2020, 11:19 AM

Please refer to the assignment details in the IS Consulting Section.

We can discuss any queries you have at the end of the session on Monday.

Figure 14.5 Announcement of assignment details.

without any face-to-face contact, there was none of this. Students utilized WhatsApp and email to connect with each other and the presentations made were "informative, well researched, and futuristic," in the words of the external moderator. Some groups went beyond what was expected of them and experimented with the use of PowToon for their presentations,

Welcome
by Upasana Gitanjali Singh - Tuesday, 15 September 2020, 7:53 PM

Dear Students,

Welcome to ISTN3PS.

Our first online session is on Monday 21st September 2020, from 9am to 10.30am on Zoom.

Please register, using the format of StudentNo_Surname (216789349_Singh) to attend your online lectures using the link below:

https://ukzn.zoom.us/meeting/register/tJ0rf-ivrDorG9GfNm6p4WtKxEKD2pMctDKO

After registering, you will receive a confirmation email containing information about joining the meeting.

I look forward to seeing you all on Monday.

Regards,

Dr Upasana Singh

Content for self study
by Upasana Gitanjali Singh - Wednesday, 23 September 2020, 1:57 PM

Dear Students,

You are expected to work through IT Strategy lecture slides Ch1, 2 and 6 this week, in preparation for Monday's interactive live lecture session.

Have a lovely week ahead.

Dr Singh

Reminder: Live session today
by Upasana Gitanjali Singh - Monday, 28 September 2020, 8:28 AM

Dear Students,

A reminder that we have our special guests from KPMG today and they will be including live group sessions, which require both your video and audio to be on.

Please ensure that you have these facilities available, even if its on your mobile phone...And don't forget to change out of your pyjamas.

Zoom login details are the same as last week.

See you @ 9.

Dr Singh

Figure 14.6 Regular communications with students.

while others mastered the use of the remote control feature in Zoom to ensure seamless presentations. Upon reflection, I believe that if students are given the opportunity to work independently of the lecturer, and collaborate with each other, their imagination and creativity blossoms.

Sharing highlights of the student's presentations in an edited 3-min video clip on LinkedIn provided encouragement to the students, and a sense of reward for their dedicated efforts, which was well appreciated.

Regular and informative communication (see Fig. 14.6) assisted in keeping students connected with the lecturer, while clear guidelines on interaction with the lecturer and students helped foster mutual respect.

14.8 Implications

While 2020 has been a year of the unexpected, I believe that it is the year that has provided the greatest impetus to adopting technology in education. Through the above journey, I have learnt from the students in the class; engaged with colleagues, experts, and the Internet for ways to make the online class a more "connected" experience; and enjoyed the experimentation with new tools and methods for engagement, interaction, and collaboration in the online space. While the future face of education is still unknown in the light of the second wave of the pandemic in South Africa, I strongly believe that this pandemic has reshaped HEIs forever, and the compromise is probably going to lie in a blended approach to teaching, learning, and assessment in 2022 and beyond. This pandemic has clearly shown us the power of technology as an enabler, in particular, the ability to create "connection in the online classroom."

References

Aderibigbe, S., Dias, J., & Abraham, M. (2021). *Understanding issues affecting students' commitment to online discussion forums in undergraduate courses*. International Association of Online Engineering. Retrieved from <https://www.learntechlib.org/p/218694/> Accessed 25.01.21.

Baber, H. (2021). "*Social interaction and effectiveness of the online learning − A moderating role of maintaining social distance during the pandemic COVID-19.*" Asian Education and Development Studies Vol. ahead-of-print No. ahead-of-print. Available from <https://doi.org/10.1108/AEDS-09-2020-0209>.

Chick, N., & Hassel, H. (2009). Don't hate me because I'm virtual, Feminist Pedagogy in the Online Classroom *Feminist Teacher*, *19*(3), 195−215. Available from http://www.jstor.org/stable/40546100.

Cooper, C. (2015). Critical pedagogy in higher education. In C. Cooper, S. Gormally, & G. Hughes (Eds.), *Socially just, radical alternatives for education and youth work practice*. London: Palgrave Macmillan. Available from https://doi.org/10.1057/9781137393593_3.

Cooper, A. (2016). 'Youth amplified': Using critical pedagogy to stimulate learning through dialogue at a youth radio show. *Education as Change, 20*(2). Available from http://doi.org/10.17159/1947-9417/2016/732.

Giroux, H. A. (2020). *On critical pedagogy.* Unites States: Bloomsbury Academic. Available from <https://books.google.co.za/books?hl = en&lr = &id = kavFDwAAQBAJ&oi = fnd&pg = PP1&dq = critical + pedagogy&ots = dvZkn1oUXc&sig = H5VRiOTAq-D5NTHFXxXmcu3WTCL8&redir_esc = y#v = onepage&q = critical%20pedagogy&f = false> Accessed 16.12.20.

Jeyaraj, J. (2020). Possibilities for critical pedagogy engagement in higher education: Exploring students' openness and acceptance. *Asia Pacific Education Review, 21*, 27–38, 2020. Available from https://doi.org/10.1007/s12564-019-09605-0.

Judy, P., & Eleanor, H. (2020). *Student pedagogic voice in the literacy classroom: A review.* Research Papers in Education. Available from https://doi.org/10.1080/02671522.2020.1864769.

Maboloch, C. R. (2020). Critical pedagogy in the new normal. *Voices in Bioethics, 6*(2020). Available from. Available from https://www.researchgate.net/publication/343510274_Critical_Pedagogy_in_the_New_Normal.

Molele, C. (2020). *Women in STEM fields: Bridging the gender digital divide in South Africa.* Inside Education. Available from <https://insideeducation.co.za/2020/08/31/women-in-stem-fields-bridging-the-gender-digital-divide-in-south-africa/> Accessed 25.01.22.

Perumal, J. (2014). Enacting critical pedagogy in an emerging South African and urban society democracy: Narratives of pleasure and pain. *Education and Urban Society.* Available from https://doi.org/10.1177/0013124514541466.

Rosso, J. D. (2021). *How loss teaches: Beyond "pandemic pedagogy."* Humanity and Society. Available from https://doi.org/10.1177/0160597620987008.

Shrewsbury, C. (1993). What is feminist pedagogy? *Women's Studies Quarterly, 21*(3/4), 8–16. Available from. Available from http://www.jstor.org/stable/40022001.

Singh, U. G. (2020a). *Women in STEM fields: Bridging the gender digital divide in South Africa.* Available from <https://insideeducation.co.za/2020/08/31/women-in-stem-fields-bridging-the-gender-digital-divide-in-south-africa/> Accessed 16.12. 20.

Singh, U. G. (2020b). *UKZN academic develops framework for online learning.* ASSET© (Academic SkillSET). Available from <https://yiba.co.za/ukzn-academic-develops-framework-for-online-learning-asset-academic-skillset> Accessed 16.12.20.

Singh, U. G., & Nair, C. S. (2020). *Teaching, learning and assessment during the Covid-19 pandemic: An African Perspective,* IGI (accepted for publication).

Singh, U. G., Proches, C. G., Blewett, C., & Leask, C. (2020). *Emergency online learning (EOL) during the COVID-19 pandemic: Postgraduate students' perspectives.* In: digiTAL 2020 conference proceedings. Durban, South Africa.

Young, J. R. (2020). *What is critical digital pedagogy, and why does higher Ed need it?* EduSurge newsletter, June 4 2020. Available from <https://www.edsurge.com/news/2019-06-04-what-is-critical-digital-pedagogy-and-why-does-higher-ed-need-it> Accessed 16.12.20.

Index

Note: Page numbers followed "*f*" and "*t*" refer to figures and tables, respectively.

A

AA. *See* Authentic assessment (AA)
AAGs. *See* Automatic Article Generators (AAGs)
AAO. *See* American Academy of Ophthalmology (AAO)
Academic curriculum model, 244–245
Academic integrity, 163–164
Accessibility, 101
Accounting education program, 185–187
Adapting assessments, 91*t*
Adaptive learning, 31
Adoption, 253, 259
AI. *See* Artificial intelligence (AI)
ALP. *See* Authentic learning pedagogy (ALP)
American Academy of Ophthalmology (AAO), 245–246
Apple Inc, 57–58
  Apple Incorporated, 58
Artificial intelligence (AI), 21–22, 26–28, 166, 243
  applications, 35–38
    artificial intelligence–assisted teaching plan and evaluation, 36–37
    artificial intelligence–assisted tutor, 35–36
    artificial intelligence–powered chatbots, 35
    virtual reality and augmented reality in education, 37–38
  in assessment, 32–34
    online courses using virtual learning environment, 34*f*
    students' online behavior and grading for classroom participation, 33*f*
  decision support system, 27
  deep learning, 28
  in education, 26*f*
  intelligent assistance for education, 28–34

in learning, 31–32
  ESE performance, 31*f*
  test preparation on students' performance, 32*f*
machine learning, 27
reinforcement learning, 27–28
role of artificial intelligence in education, 28–38
in teaching, 29–31
  student's math scores for different teaching styles, 30*f*
Asia-Pacific University Community Engagement Network (APUCEN) regional partner network, 48
Assessment (A), 38
  artificial intelligence in, 32–34
  findings, 131–140
    learning and assessment in higher education institutions, 131–140
    scientific papers on learning and assessment in times of disruption in literature, 132*t*
  innovative formative assessment adopted in higher education institutions, 140
  literature, 123–130
    blended learning and blended assessment and post COVID-19 era, 129–130
    higher education institutions' online assessment, 125–126
    innovative formative assessment adopted during COVID-19 pandemic, 126–127
    online learning and assessment, 123–125
    summative assessment currently adopted and in education sector, 127–129
  methods, 121–122, 126
  online, 179–180

Assessment (A) (*Continued*)
   study, 122−123
   summative assessment currently adopted
      and in higher education institutions,
      140−142
     recommendations, 141−142
   technology, 253
ASSET Framework, 255−256
Augmented reality in education, 37−38
Authentic assessment (AA), 53
   design, 53
Authentic learning pedagogy (ALP), 217
Autoethnography
   approach, 80−81
   reflections, 80−81
Automated homework grading systems,
   181
Automatic Article Generators (AAGs), 40

B
Bachelor of Education (B. Ed), 179−180
Banking education system, 67−68
Big data analytics, 21−22
Birley place
   building, 102−105
   evaluating, 108
   evaluation findings, 109−114
     authentic learning experiences,
      109−110
     digital place-based education,
      110−111
     flexibility and convenience, 112−114
     opportunities for collaboration,
      111−112
   interactive digital placements, 105−107
   interprofessional education, 107−108
Blackboard learning management system,
   166
Blended learning, 25, 123, 152, 221,
   223−224
   approaches, 166
   and blended assessment and post
     COVID-19 era, 129−130
Blending the classroom, 223−224
Bodyswaps platform, 38
Bridge course, 222−223
Business master's program, 81−82

C
Cameras on in Zoom, 52
CARES Act research, 14
CEO Faculty program, 48
Chatbots in education, 35
Clinical educators, 112
Coca Cola company, 57−59
Collaboration, 1, 18, 88−89
   opportunities for, 111−112
Collaborative-learning techniques, 4
Communication, 105, 258, 265
   landscape, 84
   materials, 222
   synchrony, 201−202
Community, 260
Computer laboratories, 162
Computer operations, 230
Computer technology, 151
Computerized adaptive test, 37
Conceptualization, 68−69
Constructivism learning, 165
Content management system, 104−105
Conventional education, 121−122
COVID−19 pandemic, 46, 48, 50, 52−53,
      56−57, 65−66, 79, 99−100,
      121−122, 147, 161, 164, 179,
      190−191, 199, 204, 228−229,
      241−242, 253
   education, 57
   employment and labor law, 57
   health, 56
   innovative formative assessment,
     126−127
   management and leadership, 57
Cramer's rule, 230−231
Creation process, 253
Creativity, 126
Critical digital pedagogy, 67−68
Critical learning processes, 148
Critical pedagogy, 67−68, 256−257
Curricula, 243−244
Customizable technology, 105

D
Data, 29−30, 151
   access, 263
   analysis, 167, 202

collection, 226−227
 and analysis, 167
 methods, 108
 presentation, 186−194, 226
Decision support system (DSS), 26−27
Decision-making, 165, 247−248
 processes, 70−71
Deep learning (DL), 21−22, 26, 28
Demographic data, 186
Dermal wound healing process, 11−12
Design justice, 68−73
 design thinking and, 69−71
 diverse design teams at work, 71−73
 framework, 72−73
Design processes, 68−69
Design Thinking (DT), 66, 69−71
Development course design pedagogy,
 66−73
 critical digital pedagogy, 67−68
 design justice, 68−73
 design thinking and design justice,
 69−71
 diverse design teams at work,
 71−73
 open educational resource, 67
Dialogic process, 148, 155
Diffusing online learning, 50−52
DigiFEM framework, 254
Digital community, 100
Digital delivery methods, 16−18
Digital deprivation, 124
Digital development of prototype of
 innovative technology, 14−15
Digital divide, 2
Digital education, 21−22, 24−25, 40−41,
 151, 250−251
 emerging need for, 24−25
 role of artificial intelligence in education,
 28−38
 strengths, weaknesses, opportunities, and
 challenges, 38−40
 technologies for, 25−28
 artificial intelligence, 26−28
 internet of things, 25
 technology-enhanced learning, 23−24
Digital exams, 162
Digital integrative approach, 17

Digital knowledge acquisition and
 transfer, skill development through,
 13−14
Digital learning, 3, 7−10, 17−18, 25,
 122−123
 digital tool applications in holistic FUEL
 program, 8t
 experiences, 1
 resources, 100
 tools, 3
Digital literacy, 40−41
Digital models, 66−67
Digital online community, 110−111
Digital pedagogy, 66
Digital place-based education, 110−111
Digital platforms, 11, 99
Digital resources, 113
Digital shift, 40
Digital support
 for students during pandemic, 3
 systems, 179−180
Digital teaching
 platforms, 244
 program, 244−247
Digital technologies, 16, 23−24, 68, 95,
 99−101, 147, 241
 for learning, 2
Digital tools, 6−7, 10
 applications in holistic FUEL
 program, 8t
 for student success, 3−4
Digital transformation, 179, 241−242
Digitization process, 65−66
Diverse design teams at work, 71−73
Diversity, 156, 258
 students feedback on role of, 260f
DL. See Deep learning (DL)
Drug Transport and Cancer Treatment, 14
DSL technology, 51
DSS. See Decision support system (DSS)
DT. See Design Thinking (DT)
Dynamic coding, 104−105
Dynamic interaction, 150

E
E-learning, 25, 121, 179−180, 241
E-proctoring tool, 52−53

E-textbooks, 181
  factors influencing adoption of, 190*f*
  features, 188*f*
  pedagogy, 180
    data presentation and discussion,
      186–194
    literature, 180–184
    before pandemic, 186–187
    during pandemic, 187–192
    beyond pandemic, 192–194
    research methodology, 185–186
    theoretical framework, 184–185
ECTs. *See* Education communication
    technologies (ECTs)
EDI. *See* Equity, Diversity, and Inclusivity
    (EDI)
Education, 23–24, 57, 66, 99, 121–122,
    148, 192
  applications of artificial intelligence,
    35–38
  core modules, 187
  intelligent assistance for education,
    28–34
    artificial intelligence in assessment,
      32–34
    artificial intelligence in learning,
      31–32
    artificial intelligence in teaching,
      29–31
    intelligence assistance in teaching,
      learning, and assessment, 29*t*
  role of artificial intelligence in, 28–38
  system, 21–22, 222
  technology, 25
  virtual reality and augmented reality in,
    37–38
Education 4.0, 24–25
Education communication technologies
    (ECTs), 48, 50, 61
Educational environment, 23–24
Educational institutions, 121–122
Educational technologies, 68, 150,
    155–156
Educators, 21–22, 55, 59–61
Electricity, 179–180, 263
Electro-Assisted Wound Healing, 14
Electronic format, 162

Electronic resources, 174, 228–229
Electronic tools, 163
Emergency remote teaching (ERT), 3–4
Emergency remote teaching and learning
    (ERTL), 199–200
Empirical studies, 124–125
Employee selection processes, 37
End-semester exam (ESE), 31
  performance, 31*f*
Endured understanding, 60
  alternative paradigms in online learning
    design, 46
  Apple Inc, 57–58
  Apple Incorporated, 58
  authentic assessment, 53
  Coca Cola company, 57–59
  COVID-19 pandemic, 56–57
  diffusing online learning, 50–52
  endured understanding of learning,
    53–54
  essential questions should inspire
    endured understanding of learning,
      55–56
  of learning in online assessments, 45
  limitations of study, 61
  McTighe and Wiggins test to confirm
    essential question, 54–55
  online learning, 52–53
  recommendations, 59–61
  recommendations, dilemmas, and
    challenges, 59
  United Nations Educational, Scientific,
    and Cultural Organization, 46–48
Environmental concerns, 184–185
Equity, Diversity, and Inclusivity (EDI),
    49–50
ERT. *See* Emergency remote teaching
    (ERT)
ERTL. *See* Emergency remote teaching
    and learning (ERTL)
ESE. *See* End-semester exam (ESE)
Essential questions, 53–54, 59–60
  endured understanding of learning,
    55–56
  McTighe and Wiggins test, 54–55
Evaluative data, 12–13
Examination platforms, 175–176

Experimentation, 265
External partners, 112
Extracurricular research-focused
    program, 4

F

F2F. *See* Face-to-face (F2F)
Face-to-face (F2F), 147, 223−224
    interactions, 79
    interventions, 211
Facilitation, 112−113
Familiarization, 168
Faux-flip model, 224
5G networks, 51
Flexibility, 151, 164, 216
    and convenience, 112−114
Flexible approach, 101, 192
Flexible nature, 112−113
Formative assessments, 126, 149−150, 175
    online, 150−151
    systems, 233
Foundry innovation, 5−6
Foundry model, 7
Foundry Undergraduate Engaged Learners
    program (FUEL program), 1
    digital divide, 2
    digital support for students during
        pandemic, 3
    evaluative analysis, 12−13
    evaluative findings, 13−15
        digital development of prototype of
            innovative technology,
            14−15
        skill development through digital
            knowledge acquisition and transfer,
            13−14
    Holistic FUEL program, 4−12
    implications, 15−17
        innovative delivery approach,
            15−16
        student learning, 16−17
    lasting digital tools for student success,
        3−4
Foundry-guided approach, 7−10
FUEL program. *See* Foundry
    Undergraduate Engaged Learners
    program (FUEL program)

G

Gamifying assessments, 127
Gender digital divide, 258
Geographic isolation, 82
Global learning environment, 241−242
GoI. *See* Government of India (GoI)
Government of India (GoI), 40
Graduate Management Admission Test, 37
Grammarly tool, 21−22
Group management, 104−105

H

Half-and-half model, 224−226
Hattie and Timperley's feedback model,
    148, 152−154
    applying, to hybrid learning
        environments, 154−157
        design considerations, 156−157
        dialog, 155
        individual learning, 156
        learning outcomes, 156
        time and immediacy of response,
            155−156
    examples of feedback questions,
        153−154
        at level of self-regulation, 154
        at personal level, 154
        at process level, 154
        at task level, 153−154
    feed forward, 153
    feed up, 152
    feedback, 153
HE. *See* Higher education (HE)
Health care, 47
    professionals, 101−102
HEIs. *See* Higher education institutions
    (HEIs)
Higher education (HE), 24−25, 99.
    See also Digital education
    implications for future delivery of higher
        education programs, 92−95
Higher education institutions (HEIs),
    23−24, 121, 174, 179, 199
    implications and way forward, 216−217
    learning and assessment in, 131−140
    literature, 201−204
        online learning, 201−202

Higher education institutions (HEIs)
(*Continued*)
   personalized learning, 203–204
online assessment, 125–126
research methodology, 204–207
   ethical considerations, 206–207
   focus groups, 206
   informal WhatsApp chats,
      205–206
   online surveys, 205
   qualitative data analysis, 206
   quantitative data analysis, 206
   YouTube analytics, 204–205
results, 207–215
   student learning, 207–215
student-centric framework for
   personalized learning, 215–216
personalized learning framework for
   higher education, 215*f*
summative assessment currently adopted
   and in, 140–142
Higher order thinking skills (HOTS),
   223–224
HMH. *See* Houston Methodist Hospital
   (HMH)
Holistic approach, 222
Holistic FUEL program, 1, 4–12
   description of program, 6–7
   digital learning focus, 7–10
   foundry innovation, 5–6
   illustrated examples of implementation,
      10–12
      research project example 1, 10–11
      research project example 2, 11
      research project example 3, 11–12
HoloAnatomy, 38
Homographs, 226
Homophones, 226
HOTS. *See* Higher order thinking skills
   (HOTS)
Houston Methodist Hospital (HMH),
   244–245
   Summer Research Internship program,
      246
HREC. *See* Human Research Ethics
   Committee (HREC)
HTML elements, 228–229

Human Research Ethics Committee
   (HREC), 166
Hybrid learning, 152, 223–224, 246–247.
   See also Online learning
   applying Hattie and Timperley's model
      to hybrid learning environments,
      154–157
      design considerations, 156–157
      dialog, 155
      individual learning, 156
      learning outcomes, 156
      time and immediacy of response,
         155–156
   environments, 149, 244
   formative assessment and online
      formative assessment, 149–150
   using formative assessments online,
      150–151
   Hattie and Timperley's feedback model,
      152–154
      examples of three feedback questions,
         153–154
      feed forward, 153
      feed up, 152
      feedback, 153
   key concepts, 151–152
   mode, 126, 129
   need for conceptual framework,
      148–149
   relevant model for implementing online
      formative assessment in ways
      increase self-regulation by learners,
      148
HyFlex
   learning, 130–131
   model, 88–89

I

ICTs. *See* Information and communication
   technologies/training (ICTs)
IHEIs. *See* International higher education
   institutions (IHEIs)
Imagination, 265
IMF. *See* International Monetary Fund
   (IMF)
Industrial Revolution 4.0 (IR4.0), 23–24
Industry 4.0, 21–22, 24–25, 40

Information, 112, 214–215, 227
  techniques, 125
Information and communication
    technologies/training (ICTs),
    23–24, 221
  class, 228–230
    classroom processes, 229–230
    components of syllabus, 228–229
    sample task from information and
      communication training class, 230
  educational tools, 85*t*
  tools, 79
  video lesson based on operating systems,
    230*f*
Information Systems and Technology
    (IST), 257
Information Technology (IT), 257
Innovation, 191
  diffusion, 50–51
  innovation-driven learning platform,
    5–6
Innovative assessment, 80–81
Innovative formative assessment, 123
  adopted COVID-19 pandemic, 126–127
  adopted in higher education institutions,
    140
  tool, 127
Innovative online assessment, 121
Innovative technology, 5–6
  digital development of prototype of,
    14–15
Inspera, 87–88
Institutional review board (IRB), 245–246
Intelligent algorithm, 27
Intelligent tutoring robots (ITR), 36
Intelligent tutoring systems (ITSs), 22–23
Interaction with learners, 233
Interactive digital placements, 105–107
International Foundation Programme,
    221–222
International higher education institutions
    (IHEIs), 45, 52–53
International Monetary Fund (IMF),
    49–50
Internet, 164, 179–180
  access, 183
  connection, 168–169

Internet of things (IoT), 21–22, 25, 201,
    228–229
Interprofessional education (IPE), 107–108
Intranet monitoring system, 229–230
IoT. *See* Internet of things (IoT)
IPE. *See* Interprofessional education (IPE)
IR4.0. *See* Industrial Revolution 4.0
    (IR4.0)
IRB. *See* Institutional review board (IRB)
ISIS. *See* Islamic terrorism (ISIS)
Islamic terrorism (ISIS), 60–61
IST. *See* Information Systems and
    Technology (IST)
IT. *See* Information Technology (IT)
ITR. *See* Intelligent tutoring robots (ITR)
ITSs. *See* Intelligent tutoring systems (ITSs)

K

Klyukanov's approach, 49
Klyukanov's problem questions, 53–54
Knowledge dissemination process, 224

L

Language teachers, 65–66
Laptop, 234–235
Learners, 55, 59–61
  communication skills, 82
  experiences of online exams, 163–164
  flexibility, 241
  learner-centered teaching strategies,
    254–255
Learning (L), 38
  approach, 217
  artificial intelligence in, 31–32
  endured understanding, 53–54
    of learning in online assessments, 45
  engagement, 180
  environment, 16
  essential questions inspire endured
    understanding of, 55–56
  experiences, 101
  outcomes, 156
  pedagogy, 201
  process, 68, 153, 234, 255–256
  resources, 201, 210
  technologies, 99

Learning management system (LMS), 90,
    166, 188–189, 200, 223–224, 258
Linear equations, 230–231
Linear process, 153
LMS. *See* Learning management system
    (LMS)
Lockdown regulations, 121–122

M

m-learning. *See* Mobile learning (m-
    learning)
Machine learning (ML), 21–22, 26–27
Material resources, 130
McTighe test to confirm essential question,
    54–55
MDGs. *See* Millennium Development
    Goals (MDGs)
Meaning-making processes, 92–93
Med-student minute, 247–248
Medical education, 241
Medical programs, 166
Medicine, 166
Memorization skills, 249–250
Memory, 149
Microsoft Teams (MS Teams), 11, 225
Mid-semester exam (MSE), 31
Millennium Development Goals (MDGs),
    46–47
Mitigation, 163–164
ML. *See* Machine learning (ML)
Mobile learning (m-learning), 201
MobyMax tool, 21–22
Modes, 69
Moodle Learning Management Systems,
    186–187
MS Teams. *See* Microsoft Teams (MS
    Teams)
MSE. *See* Mid-semester exam (MSE)

N

NANOS. *See* North American Neuro-
    ophthalmology Society (NANOS)
National Council for Accreditation of
    Teacher Education (NCATE), 125
Network connectivity, 188–189
Network coverage, 193

Neuro-Ophthalmology Virtual Education
    Library (NOVEL), 247
New normal, implications for
    context of the programs, 81–83
    implications for future delivery of higher
        education programs, 92–95
    preparation and delivery challenges,
        83–87
    reflections on delivering classes
        during COVID-19 lockdowns,
        87–90
    reshaping assessments, 90–92
New Zealand (NZ), 79–80
North American Neuro-ophthalmology
    Society (NANOS), 247
NOVEL. *See* Neuro-Ophthalmology
    Virtual Education Library
    (NOVEL)

O

OERs. *See* Open educational resources
    (OERs)
Online assessments, 122–125, 128, 161,
    165, 201–202
    endured understanding of learning in, 45
Online clinical assessment, 173–174
Online delivery methods, 1, 3–4, 15–16
    blending the classroom, 223–224
    English class, 226–228
        classroom processes, 227
        components of syllabus, 226–227
        sample task from English class, 228
    half-and-half model, 225–226
    information and communication training
        class, 228–230
        classroom processes, 229–230
        components of syllabus, 228–229
        sample task from information and
            communication training class, 230
    mathematics class, 230–232
        classroom processes, 231–232
        components of syllabus, 230–231
        sample task from mathematics class,
            232, 232f
    results, 233–237
        access to resources, 234
        aversion to new technology, 236

different digital tools simultaneously, 233

greater involvement of online learners, 234–235

in-class practices, 236–237

interaction with learners, 233

limited exposure to learners, 235

mode of instruction, 236

motivating students, 235

movement of teacher in classroom, 234

study, 222–223

Online education, 25, 164, 253–254

analysis, 260–265

announcement of assignment details, 263*f*

extracts of assignment details, 263*f*

regular communications with students, 264*f*

implications, 265

journey, 257

literature, 255–257

methodology, 257–259

positionality, 254–255

South African context, 253–254

Online examinations, 129

Online exams, 162

learners' experiences of online exams, 163–164

literature, 162

results, 170–171

students need for authenticity in, 171–174

Online formative assessment, 148–150

in ways increase self-regulation by learners, relevant model for implementing, 148

Online invigilation, 171

Online language teacher education design, 71–72

Online learners, greater involvement of, 234–235

Online learning, 48–49, 52–53, 60, 121–125, 161, 201–202, 241–242, 253. *See also* Personalized learning

alternative paradigms in online learning design, 46

environments, 68

opportunities, 92

platforms, 45, 59

Online Learning Consortium, 223–224

Online resources, 205

Online sessions, 259

highlights of, 262*f*

Online surveys, 205

Online teaching, 83–84, 123–124, 202

Online testing environment, 168

Open educational resources (OERs), 67, 193–194

Operating system, 175

Ophthalmology education

clinical knowledge, 247

digital teaching program one, 244–246

digital teaching program two, 246–247

grand rounds, 248

morning report, 247–248

oral examination, 249–250

patient encounters, 249

research experience, 248–249

Ophthalmology graduate medical education, 241–242

Oral examination, 249–250

Organisation for Economic Cooperation and Development (OECD), 121

Organizational barriers, 104

Outcome-based taught curriculum model, 53

P

Pandemic learning environment, 84–87

Patient encounters, 249

Pedagogical approach, 130

Peer-to peer learning, 245

Peer-to peer teaching, 245

Peer-to-near-peer teaching, 245

Personalization, 193–194

Personalized learning, 32, 203–204

approach, 203

student-centric framework for, 215–216

PHEI. *See* Private HEI (PHEI)

Physiotherapy, 105, 109, 113

Platformization, 66–67

Political economy, 57–58

Pop quiz techniques, 227
Post-COVID-19, 36–37
PowerPoint presentation, 152, 186–187
Precision education, 24–25
Preferred Reporting Items for Systematic
    Review (PRISMA), 130–131
Preparation and delivery challenges, 83–87
Presentation, 248
PRISMA. *See* Preferred Reporting Items
    for Systematic Review (PRISMA)
Private HEI (PHEI), 200
Professional masters, 81
Professional program, 94–95
Program design processes, 94
Protocols, 167, 181, 226
Prototype, 71

Q
Qualifications, 94–95, 166
Qualitative data analysis, 206
Qualitative descriptive research, 226
Quality care provision, 111–112
Quantitative and qualitative data, 13
Quantitative data analysis, 206
Quarter system, 81
Quizlet tool, 21–22

R
Realistic learning, 111
Reflective strategies, 165
Reinforcement learning (RL), 26–28
Remote invigilation systems, 175–176
Remote learning, 125–126
    tools, 79–80
Remote proctoring software, 164
Renewable assessment, 67
Replication, 111
Research experience, 248–249
Research-based learning, 4
Research-focused program, 4
Reshaping assessments, 90–92
Resources, access to, 234
RL. *See* Reinforcement learning (RL)
Robotic process automation, 228–229
Rogers' diffusion innovation, 45

S
s-learning. *See* Smart learning (s-learning)
Scenarios, 102–103
School of Education (SoE), 179
SchooLinks tool, 21–22
Science, technology, engineering, and
    mathematics (STEM), 1, 254–255
SDG4. *See* United Nations Sustainable
    Development Goals 4 (SDG4)
SDGs. *See* Sustainable Development Goals
    (SDGs)
Self-regulatory processes, 148
SharePoint, 11
Smart evaluation system, 122
Smart learning (s-learning), 201–202
Smart television, 209
Smartphone, 88, 209
Social isolation, 259
Social justice, 256–257
Social problem-solving processes, 92–93
Socioeconomic factors, 102
Socratic method learning, 245
SoE. *See* School of Education (SoE)
Soft skills, 38
Standard flipped model, 224
Standardized assessments, 122
STEM. *See* Science, technology,
    engineering, and mathematics
    (STEM)
Stereotypes, 113
Strengths, weaknesses, opportunities, and
    challenges (SWOC), 22–23
    of digital education, 38–40
        analysis, 38f
        challenges, 40
        opportunities, 40
        strength, 39
        weakness, 39
Student collaboration, 254–255
Student engagement, 254–255
Student experience of online exams in
        professional programs
    literature, 162–165
        challenges faced and trends in
            transforming traditional exams,
            164–165

learners' experiences of online exams, 163—164
online exams, 162
theoretical framework, 165
methodology, 165—167
data collection and analysis, 167
study setting, 166
results, 167—174
fear of being disadvantaged, 168—170
online exams, 170—171
students need for authenticity in online exams, 171—174
Student learning, 16—17
process, 153
Student responsibility learning, 261
Student-centric framework for personalized learning, 215—216
for higher education, 215*f*
Students blend resources, 209
Summative assessment
in education sector, 127—129
in higher education institutions, 140—142
tools, 128—129
Support systems, 124
Sustainable Development Goals (SDGs), 46—47
UNESCO 2030, 46—48
Sustainable learning, 105—106
SWOC. *See* Strengths, weaknesses, opportunities, and challenges (SWOC)

T

TA. *See* Traditional assessment (TA)
TAM. *See* Technological acceptance model (TAM)
TBL sessions. *See* Team-based learning sessions (TBL sessions)
Teaching (T), 38
artificial intelligence in, 29—31
methods, 147
strategies, 254—255
systems, 122—123
teaching-learning materials, 224
teaching—learning process, 223—224, 228—229, 233

Team-based learning sessions (TBL sessions), 81—82
Technical documentation, 210—211
Technical issues, 164, 168, 263
Technological acceptance model (TAM), 180
Technology failures, 175
Technology-enhanced learning (TEL), 21—24, 201
TEL. *See* Technology-enhanced learning (TEL)
Tele-education, 242—243
Telecommunication technology, 243
Telephonic conversations, 185—186
Texas Medical Center (TX), 246
Thematic analysis, 108
3D functionality, 184
Time
and immediacy of response, 155—156
management, 236
Traditional assessment (TA), 53, 121
Traditional design approaches, 68
Traditional education system, 121
Traditional semester system, 81
Transition process, 125—126
TX. *See* Texas Medical Center (TX)

U

UDL. *See* Universal design for learning (UDL)
Unconventional learning design, 46
UNESCO. *See* United Nations Educational Scientific and Cultural Organization (UNESCO)
UNICEF, 222, 228
United Kingdom (UK), 125
United Nations Educational Scientific and Cultural Organization (UNESCO), 46—48, 122, 193—194
UNESCO 2030 sustainability development goals, 46—48
United Nations Sustainable Development Goals 4 (SDG4), 66
Universal design for learning (UDL), 216—217
University life cycle, 104—105
Uzbekistan, 221—222

V

Virtual assessments, 127–128
Virtual COVID-19 ophthalmology
    rotation (VOR), 246–247
Virtual format, 247–248
Virtual learning, 25
  experience, 1
Virtual learning environment
    (VLE), 52
Virtual ophthalmic training curricula, 243
Virtual ophthalmology rotation (VOR),
    244
Virtual platforms, 17–18
Virtual reality (VR), 21–22
  in education, 37–38
Virtual teaching, 250
Virus, 255–256
VLE. *See* Virtual learning environment
    (VLE)

VOR. *See* Virtual ophthalmology rotation
    (VOR)
VR. *See* Virtual reality (VR)

W

Wastewater Treatment Plant, 14–15
Water treatment, photocatalysis in, 15
WCTE PBS Cohort, 14
Web designing tools, 228–229
Wiggins test to confirm essential question,
    54–55
WordPress, 104
World Health Organization (WHO), 124
World Wide Web, 228–229
Wound healing processes, 10–11

Z

Zoom, 52

Printed in the United States
by Baker & Taylor Publisher Services